DISABILITY AT A GLANCE 2021

The Shaping of Disability-Inclusive Employment in Asia and the Pacific

ST/ESCAP/2981
Language: English
Printed in Bangkok
Sales no: E.22.II.F.3
ISBN: 9789211208351
eISBN: 9789210011594
Print ISSN: 2411-8303
Online ISSN: 2411-8311

Preface

Disability-inclusive employment has yet to be achieved in the Asia–Pacific region, where 472 million working-age persons with disabilities live. Data on persons with disabilities and their employment situation are scarce in almost every country in the region. What little data are available reveal that persons with disabilities fare worse than persons without disabilities throughout the labour market. Persons with disabilities – particularly women, youth and rural inhabitants – experience higher rates of unemployment and economic inactivity and are at greater risk of vulnerable employment and insufficient social protection than others without disabilities. The lack of economic resilience exposed them to even greater and more complex vulnerabilities when the COVID-19 pandemic hit and brought about prolonged public health and socioeconomic crises across the region.

By this publication, the United Nations Economic and Social Commission for Asia and the Pacific (ESCAP) offers a regional review of the employment status of persons with disabilities. The intent is to galvanize stakeholders into action and to inspire effective and innovative solutions. *Disability at a Glance 2021: The Shaping of Disability-Inclusive Employment in Asia and the Pacific* proposes a range of recommendations to Governments and other stakeholders in the region towards upholding the rights of persons with disabilities to employment that are enshrined in the Convention on the Rights of Persons with Disabilities, the 2030 Agenda for Sustainable Development and the Incheon Strategy to "Make the Right Real" for Persons with Disabilities in Asia and the Pacific.

The world of work that governments have committed to building through the international treaties and regional instruments is imperative to the full and equal participation in society and enjoyment of a dignified and adequate standard of living for the 15 per cent of us who live with disabilities. But every worker, regardless of their disability status, benefits from and works more productively in an accessible and inclusive work environment that accommodates and appreciates diversity. Businesses with an inclusive workforce deliver more innovative and accessible products and services. Business champions now realize the importance of the untapped talent resources and consumer markets that persons with disabilities represent, as illustrated in this publication.

In the journey to disability-inclusive employment, the Asia–Pacific region must cope with new challenges and leverage the strategic opportunities presented by latest developments in the world of work: technological advancement, the gig economy and the labour market reforms triggered by the COVID-19 pandemic.

To create better employment prospects and decent work conditions for persons with disabilities requires greater investment in productive employment. Such a leap would enable countries to make substantial progress on their national, regional and international commitments to inclusive development while building back from the COVID-19 pandemic. This mission cannot be achieved without concerted action. A critical momentum has emerged for aligning investment and action by governments, the business community and organizations of persons with disabilities. At ESCAP, we call for joining forces to promote the inclusive employment of persons with disabilities for a more inclusive, resilient and prosperous Asia-Pacific for all.

Acknowledgements

This publication, *Disability at a Glance 2021: The Shaping of Disability-Inclusive Employment in Asia and the Pacific*, was prepared under the overall guidance of Srinivas Tata, Director of Social Development Division, ESCAP. Cai Cai, Chief of Gender Equality and Social Inclusion Section, ESCAP Social Development Division, led the drafting team comprising Li Stephanie Choo, Zian Cao and Tingting Chen. The drafting team express our gratitude to the Executive Secretary of ESCAP, Armida Salsiah Alisjahbana, for providing inspiration and leadership to the work on supporting and empowering persons with disabilities.

Special thanks to Professor Sophie Mitra and Jaclyn Yap of Fordham University; Esteban Tromel, Senior Disability Specialist, and Valentina Stoevska, Senior Statistician, both with the International Labour Organization; Emeritus Professor Ryo Matsui of Hosei University; and Barbara Murray, Senior Consultant on Disability-Inclusive Employment, for their peer review and valuable suggestions on the draft report. Barbara Murray also co-developed with ESCAP team a technical paper that fed into this report.

Aiko Akiyama, Alexandre Cote, Andrew Byrnes, Anthony Chong, Daniel Mont, Deborah Wan, Fumihiro Kojima, Gayane Panosyan, Jessica Murphy, Jung Min Jeon, Joni Simpson, Kamal Lamichhane, Kazuo Kubotera, Kishore Singh, Kyoko Sakai, Linda Steele, Ma Xingcan, Manique Gunaratne, Michael Szporluk, Min Kyong Kim, Nicky Chan, Phyllis Choo, Ramya Prajna Sahisnu, Rick Kane, Sam Sondhi, Samrerng Virachanang, Sherol George, Song Moon Hyun, Suporntum Mongkolsawadi, Thakur D. Dhariyal, Tricia Malowney, Yeo Swee Lan and Zhou Kai also provided valuable inputs to the draft, including the contribution of case studies and good practice examples.

ESCAP interns Rosemary Plummer and Srivatsan Manivannan provided research assistance.

Karen Emmons edited and Wut Suthirachartkul designed the publication.

Executive summary

Productive employment and decent work are central to enabling persons with disabilities to participate fully and equally in society and to enjoy an adequate standard of living. The unemployment, underemployment and exclusion of persons with disabilities from the labour market also incur significant social and economic losses.

Disability at a Glance 2021: The Shaping of Disability-Inclusive Employment in Asia and the Pacific is a compendium of the current state of employment of persons with disabilities in the region. It has collated the latest data, policy developments, strategies and practices undertaken by governments, service providers and private companies in member States and associate members of the United Nations Economic and Social Commission for Asia and the Pacific (ESCAP). Based on analysis of the latest situations and progress made, the publication recommends a range of actions for the region's governments to take, in partnership with organizations of persons with disabilities and other stakeholders, to further promote disability-inclusive employment. The publication draws on labour data consolidated by the International Labour Organization and the Disability Data Initiative through the Fordham Research Consortium on Disability. Desk research and the virtual Expert Group Meeting: Promoting Inclusive Employment for Persons with Disabilities in Asia and the Pacific in July 2021 afforded all additional data, policy information, useful strategies and good practices.

The current state of employment of persons with disabilities

Persons with disabilities in Asia and the Pacific – 472 million of whom are of working age – fare worse than persons without disabilities in the labour market. Although comprehensive and comparable data sets are lacking, data available from countries in the region indicate critical disability gaps in employment-to-population ratios, labour force participation rates, engagement in informal work and youth idle rates. When compared with persons without disabilities, persons with disabilities are significantly less likely to be employed and participating in the labour force. They are more likely to engage in informal work and be idle – neither in school nor employed – when they are young. The disability gaps generally widen as the severity of disability increases. Women with disabilities and persons living in rural areas face additional challenges in employment.

To improve the employment situation of persons with disabilities, relevant policymaking needs to account for the diverse profiles that persons with disabilities have. This includes the varying types and levels of impairments they live with and the different socio-economic circumstances in the region. Policymakers need to pay attention to the opportunity to work, the earnings and working conditions. The critical gaps in disability-disaggregated data need to be filled across the region to enable and inform more effective and efficient policymaking.

Shift in policy focus from sheltered employment to supported employment

The policy focus and approach to promoting employment of persons with disabilities have been influenced by the transformed understanding of disability from the medical model to the social and human rights models. The latter models are embedded in the Convention on the Rights of Persons with Disabilities and the Incheon Strategy to "Make the Right Real" for Persons with Disabilities in Asia and the Pacific. The Convention has been ratified by 47 of the 53 ESCAP member States . Five member States have signed it. The transformed understanding of disability has catalysed a fundamental shift in the approach to promoting work and employment opportunities for persons with disabilities, from sheltered employment to supported employment in inclusive settings. Good practices have been established in some countries to promote supported employment through social enterprises and private firms.

Strategies to promote productive employment and decent work for persons with disabilities

Overarching legal frameworks are established at the national levels to protect the rights of persons with disabilities to work. At least nine countries have explicit provisions in their constitutions to address basic needs, ensuring social protection, prohibiting discrimination against and/or promoting inclusion of persons with disability in mainstream society. The majority of countries in the region have also adopted employment equity and non-discrimination laws to make discriminatory treatments of persons with disabilities by employers unlawful. Many of these laws require employers to provide reasonable accommodation in the jobs and the work environment. Challenges remain to ensure and monitor the implementation and enforcement of these laws.

Governments have also deployed various laws, policies and programmes to support the employment of persons with disabilities. These include employment quota schemes, preferential contracting, job retention, return-to-work (for workers who acquire a disability) provisions, disability-related social protection benefits, and measures to reduce the costs of employment for both employers and employees with disabilities. A range of country cases demonstrate good practices of implementing these strategies and affirmative action. More action should be explored that motivates implementation and mitigates potential disincentives.

Countries in the region have various programmes to equip persons with disability with skills and information needed for the labour market. Governments work with technical and vocational education and training (TVET) institutions and employment service providers to deliver vocational training, job coaching and jobseeking skills training that target persons with disabilities. More efforts are in demand to include persons with disabilities in mainstream TVET institutions and to ensure that TVET programmes are relevant and cater to learners with disabilities. Employment services are also provided to jobseekers with disabilities and employers, either through dedicated service providers or through mainstream employment service centres. Information-sharing and coordination among policy advocacy, training provision and employment service provision have proven to be important.

Support to entrepreneurs with disabilities is another meaningful strategy, given the wide engagement in self-employment of persons with disabilities in the region. Some countries have laws, policies and programmes to support entrepreneurs with disabilities. These include measures to facilitate the provision of business development skills training, credit and microcredit services and access to market and business networks for entrepreneurs with disabilities. Many of these policies and services require mainstream services and information to be inclusive and accessible. Others require aligning support from governments, the private sector and business associations.

Improving accessibility in the general environment, through the adoption of universal design, and enhancing public awareness remain highly relevant and critical. Given the uneven development of accessibility across the region, countries need to continue improving accessibility and promoting universal design in the built environment and public facilities. They also need to make services, knowledge, information and communication technologies accessible enablers for the employment of persons with disabilities. Misconceptions of the employability of persons with disabilities remain, and the medical approach to disability persists. Governments need to do more to improve awareness and to leverage the power of the media.

Latest changes in the world of work and associated impact on the employment of persons with disabilities

Technological transformations have been rapidly displacing low-skilled jobs, including many that are occupied by workers with disabilities. They are also creating new jobs and assistive technologies that are increasing employment opportunities for persons with disabilities. Advances in information and communications technology (ICT) have opened up telework, e-commerce and distance learning options for persons with disabilities. Yet, the cost of ICT equipment and sophisticated assistive devices remains prohibitive for many, particularly people living in developing countries.

The gig economy, especially digital gig work, has the potential to lower discriminatory barriers and enable persons with disabilities to enter full-time employment. It provides them with much-needed flexibility in working hours and location and usually requires lower overhead costs associated with employment. The challenges lie in the lack of employment benefits and protection for gig workers, which are to be tackled by governments in the region.

The COVID-19 pandemic has added to the vulnerability of persons with disabilities in employment while catalysing emergency measures taken by governments to safeguard income and livelihoods of people, including persons with disabilities. This has created opportunity for governments to transform and institutionalize some of the temporary measures to the benefit of persons with disabilities.

Recommendations

For governments to address the large gaps that remain in employment of persons with disabilities in the Asia–Pacific region, the following broad recommendations are proposed:

- Strengthen rights-based national legislative frameworks and sector-based laws and policies to provide a legal foundation and define obligations for the employment of persons with disabilities, mitigate disability-related discrimination and create incentives for employees with disabilities and employers. This may also include transforming social protection programmes (such as disability-specific benefits and allowance) to support rather than discourage persons with disabilities to pursue employment.
- Support current and future workers with disabilities to obtain practical technical and vocational education and training through disability-inclusive mainstream TVET institutions, job coaching and one-stop shop employment services.
- Support persons with disabilities with entrepreneurial aspirations to acquire business development skills, credit services and access to markets and networks; ensure that mainstream entrepreneurship development policies, programmes and services are inclusive and accessible.
- Improve buy-in of employers by providing financial incentives (such as tax exemption and wage subsidies) and technical support on job analysis, matching, placement, coaching and reasonable accommodation.
- Continue to improve accessibility in the general society and transform awareness and attitudes towards persons with disabilities and their employment.
- Leverage the momentum presented by technological advancements, the rise of the gig economy and employment-related responses to the COVID-19 pandemic to create new employment opportunities for persons with disabilities and make mainstream employment policies disability-inclusive.
- Improve the regular collection and quality of data on the employment of persons with disabilities across the region as part of the overall labour market surveys or employment-related population censuses; and promote disability-disaggregation for administrative data across sectors.

Investing in productive employment and decent work for persons with disabilities also presents an opportunity for governments to make substantial progress on national and regional commitments to inclusive development, particularly while building back from the COVID-19 pandemic. Recent developments in the world of work have presented new challenges but, more importantly, opportunities that the region could leverage to create better employment prospects and conditions for persons with disabilities. Concerted actions are required from governments, businesses and organizations of persons with disabilities to make this happen.

Contents

Annexes

Figures

Boxes

Tables

Introduction

Productive employment and decent work[1] are central to enabling persons with disabilities to participate fully and equally in society and to enjoy an adequate standard of living. They feature strongly in international commitments on disability rights and disability-inclusive development. They are the core of a dedicated article in the Convention on the Rights of Persons with Disabilities and of the first goal of the Incheon Strategy to "Make the Right Real" for Persons with Disabilities in Asia and the Pacific.

This publication seeks to equip members and associate members of the United Nations Economic and Social Commission for Asia and the Pacific (ESCAP) with updated information and insights on promoting employment for persons with disabilities in the region. It offers snapshots of the latest figures, trends, policy developments, strategies and inspirational practices. Due to limitations in the available data, the publication focuses the descriptions on the current state of participation in employment and the labour force. It does not discuss earnings and working conditions, although it recognizes they are equally important to productive employment and decent work for persons with disabilities.

The publication contains five chapters:

- Chapter 1 introduces the employment status of persons with disabilities in the region, based on the latest available figures, and discusses the critical issue of strengthening disability-disaggregated employment data for evidence-informed policymaking.
- Chapter 2 summarizes the evolution of the understanding of disability and disability rights over the years, including policy commitments at the international and regional levels that have accompanied these changes. It analyses the resulting transformation in the approach to promoting employment opportunities for persons with disabilities.
- Chapter 3 lays out the strategies available to Asia–Pacific governments and other stakeholders in promoting productive employment and decent work for persons with disabilities and showcases interesting initiatives and practices undertaken to this end.
- Chapter 4 discusses the latest developments in the world of work brought about by technological change, the rise of the gig economy and, more recently, the COVID-19 pandemic. It then explores the impact of these changes on employment opportunities for persons with disabilities.
- Chapter 5 closes with proposed recommendations for further action by governments to promote productive employment and decent work for persons with disabilities in Asia and the Pacific.

1 For this publication, "productive employment" is defined as employment yielding sufficient returns to labour that permits a worker and their dependants a level of consumption above the poverty line. "Decent work" is defined as productive work for women and men in conditions of freedom, equity, security and human dignity. The International Labour Organization's Decent Work Agenda comprises four pillars: employment creation and enterprise development; social protection; standards and rights at work; and governance and social dialogue. See ILO, *Understanding Deficits of Productive Employment and Setting Targets: A Methodological Guide* (Geneva, 2012) and ILO, *Toolkit for Mainstreaming Employment and Decent Work* (Geneva, 2007).

Chapter 1

Employment status of persons with disabilities in Asia and the Pacific

Persons with disabilities generally fare worse than persons without disabilities in the labour market. Although comprehensive data sets that are fully comparable across countries and time are lacking, data from around the world provide enough evidence of a clear disability gap in employment.[2] Countries in Asia and the Pacific show similar disparities in employment performance.

This chapter analyses the employment status of persons with disabilities in Asia and the Pacific using data from two repositories:[3] ILOSTAT[4] and the Disability Data Initiative.[5] These two repositories are the main sources for the most comprehensive and nationally representative data on employment-related indicators. However, data from different countries are not always comparable in terms of latest year of data collection,[6] definition of disability and methodology used. Hence, results based on the two data sets are not meant to be directly comparable. Instead, the intention is to underscore the clear and consistent existence of disability gaps apparent across different data sets.

Four relevant indicators were selected for the analysis: (i) employment-to-population ratio, (ii) labour force participation rate, (iii) share of adult population in the informal economy and (iv) the youth idle rate.[7] ILOSTAT offers data on indicators (i) and (ii), while the Disability Data Initiative offers data on indicators (i), (iii) and (iv). Where possible, analysis was done to understand the intersectional impacts of disability and gender and of disability and rural–urban disparity on the indicators.

Analyses of data from both repositories show a clear disability gap[8] across all employment-related indicators presented in this chapter, with intersectionality worsening the employment situation of women with disabilities and persons with disabilities living in rural communities. The results on the employment-to-population ratio, based on data from the two sources, corroborate each other. The disability gap on this indicator widens significantly alongside the increase in severity of disability while varying by type of disability.

2 Based on data from 91 countries and territories across the globe, the employment rate of persons with disabilities is 24 per cent lower than that of persons without disabilities. Employed persons with disabilities also tend to earn less than their counterparts without disabilities. See DESA, *Disability and Development Report: Realizing the Sustainable Development Goals by, for and with Persons with Disabilities 2018* (New York, 2019).

3 Please refer to Annex A for details on the use of data for Chapter 1, including a description of the data sets and the rationale for using these datasets, as well as the differentiated definitions of similar terms (such as "disability" in ILOSTAT datasets and "functional difficulty" in the Disability Data Initiative datasets).

4 ILO, "ILOSTAT". Available at https://ilostat.ilo.org/.

5 Disability Data Initiative, "Disability Data Initiative". Available at https://disabilitydata.ace.fordham.edu/.

6 See Annex B table 3 on data sources.

7 Considerations regarding the choice of indicators are elaborated in Annex A.

8 See Annex A for explanation on the definition of the term "disability gap" used in this chapter.

1.1 Employment-to-population ratio

There are an estimated 472 million persons with disabilities of working age[9] in Asia and the Pacific.[10] Persons with disabilities are less likely to be employed than persons without disabilities in the region, as indicated by data on the employment-to-population ratios[11] from both the ILOSTAT and Disability Data Initiative repositories.

In all but one of the 18 Asia–Pacific countries with disability-disaggregated data in ILOSTAT, including 15 countries in special situations,[12] persons with disabilities had lower employment-to-population ratios than persons without disabilities (figure 1). The exception was Timor-Leste, where the ratio was similar for both groups. Further research is needed to explore and understand the pattern in Timor-Leste. The median employment-to-population ratio was 28 per cent for persons with disabilities, while it was 51 per cent for persons without disabilities. This represented a median disability gap of 26 percentage points. In 10 countries, the employment-to-population ratio of persons with disabilities was less than half of what it was for persons without disabilities. In two of those countries, persons with disabilities were four to five times less likely to be employed than persons without disabilities.

The analysis of sex-disaggregated data indicates that men with disabilities were less likely to be employed than men without disabilities in 16 of the 18 countries, with the exception of the Marshall Islands and Timor-Leste. Women with disabilities were less likely to be employed than women without disabilities in all 18 countries. Further research is needed to explore and better understand the distinctive findings in these two countries. On average,[13] the employment-to-population ratios for men with and without disabilities were 36 per cent and 63 per cent, respectively. For women with and without disabilities, the employment-to-population ratios were 19 per cent and 42 per cent, respectively.

Intersecting disadvantages further worsen the employment situation for women with disabilities (figure 2). In all 18 countries with available data, women with disabilities had lower employment-to-population ratios than men without disabilities, with the median gender-disability gap at 45 percentage points. In 15 of those countries, women with disabilities were at least twice less likely to be employed than men without disabilities. In seven of those countries, women were at least five times less likely than men to be in employment. In one country,

Figure 1
Employment-to-population ratio for 18 countries or territories, by disability status

Persons with disabilities are much less likely to be employed than persons without disabilities.

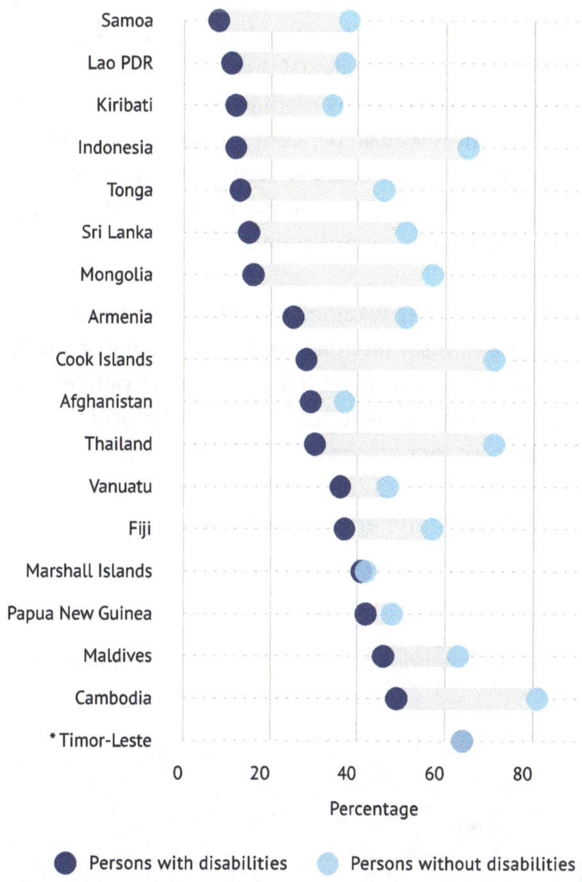

*In **Timor-Leste**, the employment-to-populationratio was similar for persons with and without disabilities.

Source: ESCAP analysis based on data from ILOSTAT (last update as of 18 July 2021).

9 Working age is defined as 15–64 years for this calculation. In the rest of this publication, "the working-age population" where ILOSTAT data are described and "the adult population" or "adults" where data from the Disability Data Initiative are described both refer to all persons aged 15 or older.

10 Calculated as 15 per cent of the ESCAP estimate that 3,144,378,848 of the Asia and Pacific population were of working age at mid-year 2020. See ESCAP, "Population and development indicators for Asia and the Pacific, 2020", Data Sheet (Bangkok, 2020).

11 The employment-to-population ratio, also called the employment rate, measures the share of the adult population who work for pay or profit (self-employed). It is Indicator 1.2 of the Incheon Strategy Target and Indicator Framework.

12 The group of countries in special situation in Asia and the Pacific comprised least developed countries, landlocked developing countries and small island developing States. See ESCAP, "Countries in special situations". Available at: www.unescap.org/our-work/countries-special-situations. Among the 15 countries referred to here, there were two least developed and landlocked developing countries (Afghanistan and Lao People's Democratic Republic), one least developed country (Cambodia), two least developed and small island developing States (Kiribati and Timor-Leste), two landlocked developing countries (Armenia and Mongolia), and eight small island developing States (Cook Islands, Fiji, Maldives, Marshall Islands, Papua New Guinea, Samoa, Tonga and Vanuatu). In this publication, the use of the term "country" or "countries" by no means implies the expression of any opinion whatsoever on the part of the Secretariat of the United Nations concerning the legal status of any country, territory or of its authorities.

13 The term "average" refers to the median throughout Chapter 1.

the employment rate for women with disabilities was 10 times lower than for men without disabilities.

The data sources used by the Disability Data Initiative define disability by functional difficulty.[14] The data corroborate the findings from the ILOSTAT data. Thirteen Asia–Pacific countries had data on the employment-to-population ratio. Of them, 10 were countries in special situations.[15] The median employment-to-population ratios was 40 per cent for persons "with functional difficulty" and 50 per cent for persons "without functional difficulty", with the median disability gap more than 4 percentage points.

The disability gap widened significantly with increased severity of disability (figure 3). The median employment-to-population ratio dropped to 46 per cent for persons with "some functional difficulty" and then to 27 per cent for persons with "at least a lot of difficulty". For seven of the 13 countries with this data, there was a gradient in the employment-to-population ratio: Persons with some functional difficulty had lower employment-to-population ratios than persons with "no difficulty", but it was higher than persons with at least a lot of difficulty. In all countries with available data except Timor-Leste, persons with at least a lot of functional difficulty were less likely than persons without difficulty to be employed. In four countries, persons with at least a lot of functional difficulty were less than half as likely to be employed than persons without difficulty. And in one of those countries, persons without functional difficulty were more than five times as likely as persons with at least a lot of functional difficulty to be employed.

The disability gap also differed by the type of functional difficulty (figure 4). The median gap was largest for persons with difficulty in self-care (at 26 percentage points), followed by communication (at 16 percentage points), mobility (at 14 percentage points), cognition (at 13 percentage points), hearing (at 5 percentage points) and seeing (at 3 percentage points).

Figure 2
Employment-to-population ratio for 18 countries or territories, by gender and disability status
Intersectional gender-disability gaps exist in employment.

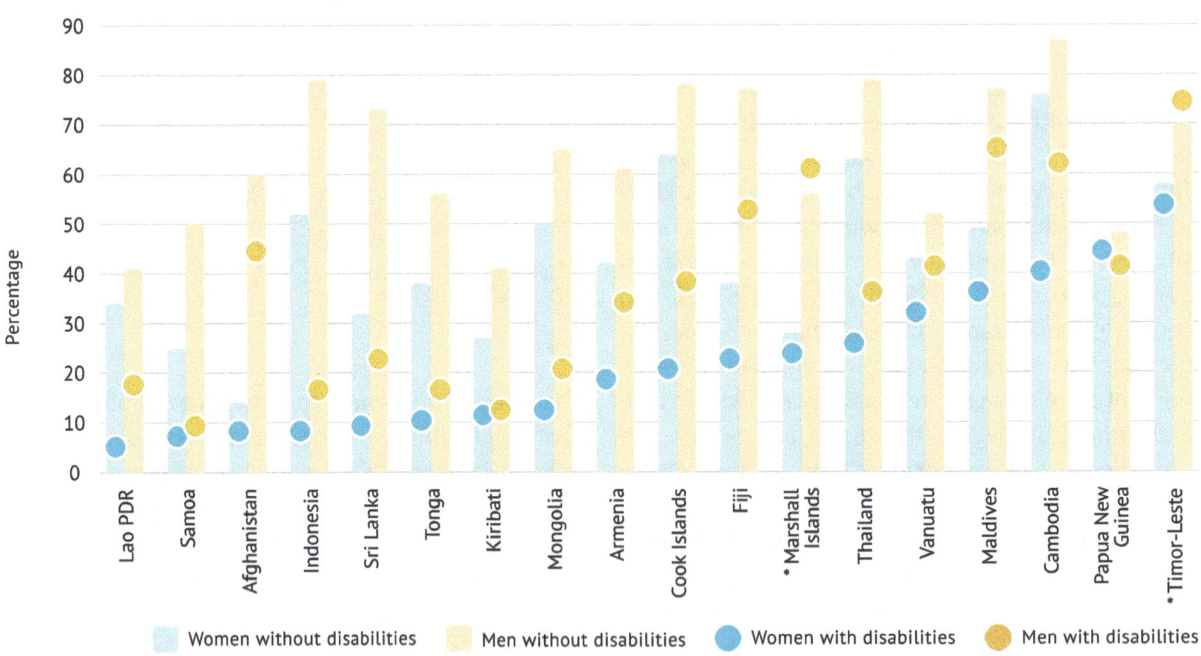

*In **Marshall Islands** and **Timor-Leste**, men with disabilities had higher employment-to-population ratio than the other three groups. Further analysis is needed to understand the reasons behind these exceptions.

Source: ESCAP analysis based on data from ILOSTAT (last update as of 18 July 2021).

14 The term "functional difficulty" is used here and elsewhere in Chapter 1 where observations are based on the Disability Data Initiative data set. This is because the data set is solely based on selected functional difficulties (in hearing, seeing, mobility, communication, cognition and self-care) and therefore does not capture all persons with disabilities, specifically those with psychosocial and mental health disabilities. When describing the level of functional difficulty, the following terms are used in the Disability Data Initiative data set: "No difficulty", "Some difficulty" and "At least a lot of difficulty". See Annex A for further explanation on the use of the term "persons with functional difficulty".

15 There was one least developed and landlocked developing country (Afghanistan), two least developed countries (Bangladesh and Cambodia), two least developed and small island developing States (Kiribati and Timor-Leste), one landlocked developing country (Tajikistan) and four small island developing States (Maldives, Papua New Guinea, Tonga and Vanuatu).

Figure 3
Employment-to-population ratio for 13 countries or territories, by extent of functional difficulty

Persons with severe disabilities are less likely to be employed than those without disabilities.

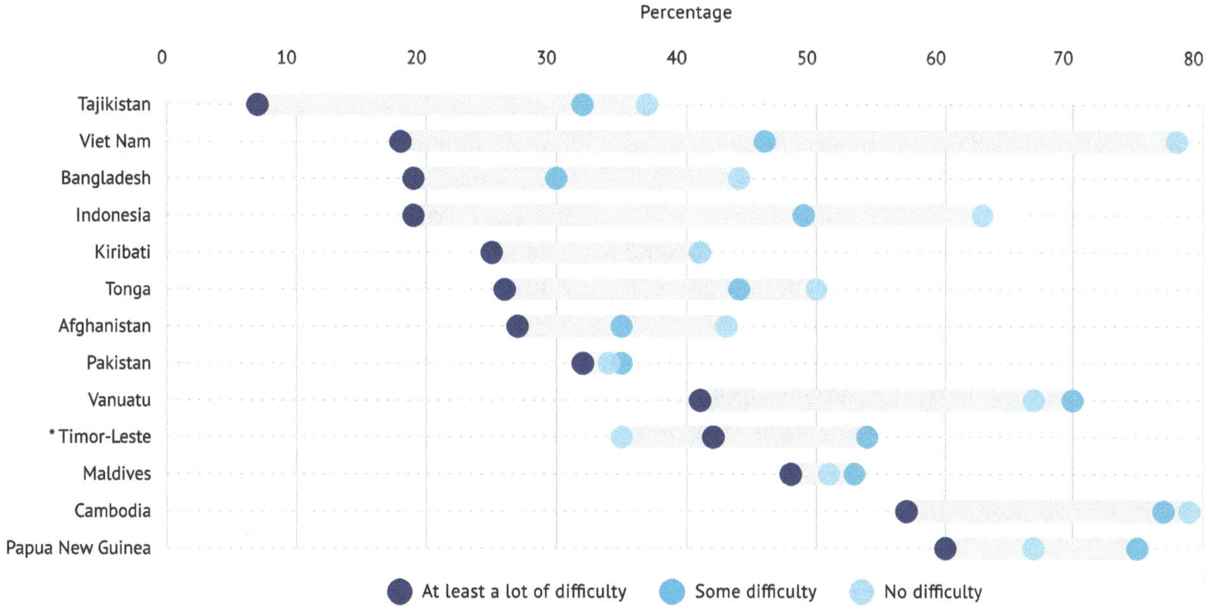

*In **Timor-Leste**, persons without difficulty had lower employment-to-population ratio than the other two groups. In this country, the group of persons with some difficulty also included older persons with a larger employment-to-population ratio.

Source: ESCAP analysis based on data compiled by Disability Data Initiative. See Sophie Mitra and Jaclyn Yap, *The Disability Data Report 2021* (New York, 2021).
Note: The difference between persons with some functional difficulty and without difficulty was not statistically significant in Cambodia, Kiribati, Maldives and Pakistan. The difference between persons with a lot of functional difficulty and without difficulty was not statistically significant in Maldives, Pakistan and Timor-Leste.

Figure 4
Disability gap in employment-to-population ratios, by type of functional difficulty

Persons with self-care difficulty are least likely to be employed, followed by persons with difficulty in communication, mobility, cognition, hearing and seeing.

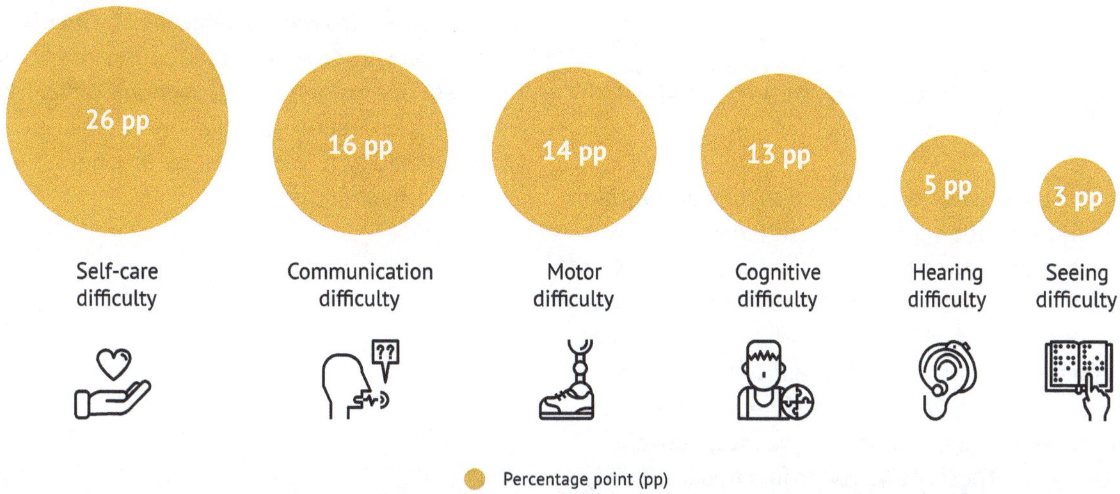

Source: ESCAP analysis based on data compiled by Disability Data Initiative. See Sophie Mitra and Jaclyn Yap, *The Disability Data Report 2021* (New York, 2021).
Note: The use of symbols in Figure 4 does not intend to represent all forms of functional difficulty in each category. Data on difficulty in cognition, mobility, hearing and seeing were available for 13 countries. There were data on difficulty in communication only for nine countries, and data on difficulty in self-care only for eight countries. Disability gap is estimated by the median gap in employment-to-population ratios between persons with each type of difficulty and persons without any difficulty across the countries with data for the respective type.

In three of the 13 countries with the data, persons with difficulty in hearing and persons with difficulty in mobility were less than half as likely to be employed as those without functional difficulty. In five of the eight countries with data, persons with difficulty in self-care were less than half as likely to be employed. In two of those five countries, they were five times less likely to be employed. In two of nine countries with this data, persons with difficulty in communication were four to five times less likely to be employed (figure 5).

The disability gap also widens with age, with a jump for the age group of 30–44 years and the age group of 45–64 years (table 1). The number of countries in which persons with functional difficulty are less likely to be in employment than those without difficulty increases significantly, alongside the size of the median gap for this age group.[16]

Table 1
Disability gap in employment-to-population ratio for 13 countries or territories, by age

	Age group		
	15 to 29	30 to 44	45 to 64
Countries in which persons with functional difficulty had lower employment-to-population ratios (of 13 countries)	8 countries	12 countries	12 countries
Median gap (in percentage points, 13 countries)	0.8 pp	10.3 pp	10.5 pp

Source: ESCAP analysis based on data compiled by Disability Data Initiative. See Sophie Mitra and Jaclyn Yap, *The Disability Data Report 2021* (New York, 2021).

When disaggregated by sex, the disability gap within the male population appeared to be larger than it was within the female population. In the 13 countries with data, the median employment-to-population ratio was 61 per cent for men with functional difficulty and 77 per cent for men without functional difficulty. For women with and without functional difficulty, the median employment-to-population ratio was, respectively, 31 per cent and 39 per cent. Men with functional difficulty had a lower employment-to-population ratio than men without difficulty in 10 of the 13 countries. A similar observation was found in only eight of the 13 countries for the female population. The median disability gap between men with and without functional difficulty was 6 percentage points. Such a gap between women with and without functional difficulty was less than 3 percentage points.

Gender gaps also appear to be significantly larger than disability gaps and were most pronounced for countries in the South and South-West Asia subregion. In the 13 countries, the median gender gap between men and women who had no difficulties was 34 percentage points. Between men and women with any functional difficulty, it was 25 percentage points. In all but Papua New Guinea, the employment-to-population ratio of women was lower than for men with and without functional difficulty (figure 6).

In terms of intersectionality, the median gender–disability gap between men without functional difficulty and women with functional difficulty was 43 percentage points in 13 countries. Among 12 of those countries, men without functional difficulties were more likely to be employed than women with disabilities. In eight countries, men without difficulty were 2 to 10 times more likely to be employed than women with functional difficulty.

In terms of urban–rural disaggregation (figure 7), in the 11 countries with available data, the median employment-to-population ratio was 44 per cent for rural residents with difficulty and 50 per cent for rural residents without difficulty, with a median disability gap of 9 percentage points. For residents in urban areas, the median employment-to-population ratio was 34 per cent among persons with functional difficulty and 48 per cent for persons without difficulty. The median disability gap was 6 percentage points. In seven of the 11 countries, rural residents with functional difficulty had a lower employment-to-population ratio than persons without difficulty. It was similar for urban residents in nine of the 11 countries.

16 For the age group 15–29, the difference between persons with and without functional difficulty was not statistically significant in five of the 13 countries (Cambodia, Maldives, Pakistan, Tajikistan and Timor-Leste). For the age group 30–44, such differences are not statistically significant in Timor-Leste. For the age group 45–64, differences between persons with and without difficulty are statistically significant (at different significance levels) in all 13 countries.

Figure 5
Employment-to-population ratio, by type of functional difficulty

Persons with difficulty in hearing, mobility, self-care and communication fare worse in employment than those without functional difficulty in some countries.

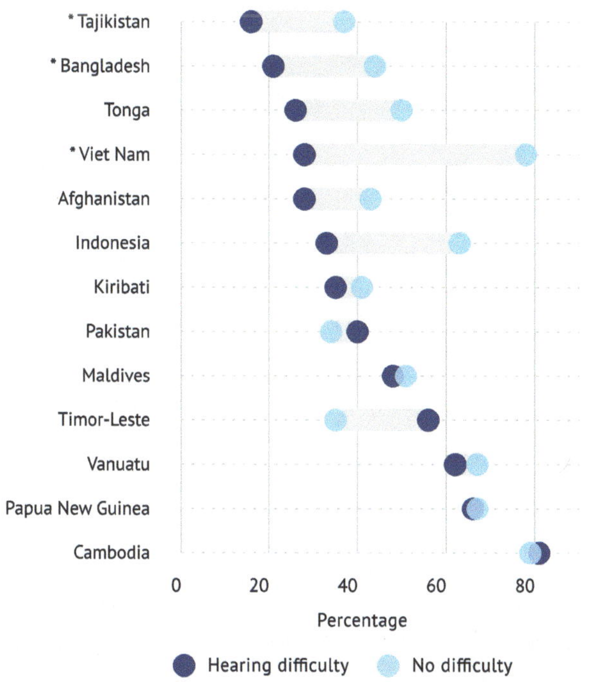

*In **Tajikistan, Bangladesh** and **Viet Nam**, persons with hearing difficulty were less than half as likely to be employed than persons without functional difficulty.

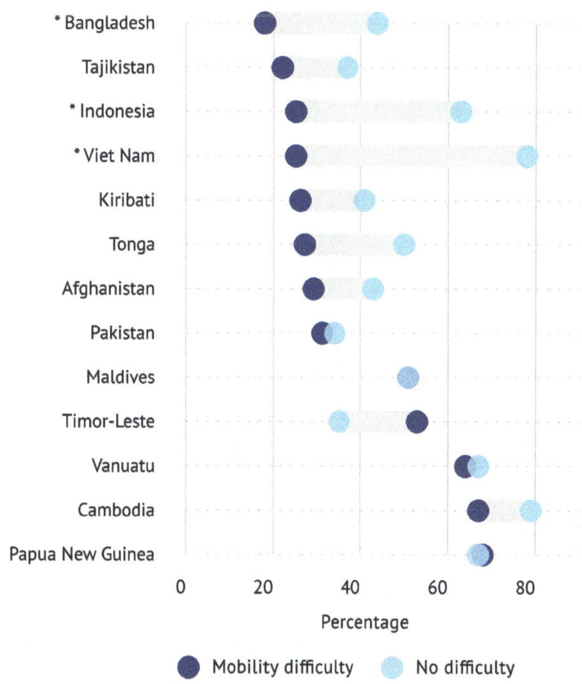

*In **Bangladesh, Indonesia** and **Viet Nam**, persons with difficulty in mobility were less than half as likely to be employed than persons without functional difficulty.

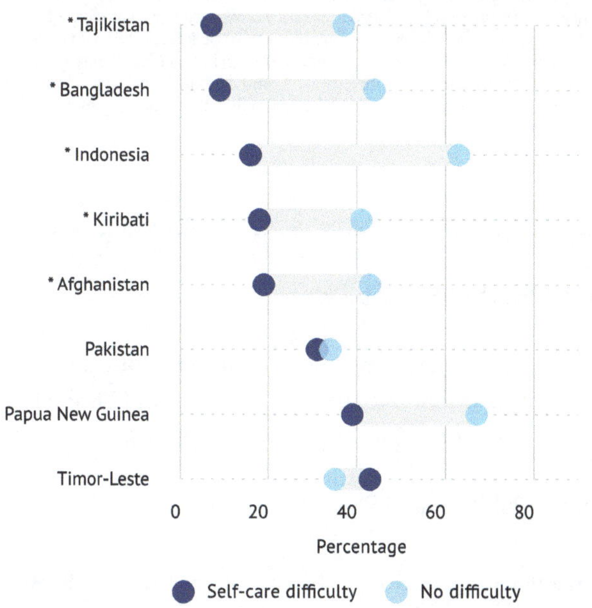

*In these five countries, persons with difficulty in self-care were less than half as likely to be employed than persons without functional difficulty.

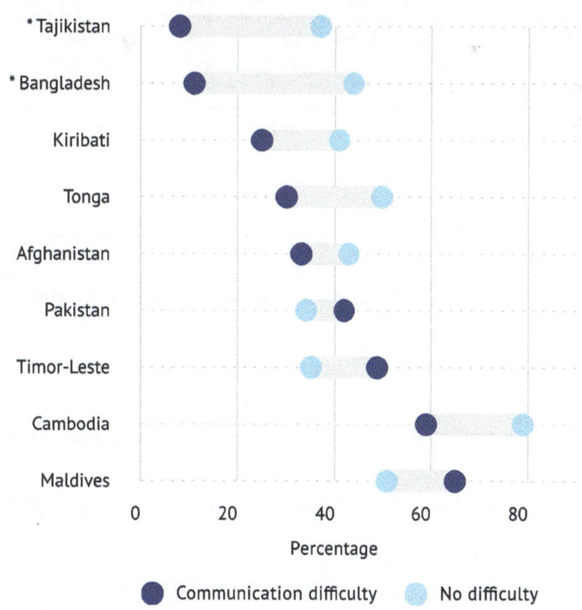

*In **Tajikistan** and **Bangladesh**, persons with difficulty in communication were four to five times less likely to be employed than persons without functional difficulty.

Source: ESCAP analysis based on data compiled by Disability Data Initiative. See Sophie Mitra and Jaclyn Yap, *The Disability Data Report 2021* (New York, 2021).
Note: Data on difficulty in mobility and hearing were available for 13 countries. There were data on difficulty in communication only for nine countries, and data on difficulty in self-care only for eight countries. The estimates by type of functional difficulty did not separate those with some difficulty and those with at least a lot of difficulty. The estimates by type largely reflected the situations of those with less severe difficulty, with a reverse gap in some countries. This was especially the case in Timor-Leste, where the group of persons with some difficulty also included older persons with a larger employment-to-population ratio. Further analysis, primarily through regression analysis, is needed to adjust for the composition of these groups based on age and gender. The estimates for Papua New Guinea also need to be interpreted with caution. The answer scale for functional difficulty questions was reversed from the Washington Group Short Set recommendation. In Papua New Guinea, the answers in the questionnaire began with "Unable to do", and was then followed by "At least a lot of difficulty", then "Some difficulty" and finally "No difficulty". This could possibly contribute to the very high prevalence rate and a larger group of persons with functional difficulties, including many with less severe difficulties.

Figure 6
Employment-to-population ratio for 13 countries or territories, by gender and functional difficulty

Intersectional gender-disability gaps exist in employment.

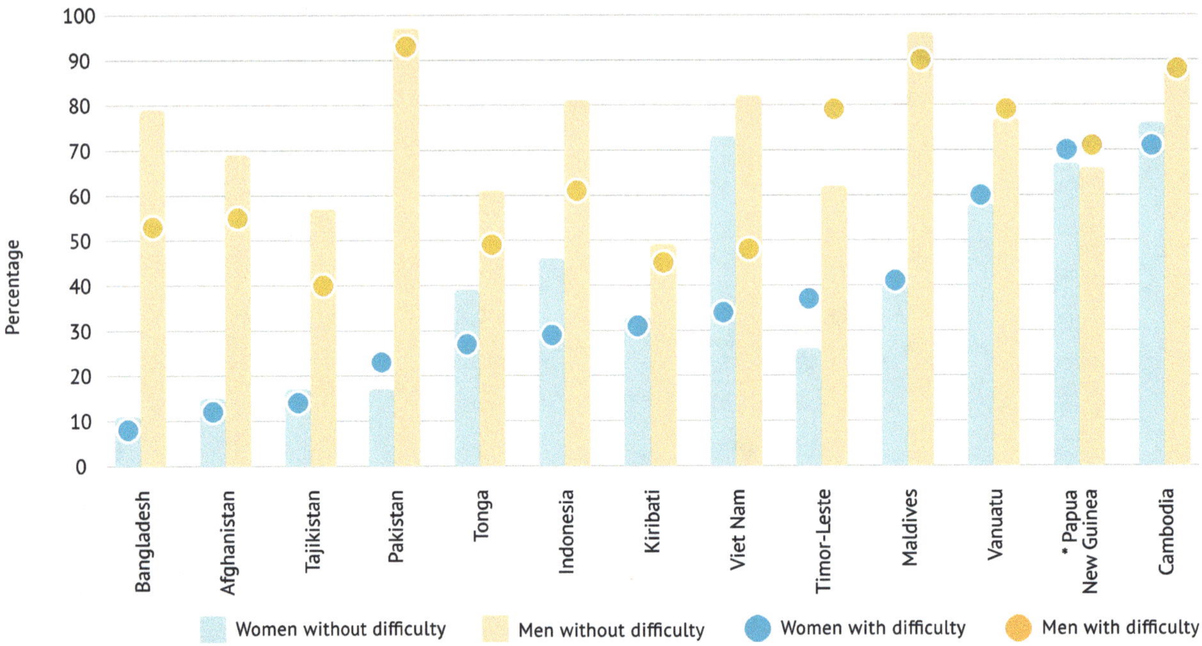

*In **Papua New Guinea**, both women and men with difficulty appeared to have slightly higher employment-to-population ratio than women and men without difficulty.

Source: ESCAP analysis based on data compiled by Disability Data Initiative. See Sophie Mitra and Jaclyn Yap, *The Disability Data Report 2021* (New York, 2021).
Note: The difference between men with and without functional difficulty was not statistically significant in Cambodia. For women with and without functional difficulty, the difference was not statistically significant in Maldives. The estimates for Papua New Guinea need to be interpreted with caution. The answer scale for functional difficulty questions was reversed from the Washington Group Short Set recommendation. In Papua New Guinea, the answers in the questionnaire began with "Unable to do", and was then followed by "At least a lot of difficulty", then "Some difficulty" and finally "No difficulty". This could possibly contribute to the very high prevalence rate and a larger group of persons with functional difficulties, including many with less severe difficulties.

Box 1
Employment-to-population ratios of persons with multiple disabilities

Findings from a study of employment-to-population ratios in **Bangladesh, Pakistan** and the **Philippines** indicate that persons with multiple disabilities have lower employment rates than persons without disability and persons with a single disability, with disability gaps ranging from 10 to 29 percentage points.

Study of employment-to-population ratios in Bangladesh, Pakistan and Philippines

Country	Persons without disability	Persons with single disability	Persons with multiple disabilities
Bangladesh	54%	40%	25%
Pakistan	52%	31%	27%
Philippines	55%	49%	44%

Source: Suguru Mizunoya and Sophie Mitra, "Is there a disability gap in employment rates in developing countries?", *World Development*, vol. 42 (February 2013).

Figure 7

Employment-to-population ratio for 11 countries or territories in rural and urban areas, by functional difficulty

Adults with functional difficulty in both rural and urban areas are less likely to be employed than adults without difficulty.

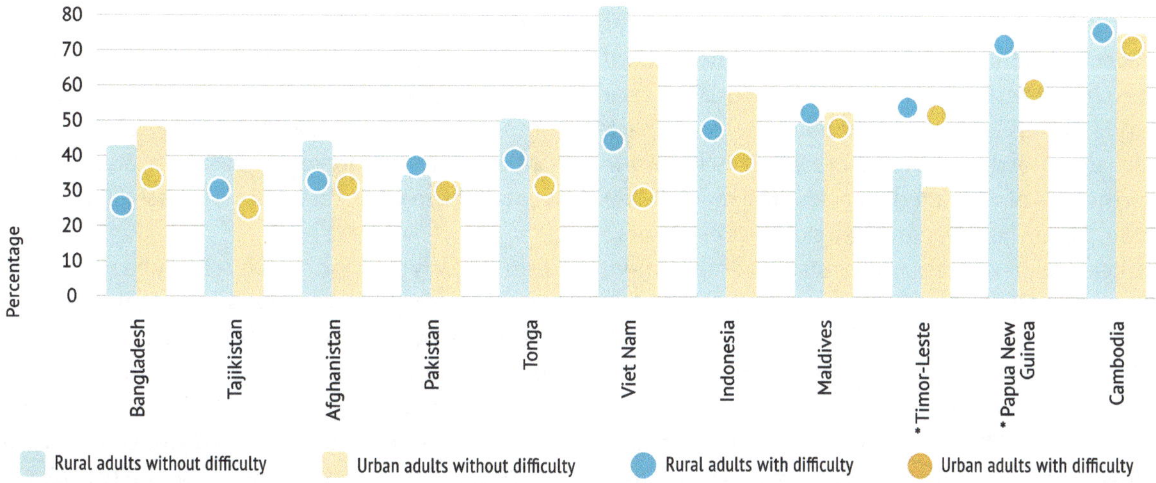

***In Papua New Guinea** and **Timor-Leste**, both rural and urban adults with difficulty appeared to have higher employment-to-population ratio than rural and urban adults without difficulty.

Source: ESCAP analysis based on data compiled by Disability Data Initiative. See Sophie Mitra and Jaclyn Yap, *The Disability Data Report 2021* (New York, 2021).
Note: The difference between rural residents with and without functional difficulty was not statistically significant in Pakistan and Papua New Guinea. For residents in urban areas, the difference was not statistically significant also in Cambodia and Maldives. The estimates for Timor-Leste and Papua New Guinea need to be interpreted with caution. In Timor-Leste, the group of persons with some difficulty also included older persons with a larger employment-to-population ratio. Further analysis is needed to adjust for the composition of these groups based on age. In Papua New Guinea, the answer scale for functional difficulty questions was reversed from the Washington Group Short Set recommendation. The answers in the questionnaire began with "Unable to do", and was then followed by "At least a lot of difficulty", then "Some difficulty" and finally "No difficulty". This could possibly contribute to the very high prevalence rate and a larger group of persons with functional difficulties, including many with less severe difficulties.

Box 2
Self-employment among the employed and disability status

Self-employment rates provide information about the proportion of employed persons in a country who run their own enterprises, with or without hired labour or who work without pay within the family unit. These workers often face higher economic risks in their work. Where a significant part of the self-employed are own-account workers (without hired labour) and contributing family workers, it may be an indication of a large agriculture sector and high informality.

When employed, persons with disabilities, were often more likely than persons without disabilities to be self-employed. Data available from 12 countries in Asia and the Pacific show that the median self-employment rate was as high as 73 per cent among employed persons with disabilities. The rate was 51 per cent for persons without disabilities. In many countries, this means that persons with disabilities have fewer opportunities for paid employment.

Percentage of employed persons for 12 countries or territories who were self-employed, by disability status

Employed persons with disabilities are more likely to be self-employed.

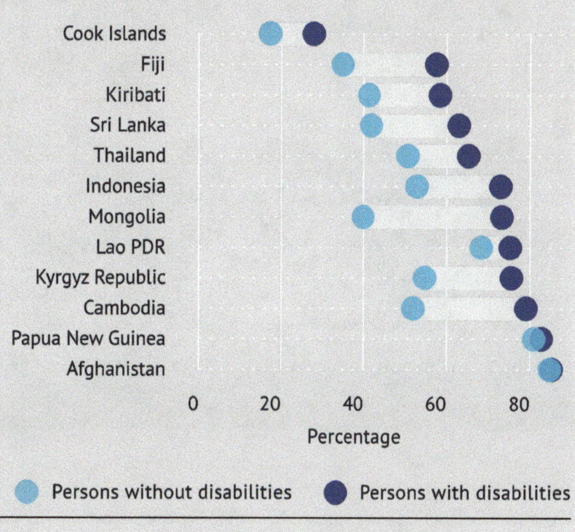

Source: ESCAP analysis based on data from ILO Department of Statistics.
Note: Self-employment jobs, as defined by the ILO, refer to employers, own-account workers, contributing family workers and members of producers' cooperatives. See ILO, "Indicator description: employment by status in employment". Available at https://ilostat.ilo.org/resources/concepts-and-definitions/description-employment-by-status/.

Box 3
Job security and earnings for employees with disabilities in Japan

Decent work concerns the opportunity to work, as reflected by the employment-to-population ratio. It also reflects other aspects of work, such as job security, earnings and working conditions. This publication does not discuss the other aspects in depth due to the lack of relevant data across the region. Data from **Japan**, however, enable a closer look into these other aspects concerning the state of employment for persons with disabilities.

The total number of persons with disabilities in Japan amounts to around 9.6 million,* representing about 7.6 per cent[a] of the total population. The Government disaggregates labour statistics to account for employment status and earnings for employed persons with disabilities.

Japan's Ministry of Health, Labour and Welfare conducts regular surveys – once every five years since the early 1960s – on the employment situation of persons with disabilities in enterprises with five or more employees. The latest survey 2018[b] found that persons with disabilities were far more likely to be non-regular employees, at 47.1 per cent of person with a physical disability, 80 per cent of persons with an intellectual disability and 74.4 per cent of persons with a psychosocial disability. Only 37.8 per cent of persons without a disability were non-regular employees.

The same pattern appears when looking at part-time employment (working for less than 30 hours per week), which accounted for 19.8 per cent of employees with a physical disability, 34.4 per cent of those with an intellectual disability and 34.4 per cent of those with a psychosocial disability.

The relatively poor job security clearly has an impact on the earnings of employees with disabilities. The average monthly wage was the lowest for employees with an intellectual disability, at around 117,000 Japanese yen (equivalent to $1,022 in 2018), followed by psychosocial disability (125,000 yen, equivalent to $1,092) and those with a physical disability (215,000 yen, equivalent to $1,878). These rates were significantly lower than the average monthly wage of employees without disabilities (306,200 yen, equivalent to $2,675).

The data from Japan draw attention to the issue of "the working poor", which includes large numbers of workers with disabilities. Without addressing gaps in job security, pay and working conditions for persons with disabilities, countries risk failing to promote the transition from sheltered employment to open market employment, as recommended by the Committee on the Rights of Persons with Disabilities in its General Comments No. 6.

Source: [a] Cabinet Office of Japan, *The White Paper on Disability* (Tokyo, 2021). Available at www.cao.go.jp/shougai/whitepaper/r03hakusho/zenbun/index-pdf.html. [b] Ministry of Health, Labour and Welfare of Japan, *Report on the 2018 Survey on Employment of Persons with Disabilities* (in Japanese) (Tokyo, 2019). Available at www.mhlw.go.jp/content/11601000/000521376.pdf.
Note: * Calculated as 7.6 per cent of the ESCAP estimate of the total population in Japan as of mid-year 2020, which was 126,476,000. See ESCAP, "Population and development indicators for Asia and the Pacific, 2020", Data Sheet (Bangkok, 2020).

1.2 Labour force participation

The labour force participation rate is a measure of the proportion of a country's working-age population that engages actively in the labour market, either by working or looking for work. It captures both persons employed and unemployed.[17] Information on the labour force participation of persons with disabilities enables insights on the share of working-age persons with disabilities who are currently working or are available and desire for work.

Disability-disaggregated data on labour force participation from the International Labour Organization (ILO) were available for 18 countries in Asia and the Pacific (figure 8), of which 15 were countries in special situations.[18] The median labour force participation rate was 31 per cent for persons with disabilities, compared with 57 per cent for persons without disabilities, with a median disability gap of 31 percentage points. In all of these countries, with the exception of Timor-Leste, persons with disabilities were less likely than persons without disabilities to be in the labour force. In 10 of these countries, the labour force participate rate of persons with disabilities was less than half the rate of persons without disabilities. And in two (of the 10) countries, persons with disabilities were five times less likely than persons without disabilities to be in the labour force.

For the male population, the median labour force participation rate of men with disabilities was 38 per cent, which was lower than that of men without disabilities, at 71 per cent. The median disability gap was 30 percentage points. In nine of the 18 countries, men with disabilities were less than half as likely as men without disabilities to participate in the labour force. And within two of those countries, the men with disabilities were less than one quarter as likely as men without disabilities to be in the labour force. Women with disabilities were less likely to be in the labour force than women without disabilities in all 18 countries: On average, it was 21 per cent for women with disabilities, and 48 per cent for women without disabilities, with a median disability gap of 25 percentage points. In 10 countries, the labour force participation rate of women without disabilities was more than double what it was for women with disabilities. And in five of those countries, the participation rate of women without disabilities was four to eight times as high as the rate for women with disabilities (figure 9).

Figure 8
Labour force participation rate for 18 countries or territories, by disability status

Persons with disabilities are much less likely to participate in the labour force.

*In **Timor-Leste** and **Papua New Guinea**, the labour force participation rates were similar for persons with and without disabilities. A minor reverse gap was observed in Timor-Leste.

Source: ESCAP analysis based on data from ILOSTAT (last update as of 18 July 2021).

Women with disabilities were further excluded from the labour force due to intersecting barriers arising from their gender and disability – with lower labour force participation rates than men without disabilities. On average, the gender-disability gap was 49 percentage points. In 15 of the 18 countries, women with disabilities were less than half as likely as men without disabilities to participate in the labour market. In four countries among them, the labour force participation rate of women with disabilities was 8 to 10 times lower than the rate for men without disabilities.

17 ILO, "Indicator description: labour force participation rate". Available at https://ilostat.ilo.org/resources/concepts-and-definitions/description-labour-force-participation-rate/.

18 There were two least developed and landlocked developing countries (Afghanistan and Lao PDR), one least developed country (Cambodia), two least developed and small island developing States (Kiribati and Timor-Leste), two landlocked developing countries (Armenia and Mongolia) and eight small island developing States (Cook Islands, Fiji, Maldives, Marshall Islands, Papua New Guinea, Samoa, Tonga and Vanuatu).

Figure 9

Labour force participation rate for 18 countries or territories, by gender and disability status

Intersectional gender-disability gaps exist in labour force participation.

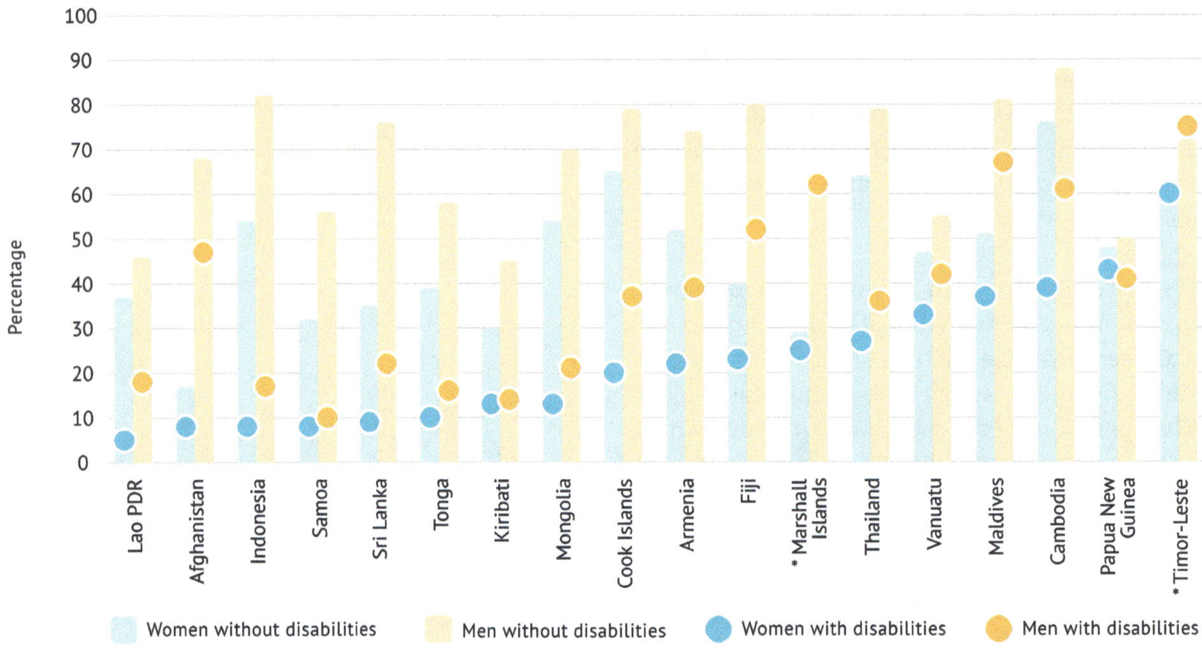

*In **Marshall Islands** and **Timor-Leste**, men with disabilities had higher labour force participation rate than the other three groups. Further analysis is needed to understand the reasons behind these exceptions.

Source: ESCAP analysis based on data from ILOSTAT (last update as of 18 July 2021).

1.3 Engagement in the informal economy

Data on adults with functional difficulty in the informal economy[19] were available from the Disability Data Initiative for 12 countries in Asia and the Pacific (figure 10), of which eight were countries in special situations.[20] The percentage of persons with functional difficulty in informality was strikingly high, with a median of 80 per cent, compared with the 66 per cent median for persons without difficulty. The median disability gap was 8 percentage points. In all countries except Pakistan, persons with any functional difficulty were more likely to be engaged in informal work than persons without difficulty.

The relationship between the severity of disability and the extent of engagement in informal work was proportional (figure 11). In 11 countries where disaggregation by extent of functional difficulty was available, the median percentage of adults in informal work was 81 per cent for persons with some difficulty and 87 per cent for those with at least a lot of difficulty. It was only 67 per cent for persons with no difficulty. The median disability gap widened with the increase in the severity of disability. It was 7 percentage points when comparing persons with some difficulty against those without difficulty. It was 9 percentage points when comparing persons with at least a lot of difficulty to those without any difficulty. In six of the 11 countries, there was a gradient in the share of adults engaged in informal work, with the share in informal work the greatest among persons with at least a lot of difficulty, followed by persons with some difficulty and then by persons with no difficulty. In nine of these 11 countries, persons with some or with a lot of functional difficulty were more likely to be engaged in informal work than persons without any difficulty.

Within both the male and female populations, persons with any functional difficulty were more likely to be engaged in informal work than persons without functional difficulty (figure 12). In the 12 countries with available data, the median percentage of men in informal work was 69 per cent for those with difficulty and 55 per

19 "Adults in informal work" measures the share of the adult population who do informal work: those who are self-employed, those who work for a micro-enterprise with five or fewer employees or in a firm that is unregistered and those who have no written contract with their employer. Family workers without pay are included as informal workers.

20 There was one least developed and landlocked developing country (Afghanistan), two least developed countries (Bangladesh and Cambodia), one least developed and small island developing country (Timor-Leste) and four small island developing States (Maldives, Papua New Guinea, Tonga and Vanuatu).

cent for those without difficulty. The median disability gap was 8 percentage points. Regarding women with and without difficulty in informal work, the median percentage was 60 per cent and 47 per cent, respectively. The disability gap was 6 percentage points. In nine of the 12 countries, the percentage of men with any functional difficulty in informal work was higher than the share among men without difficulty. It was a similar situation for women in 10 of those 12 countries.

Interestingly, a closer look at the intersection between gender and disability reveals mixed results. The median gender–disability gap stands at 13 percentage points. On average, women with functional difficulty were 20 per cent more likely than men without difficulty to engage in informal work. In seven of the 12 countries, women with functional difficulty were more likely to be in the informal economy than men without difficulty.[21] There was a significant reverse gender–disability gap in two countries, as high as 61 percentage points in Pakistan and 72 percentage points in the Maldives. In these two countries, men without functional difficulty were three to four times more likely than women with functional difficulty to be in the informal economy. The mixed picture could stem from the fact that a significant proportion of women were not in employment in some countries.[22]

In both rural and urban areas, persons with functional difficulty are more likely to be in informal work than those without difficulty within the same geographical classification (figure 13). In the 10 countries with available data, the percentages of rural residents with and without difficulty in informal work, on average, were 87 per cent and 79 per cent, respectively. The median gap was 8 percentage points. For urban residents with and without difficulty, the percentages of adults in informal work were 70 per cent and 59 per cent, respectively, with the median gap at 3 percentage points. In two countries (Tonga and Viet Nam), urban residents with functional difficulty were more than 50 per cent more likely to be working in informality than urban residents without difficulty.

Intersectionality further disadvantaged persons with any functional difficulty in rural areas. The median rural–disability gap (rural residents with difficulty compared with urban residents without difficulty) was 28 percentage points. In nine of the 10 countries with this data, rural residents with functional difficulty were more likely than urban residents without difficulties to engage in informal work. In three countries, rural residents with functional difficulty were two to five times more likely than urban residents without functional difficulty to be in informal work. The large intersectional gap stems from wide disparities between urban and rural residents engaging in informality: The median urban–rural gap (urban residents and rural residents) in 10 countries for persons with functional difficulty was 17 percentage points. For persons without difficulty, it was 20 percentage points.

Figure 10
Percentage of adults engaged in informal work for 12 countries or territories, by functional difficulty

Persons with functional difficulty are more likely to engage in informal work.

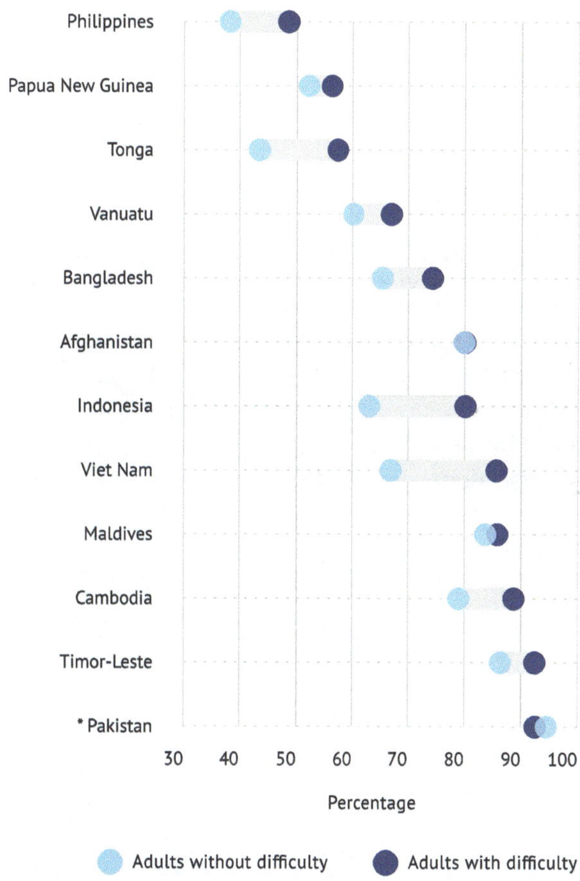

*In **Pakistan**, the share of adults engaged in informal work was higher among persons without functional difficulty than among persons with difficulty. Further analysis is needed to understand the reason behind this exception.

Source: ESCAP analysis based on data compiled by Disability Data Initiative. See Sophie Mitra and Jaclyn Yap, *The Disability Data Report 2021* (New York, 2021).
Note: The difference between the two groups was not statistically significant in Afghanistan.

21 In the same seven countries, women with and without functional difficulty were more likely to be in informal work than their male counterparts. In the 12 countries with available data, the median gender gap (percentage of female adults in informal work minus percentage of male adults in informal work) was 6 and 5 percentage points for persons with and without difficulty, respectively.

22 ILO, *Women and Men in the Informal Economy: A Statistical Picture* (third edition) (Geneva, 2018).

Figure 11
Percentage of adults engaged in informal work for 11 countries or territories, by extent of functional difficulty

Persons with a lot of functional difficulty are more likely to engage in informal work, followed by persons with some difficulty and then persons without functional difficulty.

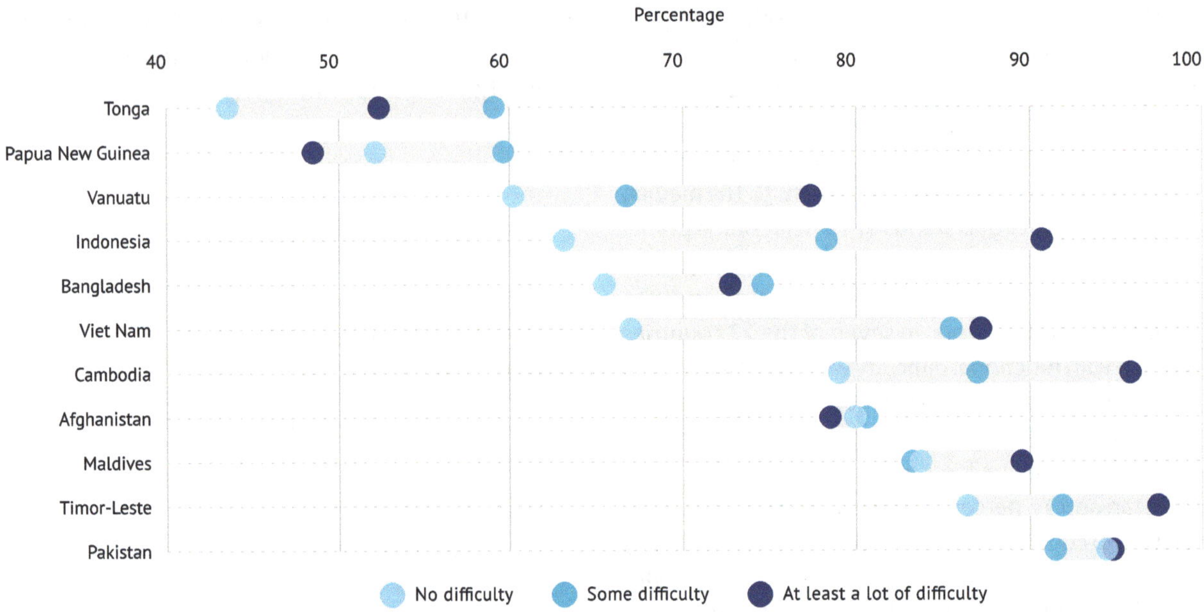

Source: ESCAP analysis based on data compiled by Disability Data Initiative. See Sophie Mitra and Jaclyn Yap, *The Disability Data Report 2021* (New York, 2021).
Note: The difference between persons with some functional difficulty and without difficulty was not statistically significant in Afghanistan and Maldives. The difference between persons with a lot of functional difficulty and without difficulty was not statistically significant in Afghanistan and Pakistan.

Figure 12
Percentage of adults engaged in informal work for 12 countries or territories, by gender and functional difficulty

Intersectional gender-disability gaps exist in informal employment.

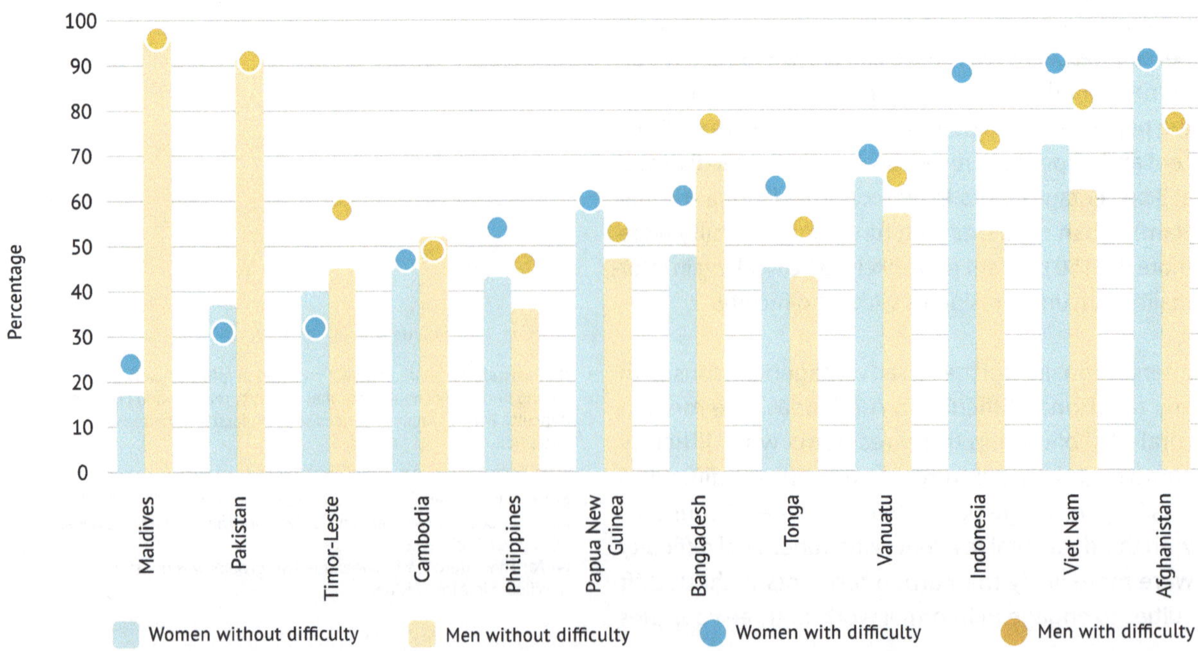

Source: ESCAP analysis based on data compiled by Disability Data Initiative. See Sophie Mitra and Jaclyn Yap, *The Disability Data Report 2021* (New York, 2021).
Note: The difference between men with and without functional difficulty was not statistically significant in Afghanistan, Cambodia, Maldives and Pakistan. For women with and without functional difficulty, the difference was not statistically significant in Afghanistan, Cambodia, Pakistan and Papua New Guinea.

Figure 13
Percentage of adults engaged in informal work for 10 countries or territories, by rural–urban locale and functional difficulty

Rural adults with functional difficulty are more likely to engage in informal work.

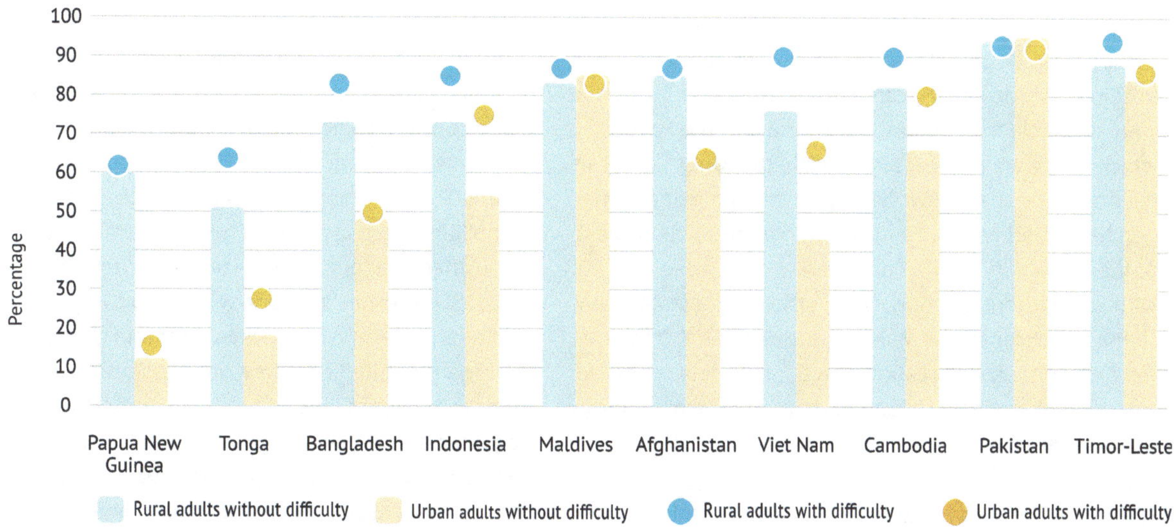

Source: ESCAP analysis based on data compiled by Disability Data Initiative. See Sophie Mitra and Jaclyn Yap, *The Disability Data Report 2021* (New York, 2021).
Note: The difference between rural adults with and without functional was not statistically significant in Pakistan and Papua New Guinea. For adults in urban areas, the difference was not statistically significant in Afghanistan, Bangladesh and Maldives.

The percentage of persons with functional difficulty engaging in informal work remained high across the life cycle, with a slight decline for persons aged 30–44. A disability gap in informality existed across all ages, with a similar dip for the 30–44 age group (table 2).[23]

Individual country studies corroborate the observation of disability gap in engagement in informal work: In Indonesia, 65 per cent of persons with mild disabilities and 76 per cent of persons with severe disabilities were reported to be working in informal jobs.[24] In Timor-Leste, 62 per cent of persons with disabilities were reported to be own-account workers, and 21 per cent employed as contributing family workers.[25] In Australia, persons with disabilities had a higher rate of self-employment (at 13 per cent) than persons without disabilities (at 10 per cent).[26] The available evidence indicated that they were involved in a range of services, such as tailoring, massage and shopkeeping.[27]

Table 2
Persons with functional difficulty for 12 countries or territories, by age group

	Age group		
	15-29	**30-44**	**45-64**
Adults with functional difficulty in informal work (median %)	72%	68%	77%
Countries in which persons with functional difficulty have higher percentages of adults in informal work (of 12 countries)	10 countries	9 countries	7 ountries
Median gap (in percentage points, 12 countries)	3 pp	1 pp	2 pp

Source: ESCAP analysis based on data compiled by Disability Data Initiative. See Sophie Mitra and Jaclyn Yap, *The Disability Data Report 2021* (New York, 2021).

23 For the age group 15-29, the difference between persons with and without functional difficulty was not statistically significant in six of the 12 countries (Afghanistan, Cambodia, Pakistan, Timor-Leste, Tonga and Vanuatu). For the age group 30-44, the difference also was not statistically significant in six of those 12 countries (Afghanistan, Bangladesh, Cambodia, Papua New Guinea, Timor-Leste and Tonga). For the age group 45-64, the difference between persons with and without difficulty was not statistically significant in five of those 12 countries (Afghanistan, Bangladesh, Maldives, Papua New Guinea and Tonga).
24 ILO, *Final Report-Mapping Persons with Disabilities in Indonesia Labor Market* (Jakarta, 2017).
25 National Statistics Directorate and UNFPA, *Timor-Leste Population and Housing Census, 2010: Analytical Report on Disability*, Vol. 10 (Dili, 2012).
26 Simon Darcy and others, *Australia's Disability Entrepreneurial Ecosystem: Experiences of People with Disability with Microenterprises, Self-employment and Entrepreneurship* (Sydney, 2020).
27 See, for example, ILO, *Disabilities and Decent Work in the Pacific: The Case for Disability Inclusive Employment* (Suva, 2012).

Box 4
Women in managerial positions

Women's representation in leadership and management is an important indicator for gender equality in employment. Disability-disaggregated data on women in managerial positions* are extremely scarce around the world. Such data were available for 11 countries in Asia and the Pacific, of which nine were countries in special situations.** In these countries, the share of working women who had a managerial position was extremely low in general, regardless of their disability status. The difference between women with and without functional difficulty was not statistically significant except in the Maldives and Viet Nam.*** Further research, notably using Labour Force Survey data, is needed to explore the potential disability gap in women's holding managerial positions.

Although data from the region are limited, the latest evidence in the United States showed that women with disabilities were less likely than women without disabilities – but more likely than men with disabilities – to work in management or in a professional or related occupation.[a]

Gender was a primary contributing factor to women's underrepresentation in managerial positions, regardless of their disability status. The findings from the 11 countries in Asia and the Pacific were consistent with general observations that significant gender gaps continue to prevail in the world of work, with a "leaking" pipeline of female talent. This leaking pipeline also applies to women with disabilities. Despite progress made on closing gender gaps in business leadership, the Asia–Pacific region is lagging: In 2018, there was only one woman to every four men in business leadership roles, while it was four women for every 10 men globally.[b] The slow progress on closing gender gaps in business leadership is disproportionate to the region's declining gender gaps in education and increasing female labour force participation.[c] Hence, efforts to support women with disabilities in the labour market and in their pursuit of leadership roles would need to be aligned with the broader call for gender equality in the world of work.

The "leaking" pipeline of female talent[d]

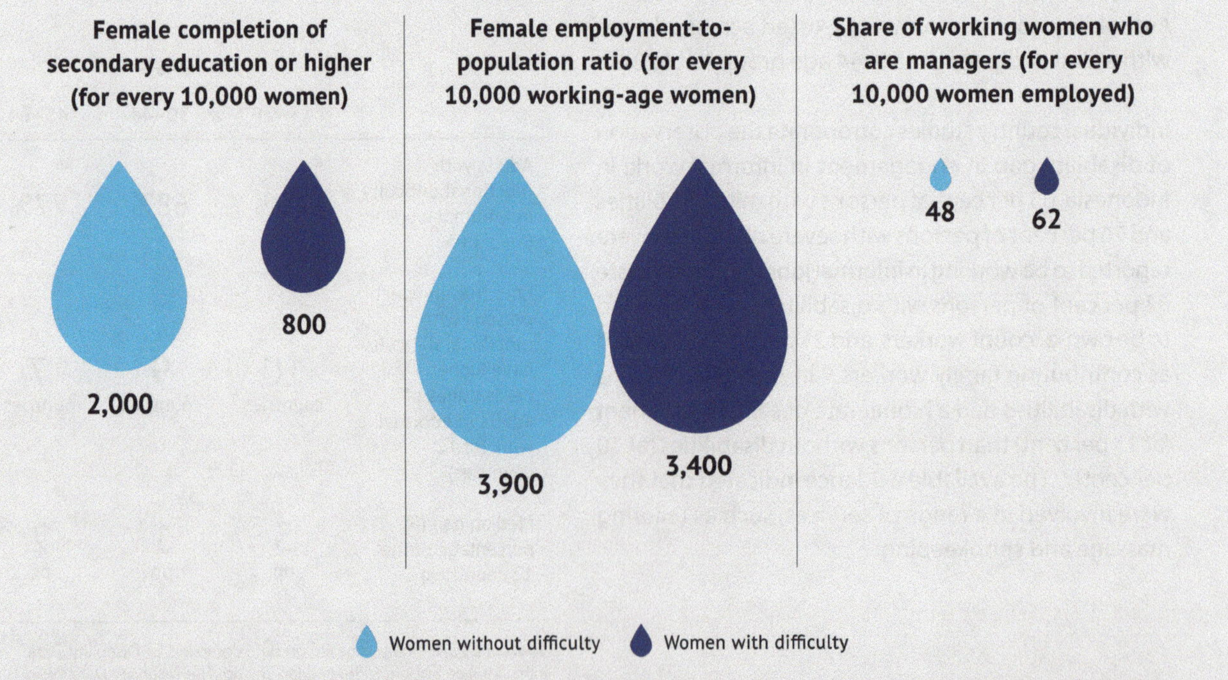

Source: [a] United States Department of Labor, Office of Disability Employment Policy, "Spotlight on women with disabilities", March 2021. Research Brief (Washington, D.C., 2021). Available at www.dol.gov/sites/dolgov/files/ODEP/pdf/Spotlight-on-Women-with-Disabilities-March-2021.pdf; [b] McKinsey Global Institute, *The Power of Parity: Advancing Women's Equality in Asia Pacific* (New York, 2018). Available at www.mckinsey.com/~/media/mckinsey/featured%20insights/gender%20equality/the%20power%20of%20parity%20advancing%20womens%20equality%20in%20asia%20pacific/mgi-the-power-of-parity-advancing-womens-equality-in-asia-pacific-full-report.pdf; [c] ibid.; [d] ESCAP analysis based on data from 11 countries in Asia and the Pacific compiled by Disability Data Initiative. See Sophie Mitra and Jaclyn Yap, *The Disability Data Report 2021* (New York, 2021). Figures presented are median values of all countries with the data.
Note: * Women in managerial positions is the share of working women who hold managerial positions. This definition varies from the relevant SDG Indicator 5.5.2, which tracks the share of managerial positions occupied by women. ** There was one least developed and landlocked developing country (Afghanistan), two least developed countries (Bangladesh and Cambodia), two least developed and small island developing States (Kiribati and Timor-Leste) and four small island developing States (Maldives, Papua New Guinea, Tonga and Vanuatu). *** Statistical significance was 10 per cent for the Maldives and 1 per cent for Viet Nam.

1.4 Youths who are out of school and not employed

Disability-disaggregated data on youth idle rates[28] were available for 12 countries in Asia and the Pacific (figure 14), of which nine were countries in special situations.[29] The median idle rate for those countries was 27 per cent for youths with functional difficulty and 18 per cent for youths without functional difficulty. The median disability gap was 5 percentage points. In 10 of those countries, the percentage of idle youths with functional difficulty was higher than for youths without functional difficulty.

A closer look at the severity of disability and youth idleness yields interesting observations (table 3 and figure 15). While the median idle rate and disability gap increased progressively with the extent of functional difficulty in the 10 countries with available data, fewer countries had disability gap for idle youths with at least a lot of difficulty than for idle youths with some difficulty.

Table 3
Median youth idle rate and disability gap for 10 countries or territories, by extent of function difficulty

	Extent of functional difficulty		
	None	**Some difficulty**	**At least a lot of difficulty**
Median youth idle rate	20%	25%	36%
Countries in which youths with functional difficulty have higher idle rates (of 10 countries)	-	9 countries	6 countries
Median gap (in percentage points, 10 countries)	-	5 pp	6 pp

Source: ESCAP analysis based on data compiled by Disability Data Initiative. See Sophie Mitra and Jaclyn Yap, *The Disability Data Report 2021* (New York, 2021).

Figure 14
Share of youths (aged 15–24) who were idle in 12 countries or territories, by functional difficulty

Youths with functional difficulty are more likely to be idle than their peers without functional difficulty.

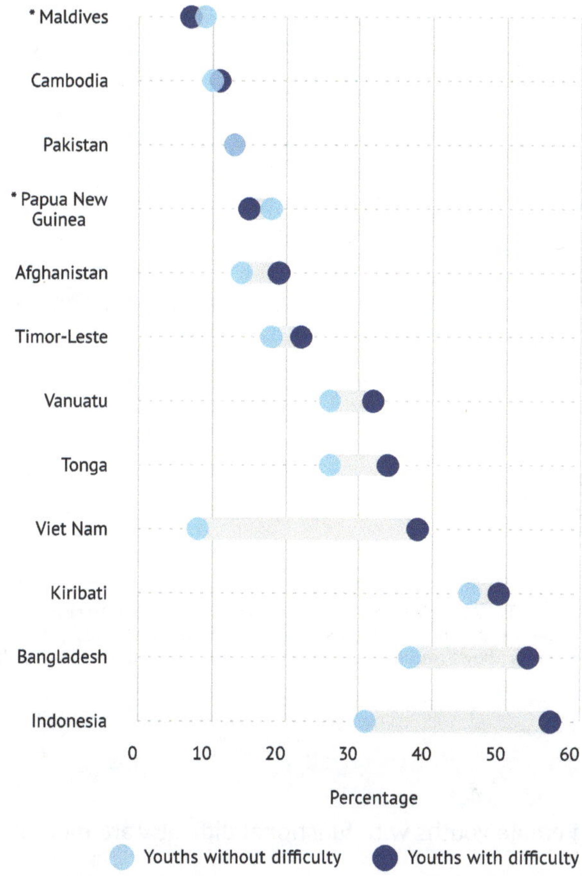

*In **Maldives** and **Papua New Guinea**, youths without difficulty appeared to have higher idle rate. Further analysis is needed to understand the reason behind these exceptions.

Source: ESCAP analysis based on data compiled by Disability Data Initiative. See Sophie Mitra and Jaclyn Yap, *The Disability Data Report 2021* (New York, 2021).
Note: The difference in the idle rate between youths with and without functional difficulty was not statistically significant in Cambodia, Pakistan, Papua New Guinea and Timor-Leste.

While there was a reverse disability gap – with youths without functional difficulty more likely to be idle than persons with at least a lot of difficulty - in four countries, in three other countries, youths with at least a lot of difficulty were more than twice as likely as youths without difficulty to be idle. And in one country (Viet Nam), the idle rate of youths with at least a lot of difficulty was almost nine times what it is for youths without difficulty.

28 The "youth idle rate" captures the share of youths aged 15–24 who are not enrolled in school or not employed. Because information on training was not consistently available, the youth idle rate does not reflect whether youths might be in training. It thus differs slightly from the rate of youth not in employment, education or training (NEET).

29 There was one least developed and landlocked developing country (Afghanistan), two least developed countries (Bangladesh and Cambodia), two least developed and small island developing States (Kiribati and Timor-Leste) and four small island developing States (Maldives, Papua New Guinea, Tonga and Vanuatu).

Figure 15
Share of youths (aged 15–24) who were idle in 10 countries or territories, by extent of functional difficulty

Youths with severer functional difficulty are more likely to be idle, but the situation varies by country.

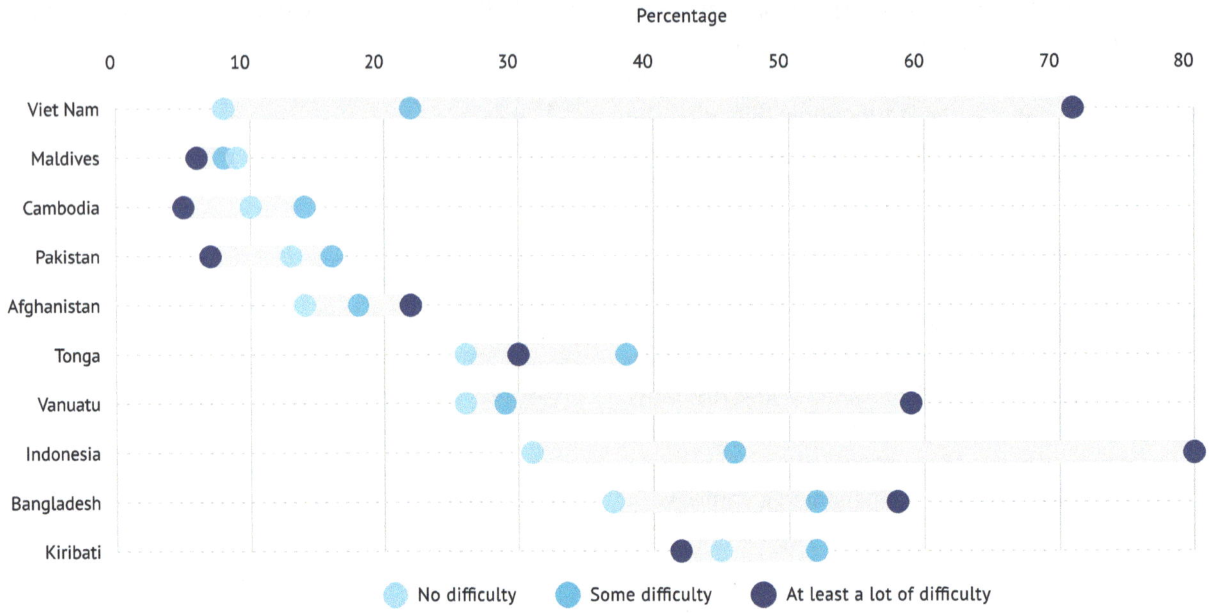

Source: ESCAP analysis based on data compiled by Disability Data Initiative. See Sophie Mitra and Jaclyn Yap, *The Disability Data Report 2021* (New York, 2021).
Note: The difference between youths with "some (functional) difficulty" and without difficulty in the idle rate was not statistically significant in Cambodia and Maldives. The difference between youths with "at least a lot of (functional) difficulty" and without difficulty was also not statistically significant in Kiribati and Tonga.

Figure 16
Share of youths (aged 15–24) who were idle in 10 countries or territories, by gender and functional difficulty

Female youths with functional difficulty are more likely to be idle.

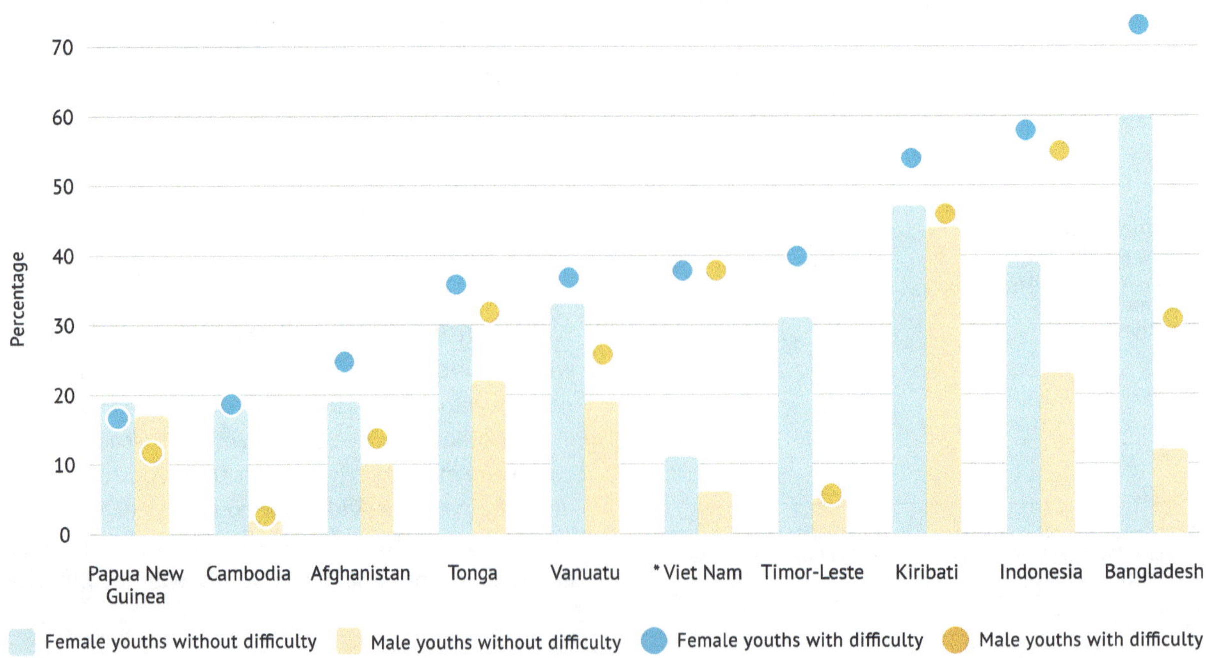

*In **Viet Nam**, the idle rates for male and female youths with functional difficulty were similar.

Source: ESCAP analysis based on data compiled by Disability Data Initiative. See Sophie Mitra and Jaclyn Yap, *The Disability Data Report 2021* (New York, 2021).
Note: The difference between male youths with and without functional difficulty in the idle rate was not statistically significant in Cambodia, Kiribati and Timor-Leste. For female youths with and without functional difficulty, the difference was not statistically significant in Cambodia and Papua New Guinea.

A disability gap also appeared within the male and female populations (figure 16). In the 10 countries with available data, the idle rate reached 28 per cent for male youths with functional difficulty but only 14 per cent for male youths without functional difficulty. The median disability gap among the male youths was 5 percentage points. For female youths with functional difficulty, the median idle rate was 38 per cent and 31 per cent for female youths without functional difficulty. The median disability gap was 7 percentage points. Nine of the 10 countries had higher idle rates for both male and female youths with functional difficulty than for youths without functional difficulty. Among the male population in four countries, male youths with functional difficulty were more than twice as likely to be idle as male youths without functional difficulty. In one of those countries (Viet Nam), the idle rate for male youths with functional difficulty was almost seven times what it was for male youths without functional difficulty. And in Viet Nam, the idle rate for female youths with functional difficulty was almost four times what it was for female youths without functional difficulty.

In terms of gender-based gaps in the 10 countries, the median gender gap between female and male youths without difficulty was 11 percentage points. It was 10 percentage points among youths with functional difficulty. The idle rate for female youths was higher than for male youths for those with and without functional difficulty, except in Viet Nam where the idle rates for male and female youths with functional difficulty were similar. Compared with male youths with functional difficulty, female youths with functional difficulty were more than twice as likely to be idle in Bangladesh, almost six times to be so in Cambodia and almost seven times in Timor-Leste.

The combined disadvantages of disability and being female increase the likelihood of youth idleness substantially. In all 10 countries with that data, the idle rate for female youths with functional difficulty was higher than for male youths without difficulty, with the median disability gap at 18 percentage points. On average, female youths with functional difficulty were more than 2.5 times likely to be idle than male youths without difficulty. The idle rate of the female youths with functional difficulty was more than six times what it is for male youths without functional difficulty in Bangladesh and Viet Nam, more than eight times in Timor-Leste and more than 12 times in Cambodia.

Figure 17
Share of youths (aged 15–24) who were idle in nine countries or territories, by rural–urban locale and functional difficulty

Youths with functional difficulty, especially those living in rural areas, are more likely to be idle.

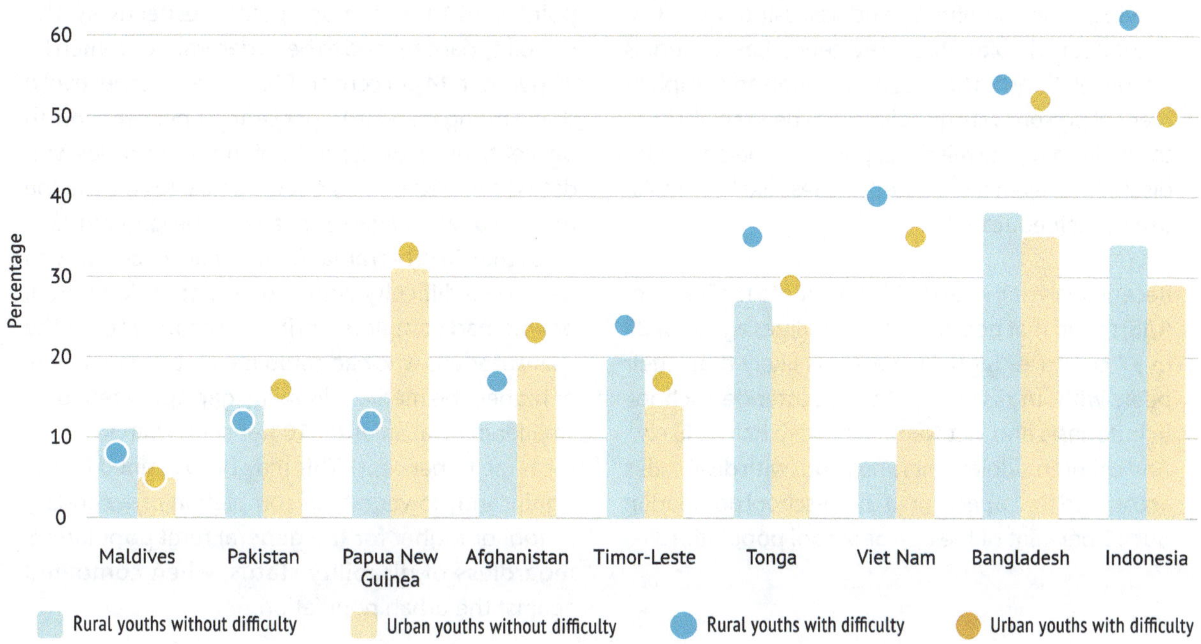

Source: ESCAP analysis based on data compiled by Disability Data Initiative. See Sophie Mitra and Jaclyn Yap, *The Disability Data Report 2021* (New York, 2021).
Note: The difference between rural youths with and without functional difficulty was not statistically significant in Pakistan, Papua New Guinea and Timor-Leste. For youths in urban areas, the difference was not statistically significant in Afghanistan, Maldives, Papua New Guinea, Timor-Leste and Tonga.

Three of the four countries with an idle rate for female youths with difficulty that was more than six times higher than what it was for male youths without difficulty were in South-East Asia. The Pacific had comparatively smaller gender-disability gaps than the other parts of the region.

When disaggregated by urban or rural residence, the findings showed a disability gap for youths with functional difficulty in both locales (figure 17). In the nine countries with available data, rural youths with and without functional difficulty had a median idle rate of 24 per cent and 15 per cent, respectively. In urban areas, the idle rates were 29 per cent for youths with functional difficulty and 19 per cent for youths without functional difficulty. The median disability gap was 5 percentage points in both areas. Rural youths with functional difficulty had a higher idle rate in six of the nine countries, while urban youths with functional difficulty were more likely to be idle in all nine countries that had that data. The disability gap was particularly high in Viet Nam, where youths with functional difficulty were more than 5.5 times likely to be idle than youths without difficulty in rural areas and more than three times than in urban areas. The disability gap also widened as a result of intersectionality, with the median rural–disability gap (rural youths with difficulty compared against urban youths without difficulty) at 11 percentage points. On average, rural youths with functional difficulty were more than 1.5 times likely to be idle than urban youths without difficulty.

Box 5

Disability-disaggregated data on academic education and technical and vocational education and training

Persons with disabilities are the most frequently identified group with vulnerabilities in constitutions, legislation and policies directly related to inclusive education. Nonetheless, interpretation of the education disability gap is challenged by the poor alignment of relevant definitions (such as age groups) in disability measures and education indicators. Also, the data – both statistical and administrative – are often not comparable across countries due to the varying ways of defining and assessing disability. The lack of reliable data and evidence-based studies on the relationship between education and employment of persons with disabilities has been an obstacle to challenging the misconception that persons with disabilities, even if educated, are less likely to make use of their education.[a]

Recent analysis by the UNESCO Institute for Statistics (UIS) found that persons with disabilities aged 15–29 in 37 countries globally were less likely than their peers without disabilities to have attended school. In Indonesia and Viet Nam, they were half as likely.[b] And children, adolescents and youth with disabilities accounted for 12 per cent of the in-school population but 15 per cent of the out-of-school population.[c]

The Disability Data Initiative compiled disaggregated education data from 14 countries in the Asia–Pacific region. The data revealed that adults with functional difficulty were generally less likely to have ever attended school, to have completed primary school or to have completed secondary school or higher education than their peers who had no functional difficulty. The median disability gap on these three indicators was 16 percentage points, 12 percentage points and 14 percentage points, respectively. The disability gaps tended to be larger among women (at 20 per cent, 14 per cent and 16 per cent, respectively) than among men (at 13 per cent, 11 per cent and 10 per cent, respectively). In 11 of the 14 countries with data disaggregated by geographical residence, the median disability gap appeared to be larger in rural areas than in urban areas for the share of adults with functional difficulty who had ever attended school or who had completed primary school. Yet, for the share of adults who had completed secondary school or higher, the median disability gap appeared to be smaller in rural areas (at 10 per cent) than in urban areas (at 17 per cent). This may be explained by the significantly lower rate of completion of secondary school or higher for the general rural population, regardless of disability status, when compared against the urban population.

Box 5 (Continued)

Share of adults with and without functional difficulty in 14 countries or territories who had obtained different levels of education[d]

Persons with disabilities are less likely to have ever attended school, have completed primary school and have completed secondary school or higher.

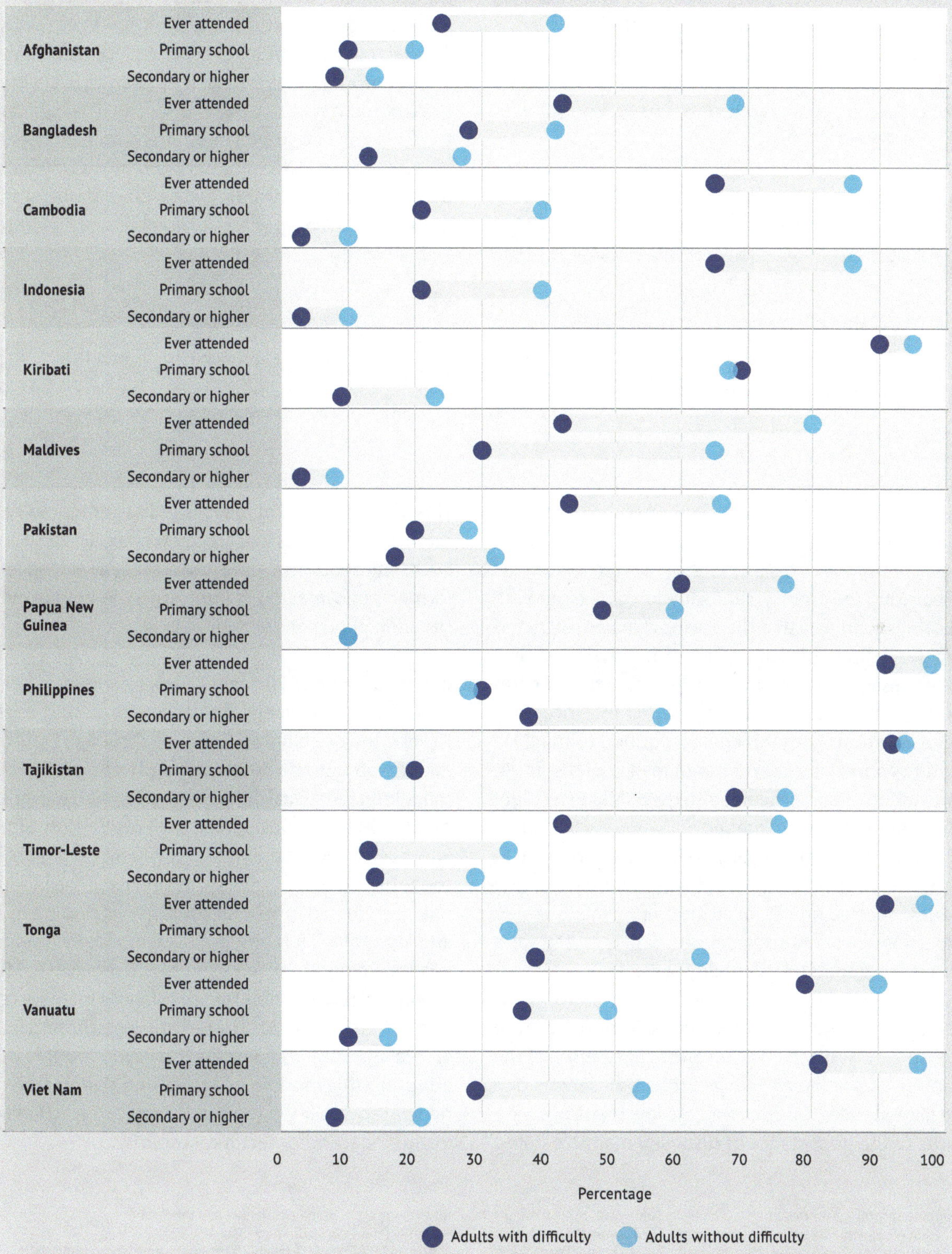

Note: The difference in completion of secondary education or higher between persons with and without functional difficulty was not statistically significant in Papua New Guinea.

Box 5 (Continued)

Technical and vocational education and training (TVET) has an important role in facilitating the transition to employment and decent work due to its links to the labour market. It thus enables social mobility for vulnerable and marginalized groups, including persons with disabilities. The fourth *Global Report on Adult Learning and Education* describes generally low participation in adult education and the slowest increase in participation since 2015 for adults with disabilities.[e]

Despite two relevant Sustainable Development Goal targets (4.3 and 4.5), disability-disaggregated statistics on participation in TVET are scarce. The data gap appears to be the largest in Asia and the Pacific, with six of the 37 countries covered by the *Global Report on Adult Learning and Education* lacking such data.[f] Where such data are collected and published, the enrolment rates for persons with disabilities are historically far below the population rate. In Australia, for example, only around 6–7 per cent of enrolment in TVET programmes between 2015 and 2018 were students who had a declared disability. The data on the transition into employment after completion also showed a great difference between those who had declared a disability and those who had not, with gaps over the same years varying between 16 and 24 per cent.[g]

Source: [a] Kamal Lamichhane, *Disability, Education and Employment in Developing Countries: From Charity to Investment* (Cambridge, 2015); [b] UNESCO Institute for Statistics, "Education and disability: analysis of data from 49 Countries", Information Paper N. 49 (Montreal, 2018); UNESCO, *Global Education Monitoring Report 2020: Inclusion and Education: All Means All* (Paris, 2020); [c] UNESCO, *Global Education Monitoring Report 2020: Inclusion and Education: All Means All* (Paris, 2020); [d] ESCAP analysis based on data compiled by Disability Data Initiative. See Sophie Mitra and Jaclyn Yap, *The Disability Data Report 2021* (New York, 2021); [e] UNESCO Institute for Lifelong Learning, *Fourth Global Report on Adult Learning and Education: Leave No One Behind: Participation, Equity and Inclusion* (Hamburg, 2019); [f] ibid.; [g] Australian Disability Clearinghouse on Education and Training, "Vocational education and training (VET) statistics". Available at www.adcet.edu.au/inclusive-teaching/understanding-disability/vet-statistics.

1.5 Improving disability-disaggregated employment data

Measuring the employment situation of persons with disabilities in Asia and the Pacific remains restricted by the limited availability and poor quality of disability-disaggregated labour data across the 58 countries and territories of the region. For instance, only 35 Asia–Pacific governments responded to the 2017 country survey for the midpoint review of the implementation of the Incheon Strategy to "Make the Right Real" for Persons with Disabilities in Asia and the Pacific (table 4).[30] Of them, several governments responded to individual indicators, but only nine countries and territories reported figures for all the employment-related questions. In a few instances, the data reported were not disaggregated by disability or sex.[31]

Data gaps often arise from the failure to capture persons with disabilities in statistical systems of the labour, education and social protection sectors due to limited data collection and the low levels of awareness of the importance of disability mainstreaming. This leads to a lack of disability-disaggregated data, particularly statistics that are comparable across sectors. Such data deficiencies limit the efficacy of evidence-informed policymaking in improving the employment situation of persons with disabilities.

In light of the need for more comprehensive information on the employment of persons with disabilities, the ILO and the Washington Group on Disability Statistics have collaborated in developing and testing a disability module on functional difficulties and barriers to employment.[32] Built on questions of the Washington Group Short Set on Functioning that is widely used globally to capture data on disability prevalence,[33] the module has been tested in several countries, including India and Mongolia.[34] It is being considered for inclusion in a forthcoming labour force survey in Bangladesh.[35] The module is now available for use in labour force surveys and other population-based surveys that include employment. Many countries, however, struggle with adopting this module or something comparable to generate disability-disaggregated data due to limited institutional and/or technical capacity.

30 See section 2.2 for details on the Incheon Strategy to "Make the Right Real" for Persons with Disabilities in Asia and the Pacific.

31 ESCAP, *Building Disability-inclusive Societies in Asia and the Pacific: Assessing Progress of the Incheon Strategy* (Bangkok, 2018).

32 Washington Group on Disability Statistics, "WG ILO Labor Force Survey Disability Module (LFS-DM)". Available at www.washingtongroup-disability.com/question-sets/wg-ilo-labor-force-survey-disability-module-lfs-dm/.

33 See Annex C for details on the Washington Group Short Set on Functioning.

34 Washington Group on Disability Statistics, *Report of the Washington Group (WG) on Disability Statistics including an Executive Summary of the 19th Annual Meeting* (Hyattsville, 2019).

35 ILO Statistics Department, personal communication, November 2020.

Table 4
Reporting on employment-related Incheon Strategy indicators by 35 participating governments (as of 2017)

Incheon Strategy indicators	No. of ESCAP member States that reported	No. of ESCAP associate members that reported
1.2 Ratio of persons with disabilities in employment to the general population in employment		
Employment-to-population ratio, by sex and disability status	18	1
Unemployment rate, by sex and disability status	17	1
Labour force participation rate, by sex and disability status	17	1
Ratio of persons with disabilities in employment to general population in employment, by sex	17	1
1.3 Proportion of persons with disabilities who participate in government-funded vocational training and other employment-support programmes as a proportion of all people trained		
Participation of persons with disabilities in government-funded vocational training programmes, by sex	14	3

Source: ESCAP, *Building Disability-inclusive Societies in Asia and the Pacific: Assessing Progress of the Incheon Strategy* (Bangkok, 2018).

Box 6
Washington Group and ILO Labour Force Survey disability module

The Labour Force Survey disability module that the International Labour Organization and Washington Group on Disability Statistics have developed has five sections:

- Disability identification, using the Washington Group Short Set on Functioning with two additional, optional questions on anxiety and depression.
- Barriers to employment, including qualification, training and skills; availability of suitable transport to and from the workplace; assistance in identifying appropriate jobs; attitudes towards persons with disabilities; availability of special equipment or assistive devices; availability of more flexible work schedules or work tasks arrangements; availability of a more accommodating workplace; and supportiveness of family members.
- Accommodations necessary for employment: whether the work schedule or work tasks have been arranged or the workplace has been modified to account for difficulties the individual has in performing certain activities.
- Attitudes: willingness of employers to hire persons with disabilities and willingness of workers to work alongside persons with disabilities.
- Social protection: whether the individual's difficulties have been officially recognized or certified and whether they receive disability-related cash benefits from the government.

Note: Additional information, including national adaptation guides, variable derivation guides and Labour Force Survey integration guide are provided on the ILO website: https://ilostat.ilo.org/resources/lfs-resources/.

1.6 Summary

The unemployment, underemployment and exclusion of persons with disabilities from the labour market led to social and economic losses estimated at between 3 and 7 per cent of gross domestic product.[36] It is therefore critical for policymakers to be cognizant of these substantial costs and to integrate disability inclusion when designing measures to promote productive employment and decent work.

In seeking to understand the employment situation of persons with disabilities and to develop appropriate policy measures, it is also important to emphasize that persons with disabilities have very diverse profiles, with different socioeconomic circumstances and varying levels of physical, sensory, intellectual and/or psychosocial impairments. In addition, depending on whether these impairments date from birth, childhood, teenage years or adulthood, their work-related profiles will differ significantly because of disparate educational, training and work experiences or lack thereof. Whether these impairments are observable or invisible also affects the extent to which persons with disabilities experience exclusion and disadvantage: Persons with invisible disabilities are less likely to face discriminatory barriers to employment. Yet, they may find it difficult to request and obtain reasonable accommodation when such support becomes required, if no prior disclosure of a disability was made to their employer.[37]

The next chapters discuss the shifts in discourse in promoting employment for persons with disabilities over the past decades. They lead to strategies and recommendations to improve the employment situation of persons with disabilities in Asia and the Pacific.

36 Based on an exploratory study of 10 low- and middle-income developing countries in Africa and Asia. See ILO, "The price of exclusion: The economic consequences of excluding people with disabilities from the world of work", Employment Working Paper No. 43 (Geneva, 2009).

37 Michael J. Prince, "Persons with invisible disabilities and workplace accommodation: findings from a scoping literature review", *Journal of Vocational Rehabilitation*, vol. 26, No. 1 (January 2017).

Chapter 2

Transformed understanding of disability and changes in promoting employment opportunities for persons with disabilities

2.1 Models of disability

In recent decades, the understanding of disability has evolved significantly. Prior to the 1980s, disability was traditionally regarded as a personal problem requiring medical and charitable actions. Under this medical model of disability, persons with a disability were typically viewed as incapable and unable to participate in society, including in the open labour market, due to their impairment. They therefore had to rely on the goodwill of others or social welfare provisions to meet their basic needs.[38] Accordingly, policies focused on the provision of social welfare and assistance, segregated medical and rehabilitation services and employment in separate centres set aside for persons with disabilities.

Since the 1980s, a social model of disability has emerged whereby barriers to the participation of persons with disabilities in society, including the labour market, are perceived as stemming from discriminatory and inaccessible social and physical environments.[39] Such an environment, in turn, is now seen as the result of laws, policies, programmes and services that perpetuate the medical or social welfare approach; the inaccessible built and communications environments; and public perceptions of disability and ensuing assumptions about persons with disabilities.

Policies now aim at prohibiting discrimination and promoting inclusion in the mainstream of society, including employment in mainstream firms. These policies include developing community-based services that provide support to persons with disabilities; promoting accessibility of the built environment and of information and communications technology; and tackling negative attitudes and mistaken assumptions about persons with disabilities.

More recently, a human rights model of disability has emerged that affirms that persons with disabilities are holders of rights and entitled to human dignity; that impairments are to be considered as aspects of human diversity; and that persons with disabilities are active stakeholders in all matters that concern them. As with the social model, the primary policy goal based on the human rights approach is the inclusion of persons with disabilities in all parts of society, including in education and training programmes and in the labour market. Because certain groups, such as women with disabilities and indigenous persons with disabilities, may experience multiple and intersecting discrimination, differentiated and targeted policy measures are required to bring about change and promote inclusion.

2.2 Development of international commitments and instruments

Since the mid-twentieth century, the movement to improve the status of persons with disabilities in society has taken root and expanded through numerous international and regional initiatives. This shift reflects the transformed understanding of disability.

The major human rights and non-discrimination instruments adopted by the United Nations between 1948 and 1966 made no mention of persons with disabilities. But there have been 16 international initiatives since 1944 specifically concerning persons with disabilities and 13 others pertaining to the general population in which persons with disabilities are explicitly mentioned.[40]

Employment issues are featured in several of these commitments, notably, the ILO Convention concerning Vocational Rehabilitation and Employment (Disabled Persons), 1983 (No. 159); the United Nations Standard Rules on the Equalization of Opportunities for Persons with Disabilities (1993); and, most recently, the United Nations Convention on the Rights of Persons with Disabilities, adopted in 2006. The 2030 Agenda for Sustainable Development, adopted by all United Nations Member States in 2015, also includes a target on achieving full and productive employment and decent work for all women and men, including young people and persons with disabilities, and equal pay for work of equal value (Sustainable Development Goal 8.5).

Of these commitments, the Convention on the Rights of Persons with Disabilities has been critical in accelerating the promotion of disability rights and disability-inclusive development, including in the area of employment. Through its dedicated article on work and employment (article 27), the Convention explicitly recognizes the right of persons with disabilities to work on an equal basis with others, including "the right to the opportunity to gain a living by work freely chosen or accepted in a labour market and work environment that is open, inclusive and accessible to persons with disabilities".[41] Other articles on equality (article 5), awareness-raising (article 8), accessibility (article 9) and education (article 24) further provide guidance

38 A/70/297.

39 Tom Shakespeare and Nicholas Watson, "The social model of disability: An outdated ideology?", *Research in Social Science and Disability*, vol. 2 (June 2001).

40 See Annex D for the full list of disability-specific and disability-related instruments.

41 United Nations, *Treaty Series*, vol. 2515, No. 44910.

Box 7

Implications of article 27 of the Convention on the Rights of Persons with Disabilities for Asian and Pacific governments

With reference to the rights of persons with disabilities to decent work and productive employment, the Convention on the Rights of Persons with Disabilities calls upon its States parties to adhere to the following principles:

Respect: ensuring that the direct actions of the State do not discriminate in employment.

Protect: ensuring that private employers do not discriminate against persons with disabilities, by providing legislative protection and access to remedies.

Fulfil and promote: taking positive legislative, policy and other steps to promote and support the employment of persons with disabilities in the public and private sectors.

All States parties are obliged to review existing laws and, where required, revise them to provide the necessary protection and undertake positive measures to this end.

Source: Andrew Byrnes, "CRPD harmonization in the context of employment in Asia and the Pacific: Reflections on the practice of the CRPD Committee", Presentation at ESCAP Expert Group Meeting on Promoting Inclusive Employment for Persons with Disabilities in Asia and the Pacific, 2021. Available at www.unescap.org/events/2021/expert-group-meeting-promoting-inclusive-employment-persons-disabilities-asia-and.

on strengthening the enabling environment for the promotion of employment opportunities for persons with disabilities.

In Asia and the Pacific, the Convention on the Rights of Persons with Disabilities has been ratified by 47 of the 53 ESCAP member States. It has been signed with a view to ratification by five other member States.[42] However, only 14 member States have ratified the Optional Protocol, which establishes a mechanism through which individuals or groups may lodge a complaint to the Committee on the Rights of Persons with Disabilities if their rights under the Convention have been denied. The region falls slightly behind the global average: 93 per cent of governments in the world have ratified the Convention, and 50 per cent have ratified the Optional Protocol.

At the regional level, the commitment to promoting employment opportunities for persons with disabilities has deepened over the three Asian and Pacific Decades for Persons with Disabilities, since 1993, with the subject of employment featured prominently as a stand-alone goal or category in the policy frameworks for all three decades. The current framework, spanning from 2013 to 2022, is the Incheon Strategy to "Make the Right Real" for Persons with Disabilities in Asia and the Pacific, adopted in 2012, which includes as its first goal the reduction of poverty and enhancement of work and employment prospects.

2.3 Shifts in policy focus: From sheltered workshops to supported employment

The transformed understanding of disability, increasingly reflected in international commitments and instruments on disability rights, has catalysed a fundamental shift in the approach to work and employment opportunities for persons with disabilities.

2.3.1 Sheltered employment

With the medical model being the predominant model of disability until the 1980s, sheltered workshops exclusively catering to persons with disabilities were their primary employment option. Often established as social service initiatives by voluntary efforts, such as charities, religious groups and family members of persons with disabilities, these segregated centres were frequently funded as charitable enterprises, with revenues dependent on the number of workers rather than sales;[43] sheltered workshops only later became subject to state regulation and eligible for public funding.[44]

42 Stocktaking as of 30 June 2021.

43 ESCAP, *Disability at a Glance 2015: Strengthening Employment Prospects for Persons with Disabilities in Asia and the Pacific* (Bangkok, 2016).

44 ILO, *Decent Work for Persons with Disabilities: Promoting Rights in the Global Development Agenda* (Geneva 2015).

Box 8

Incheon Strategy to "Make the Right Real" for Persons with Disabilities in Asia and the Pacific and the Beijing Declaration and Action Plan to Accelerate the Implementation of the Incheon Strategy

Goal 1 of the Incheon Strategy seeks to "reduce poverty and enhance work and employment prospects" through the following targets:

Target 1.A
Eliminate extreme poverty among persons with disabilities

Target 1.B
Increase work and employment for persons of working age with disabilities who can and want to work

Target 1.C
Increase the participation of persons with disabilities in vocational training and other employment-support programmes funded by governments

The Beijing Declaration and Action Plan, adopted in 2017, calls on Asian and Pacific governments to develop and implement enabling schemes that promote the employment of persons with disabilities and increase their opportunities for livelihood, decent work and entrepreneurship. It particularly refers to promoting the inclusion of persons with diverse disabilities and women with disabilities, with the provision of reasonable accommodation. This call specifies:

- creating a one-stop system of employment services for persons with disabilities to avoid fragmentation;
- providing financial or other incentives to employers to hire persons with disabilities and construct accessible facilities in the workplace;
- promoting disability-inclusive business as a new business model that is distinct from the corporate social responsibility approach to disability and incorporating disability perspectives into all stages of the business cycle;
- promoting the establishment of business-to-business networks and improving coordination across the disability employment services system to increase job opportunities, vocational training and skills development for persons with disabilities;
- promoting the provision of disability support services for employees, such as job coaching, job matching, pre-employment counselling, information in accessible formats and reasonable accommodation and assistive technologies to sustain the employment of persons with disabilities.

Source: ESCAP, *Incheon Strategy to "Make the Right Real" for Persons with Disabilities in Asia and the Pacific and Beijing Declaration including the Action Plan to Accelerate the Implementation of the Incheon Strategy* (Bangkok, 2018). Available at www.unescap.org/resources/incheon-strategy-make-right-real-persons-disabilities-asia-and-pacific-and-beijing.

Criticisms levelled at such workshops have concerned the absence of adequate working conditions, employment contracts and the right to organize, linked to the non-application of employment and occupational safety laws; and the payment of sheltered workers at less than the minimum wage, often in the form of a productivity-related top-up to their disability benefits.[45]

Since the 1980s and stemming from the emergence of the social model of disability, the importance of productive employment and decent work for men and women with disabilities has come to be recognized. It is based on the increasingly widespread view that persons with disabilities should be provided with the opportunity to live and work in the mainstream of society. Sheltered workshops in receipt of public funding in many countries have therefore been required to reorganize in terms of programmes offered, working conditions and opportunities for persons with disabilities to move to more open forms of employment, based on their own choices.

This transformation has been further accelerated by the advent of the Convention on the Rights of Persons with Disabilities and the human rights model of disability. The Committee on the Rights of Persons with disabilities, in its general comments and concluding observations to numerous States parties' reports, have urged States parties to facilitate the transition away

45 ibid.

from segregated work environments to open labour market settings for persons with disabilities, including the adoption of measures to support their engagement in the open labour market. As countries shifted to supported-employment approaches, the Committee also called for them to ensure the immediate applicability of labour rights to sheltered employment.[46]

2.3.2 Supported employment

The concept of supported employment emerged in the 1980s as an effective way of assisting persons with disabilities to move from special training centres and sheltered workshops to jobs in mainstream companies. Initially developed for persons with intellectual disabilities, this approach has expanded to be available to persons with other types of disabilities.

Supported employment seeks to empower persons with disabilities to work alongside others in open labour market settings by providing tailored support to each individual with disability so that they are able to obtain and maintain employment (table 5).

Table 5
Forms of supported employment

Individual placement	A job placement officer or job coach identifies a potentially suitable job and provides on-the-job training and/or other assistance to the individual in the workplace.
Enclave within a company	A team of persons with disabilities works on specific tasks alongside a job coach or supervisor.
Mobile work crew	Persons with disabilities perform tasks, such as gardening or cleaning, under contract from companies.
Small business	Persons with disabilities, alongside persons without disabilities, offer manufacturing or subcontracting services (such as word processing or desktop publishing) in an inclusive setting, such as a business park or a shopping mall.

Source: ILO, *Decent Work for Persons with Disabilities: Promoting Rights in the Global Development Agenda* (Geneva 2015).

Box 9
Supported Employment Service in Hong Kong, China

Since 1993, the New Life Psychiatric Rehabilitation Association in **Hong Kong, China**, has operated a supported employment service to empower persons with psychosocial disabilities to work in an open and competitive setting, based on self-directed choices according to their abilities, strengths and interests. The supported employment team, consisting of a manager, caseworkers, administrative staff and instructors, provides services for both persons with psychosocial disabilities and employers.

Persons with psychosocial disabilities may approach social workers for referral to the supported employment service, which involves individualized vocational counselling, systematic training, job matching, on-the-job support as well as various group and social rehabilitation activities. Through these services, persons with psychosocial disabilities can participate in productive employment in the open market, including in the fields of retailing, car cleaning, venue cleaning and catering. A discharge plan will be prepared when persons with psychosocial disabilities can stay in the job continuously and no longer require support services.

New Life also identifies the most suitable employees for employers who would like to offer job opportunities. Additionally, wage subsidies and mental health-related training are available for employers to encourage the employment of persons with psychosocial disabilities.

Building on more than 20 years' experience, the supported employment service has been incorporated into a one-stop vocational rehabilitation service centre that offers a range of employment assistance projects. The service centre is equipped with facilities to conduct training courses and assist persons with psychosocial disabilities in jobseeking.

Note: More information can be found on the New Life Psychiatric Rehabilitation Association website: www.nlpra.org.hk/en/our services/ses/32#supported.

46 See, for example, CRPD/C/GC/6, para. 67(a); CRPD/C/DEU/CO/1, para. 50(b); CRPD/C/EU/CO/1, para. 75; CRPD/C/KOR/CO/1 para. 49; CRPD/C/LUX/CO/1, para. 47; CRPD/C/SRB/CO/1, para. 56; and CRPD/C/SVK/CO/1, para. 74.

Following supported employment placements, some persons with disabilities continue as supported workers, requiring ongoing support from their job coach or resource person.[47] Others may be recruited as direct employees on regular employment contracts with a company. From the employer's perspective, this arrangement is beneficial because the employee with disability is able to fulfil the requirements of the position with the partnership of a job coach, whose support is available to resolve any issues that might arise during or after the period of coaching.

Over the past two to three decades, social enterprises and private companies in several countries and territories in the Asia–Pacific region have introduced supported employment as an option for jobseekers with disabilities.

Promoting supported employment through social enterprises

Social enterprises are entities operating in the open market that possess the social objective of employing

Box 10
Disability-inclusive social enterprises in Australia and Thailand

Outlook

Founded in 1970, Outlook runs the largest waste management social enterprise in **Australia.** It employs more than 200 staff, including persons with disabilities and people facing barriers to employment.

Employees with and without disabilities operate within a single workforce and are paid award-based wages.* To promote an inclusive employment setting for persons with disabilities, the following measures are in place in Outlook:

- job-matching services, to align roles and opportunities with the career ambitions and skill sets of employees;
- skills-based, on-the-job training tailored to employees' needs to advance their expressed career goals;
- provision of training materials in accessible formats, such as easy-read;
- requisite that supervisors possess both technical knowledge and case management skills to directly support persons with disabilities in the workplace; and
- requisite that employees with disabilities are represented at all levels of the staffing structure, including through an independently chaired customer advisory group and a board of governance.

Autistic Thai Social Enterprise

The Autistic Thai Social Enterprise, established in 2017, is the first social enterprise founded by a group of persons with autism in **Thailand**. The enterprise runs two major business lines – Art Story and For All Coffee, and has several stores in well-known shopping malls, government buildings and the SME Development Bank Food Centre.

The team of 31 staff at the enterprise receive a salary according to their education levels, with additional incentives paid to workers with outstanding performance. Employees with little or no education obtain a starting salary at least equivalent to the minimum wage set by law. The enterprise recruits former participants from the training and rehabilitation programmes of the Autistic Thai Foundation and further delivers customized training to staff with autism, based on their interests and aptitude.

While being a social enterprise, both business lines of Autistic Thai Social Enterprise are viable commercially. Such commercial success can be attributed to several factors, including identifying and enhancing the core competitiveness of marketable products, publicizing products through a variety of channels such as TV programmes and online marketing and establishing business partnerships with different stakeholders.

Source: Sam Sondhi, "Outlook Australia: An integrated model of supported employment", Presentation at ESCAP Expert Group Meeting on Promoting Inclusive Employment for Persons with Disabilities in Asia and the Pacific, 2021. Available at www.unescap.org/events/2021/expert-group-meeting-promoting-inclusive-employment-persons-disabilities-asia-and; Samrerng Virachanang, "Promoting employment of persons with autism through social enterprises - the case of Thai Autism Association", Presentation at ESCAP Expert Group Meeting on Promoting Inclusive Employment for Persons with Disabilities in Asia and the Pacific, 2021. Available at www.unescap.org/events/2021/expert-group-meeting-promoting-inclusive-employment-persons-disabilities-asia-and.
Note: * An award is a legal document that defines the terms and conditions of employment for a specific industry or job, such as minimum wages, overtime, penalty rates and allowances. See Queensland Government, "Awards and wages". Available at www.qld.gov.au/jobs/entitlements/wages.

47 See more details about job coaching in section 3.3.2.

persons at greatest disadvantage in the labour market. They encompass different types of community, voluntary, non-profit and for-profit activities in the form of cooperatives, mutual societies, non-profit associations, foundations and for-profit entities.[48]

Since the 1980s, social enterprises have been providing opportunities for persons with disabilities, including those with intellectual impairments and mental health conditions,[49] to work alongside persons without disabilities in open labour market settings. In recent years, the Asia–Pacific region has witnessed the growth of social enterprises that have effectively promoted and sustained the employment of persons with disabilities. Findings from country studies suggest that social enterprises can create an enabling environment that empowers persons with disabilities to meaningfully engage in the labour market.[50]

Promoting supported employment through private sector enterprises

In recent decades, employers have increasingly come to recognize the benefits to their companies of employing persons with disabilities, including improved productivity, lower employee turnover, safer workplaces and enhanced reputations.[51]

In many countries of the Asia–Pacific region, employers in the private sector have formed business and disability networks to promote the business case for employing persons with diverse disabilities and thereby effectively increasing their employment opportunities. These networks include the Australian Network on Disability; business and disability networks in Bangladesh, India, Indonesia, the Philippines and Singapore; the Employers' Network on Disability in Sri Lanka; the New Zealand Accessibility Tick Employers Network; and the Russian Business Advisory Board on Disability.[52]

Employment programmes offered by private sector employers to persons with disabilities do not necessarily constitute supported employment. But these business and disability networks advocate for employment opportunities for persons with disabilities and often take a pivotal role in establishing disability-inclusion principles and equipping employers with necessary skills and capacities to support employees with disabilities.

Box 11
ILO Global Business and Disability Network

The ILO Global Business and Disability Network is an employer-led worldwide network to promote disability inclusion in the workplace. Consisting of multinational enterprises, employer and business membership organizations, national business and disability networks, civil society organizations and academics. The Global Business and Disability Network provides technical advice on disability inclusion, particularly in developing countries, and facilitates contact with national business and disability initiatives, organizations of persons with disabilities, partners and ILO offices.

Company members have signed the Global Business and Disability Network Charter and thereby commit to its 10 disability-inclusion principles:

- respect and promotion of rights
- non-discrimination
- equality of treatment and opportunities
- accessibility
- job retention
- confidentiality
- attention to all types of disabilities
- collaboration
- evaluation and
- knowledge-sharing.

As part of the Global Business and Disability Network, employer and business membership organizations increase their capacity to address their members' needs relating to disability diversity, corporate social responsibility, human resources and adherence to laws.

Note: More information can be found at the ILO Global Business and Disability Network website: www.businessanddisability.org/.

Arising from these developments, employers have developed a range of initiatives to include persons with disabilities within their workforce. It is often in collaboration with organizations of persons with disabilities,

48 WHO, *World Report on Disability* (Geneva, 2011).

49 Social enterprises were initially established in Europe in the 1980s to support the employment of persons with psychosocial disabilities after the closure of many psychiatric institutions.

50 See, for example, Cheryl Hiu-Kwan Chui and others, "Work integration social enterprises as vessels of empowerment? Perspectives from employees", *Asia Pacific Journal of Social Work and Development*, vol. 29, No. 2 (2019); and Peter Smith and others, "Developing open employment outcomes for people with an intellectual disability utilising a Social Enterprise Framework", *Journal of Vocational Rehabilitation*, vol. 48, No. 1 (February 2018).

51 ILO, *Business as Unusual: Making Workplaces Inclusive of People with Disabilities* (Geneva, 2014).

52 See the ILO Global Business and Disability Network website at www.businessanddisability.org/.

training centres for persons with disabilities or state employment agencies.[53]

Many employers begin their involvement in disability inclusion with initiatives designed to meet legal obligations or corporate social responsibility targets and gradually strengthen their commitments to become fully disability-inclusive businesses. Some establish dedicated training and employment services for persons with disabilities. Others create employment opportunities for persons with disabilities following a period of vocational training, often organized in collaboration with a dedicated training centre for persons with disabilities.

Box 12
Employment Transition Programme of Enabling Academy, Gamuda in Malaysia

Gamuda, one of the largest infrastructure companies in **Malaysia**, set up the Enabling Academy in 2017 to prepare persons with autism for gainful and sustainable employment in the labour market. The academy offers an employment-transition programme comprising pre-employment training and job placement support. Persons with autism can attend courses to strengthen their technical and soft skills. The academy uses a simulation-based approach so that trainees can experience the corporate environment. Following the three-month training programme, participants are interviewed by a matched company. Based on the needs of successful candidates, job coaches provide on-site support to ensure employment sustainability.

Programme flow

Recruitment	Training & job matching	Job placement	Support at workplace	Post-training support
• Vocational aptitude assessment • Interview of candidates and parents or guardians	• Individualized social skills and practical skills training • Workplace assessment and consultation with partner companies	• Awareness and in-house job coaching and training • Interview at potential workplace	• Job trial, internship or probation • Full-time employment	• Ongoing social well-being support through Enabling Academy alumni network, such as online social interactions and monthly social activities

The academy also creates diverse job opportunities for persons with autism through collaboration with partner companies across a variety of industries.

Job positions of graduates	Industries involved in hiring Enabling Academy graduates
Account assistant, administrative assistant or executive, assistant manager, customer enthusiast cum marketing executive, data analyst, digital data reviewer, document controller, engineer, finance officer, global support executive, human resources assistant, IT executive, logistic database crew, reporting management officer, retail associate, quality control assistant, technical officer and test analyst	Agriculture, banking, legal sector, manufacturing, pharmaceutical industry, programming, property, construction and retail

As of April 2021, 66 persons with autism had been trained, and 79.5 per cent of graduates had secured and sustained jobs at partner companies for at least one year.

Source: Yeo Swee Lan, "Job coaching for the promotion of sustainable open employment", Presentation at ESCAP Expert Group Meeting on Promoting Inclusive Employment for Persons with Disabilities in Asia and the Pacific, 2021. Available at www.unescap.org/events/2021/expert-group-meeting-promoting-inclusive-employment-persons-disabilities-asia-and.
Note: More information can be found on the Enabling Academy web page: https://gamuda.com.my/sustainability-esg/yayasan-gamuda/enabling-academy/.

53 Workability International, *Customized Employment Guidelines* (Bangkok, 2019). Available at www.workabilityasia.com/wp-content/uploads/2019/05/WASIA Guidebook Pink En.pdf.

Chapter 3

Strategies to promote productive employment and decent work for persons with disabilities

Governments in the Asia–Pacific region have been utilizing a variety of strategies that promote productive employment and decent work for persons with disabilities in recent years. These strategies follow in tandem with the shifts in the understanding of disability and approaches to work and coupled with the rise of the private sector and social enterprises in promoting supported employment for persons with disabilities. The following framework (figure 18) outlines these strategies.

Figure 18
Strategies to promote productive employment and decent work for persons with disabilities

3.1 Overarching legal frameworks on the right to employment for persons with disabilities

3.1.1 Constitutional provisions

A constitution is the highest level of law in a country. Where persons with disabilities are explicitly mentioned within a constitution, such provisions reflect the priority attached to disability rights in the country. And it sets the framework for the development of laws to promote employment of persons with disabilities.

In the Asia–Pacific region, the commitment to disability rights is explicitly expressed in the constitution of at

Box 13
Disability-related constitutional commitments in Fiji, Nepal and Viet Nam

In addition to prohibiting discrimination, the constitutions of Fiji, Nepal and Viet Nam make further provisions to protect the rights of persons with disabilities.

The 2013 Constitution of **Fiji** covers the right of persons with disabilities to reasonable adaptation of buildings, infrastructure, vehicles, working arrangements, rules, practices or procedures to enable their full participation in society and the effective realization of their rights.

The 2015 Constitution of **Nepal** provides for the establishment of a National Inclusion Commission, with the responsibility of promoting the status of persons with disabilities as well as other marginalized groups. It also guarantees access to education for persons with physical, visual and hearing disabilities, with the provision of braille and sign language.

The 2013 Constitution of **Viet Nam** contains a commitment to providing favourable conditions for persons with disabilities to access vocational learning as well as developing a social security system to assist persons with disabilities in difficult circumstances.

Source: Government of the Republic of Fiji, "Constitution of the Republic of Fiji". Available at www.laws.gov.fj/Home/information/constitutionoftherepublicoffiji; Nepal Law Commission, "Constitution of Nepal". Available at www.lawcommission.gov.np/en/archives/category/documents/prevailing-law/constitution/constitution-of-nepal; CRPD/C/VNM/1.

least nine countries.[54] These constitutions include provisions that express a commitment to addressing the basic needs of persons with disabilities and to taking measures to ensure their social protection (Cambodia, China, Pakistan, Palau, Republic of Korea and Viet Nam); explicitly prohibit the discrimination against citizens on the ground of disability (Armenia, Fiji, Nepal and Thailand); and mandate the establishment of an agency to promote the inclusion of persons with disabilities in mainstream society (Nepal and the Philippines).

3.1.2 Employment equity and non-discrimination laws

Employment equity and non-discrimination laws make it unlawful for employers to discriminate on the basis of disability in recruitment, promotion, dismissal and other aspects of employment. Many of these laws require employers to provide reasonable accommodation involving adaptation of the job and work environment to facilitate the employment of persons with disabilities. The laws also note that the accommodation should not involve an undue cost burden to employers. The denial of reasonable accommodation is considered in many laws to be a form of discrimination and therefore illegal. Some non-discrimination and employment equity laws require employers to develop and implement affirmative action plans to give effect to their legal obligations. In some cases, companies are required to comply with employment equity and non-discrimination laws as a requisite for being eligible to provide goods or services to public entities.

Box 14
Aligning employment equity and non-discrimination laws with the Convention on the Rights of Persons with Disabilities

In General Comment No. 6 (2018) on equality and non-discrimination, the Committee on the Rights of Persons with Disabilities urged States parties to undertake the following actions to achieve equality in employment among persons with and without disabilities:

(a) Facilitate the transition away from segregated work environments for persons with disabilities and support their engagement in the open labour market, and in the meantime, also ensure the immediate applicability of labour rights to those settings;
(b) Promote the right to supported employment, including to work assistance, job coaching and vocational qualification programmes; protect the rights of workers with disabilities; and ensure the right to freely chosen employment;
(c) Ensure that persons with disabilities are paid no less than the minimum wage and do not lose the benefit of disability allowances when they start work;
(d) Expressly recognize the denial of reasonable accommodation as discrimination, and prohibit multiple and intersectional discrimination and harassment;
(e) Ensure proper transition into and out of employment for persons with disabilities in a non-discriminatory manner. States parties are obliged to ensure equal and effective access to benefits and entitlements, such as retirement or unemployment benefits. Such entitlements must not be infringed upon by exclusion from employment, thereby further exacerbating the situation of exclusion;
(f) Promote work in inclusive and accessible, safe and healthy working environments in the public and private sectors;
(g) Ensure that persons with disabilities enjoy equal opportunities regarding career advancement opportunities through regular assessment meetings with their managers and by defining the objectives to be achieved, as a part of a comprehensive strategy;
(h) Ensure access to training, retraining and education, including vocational training and capacity-building for employees with disabilities, and provide training on the employment of persons with disabilities and reasonable accommodation for employers, representative organizations of employees and employers, unions and competent authorities;
(i) Work towards universally applicable occupational health and safety measures for persons with disabilities, including occupational safety and health regulations that are non-discriminatory and inclusive of persons with disabilities; and
(j) Recognize the right of persons with disabilities to have access to trade and labour unions.

Source: CRPD/C/GC/6

54 ILO, *Achieving Equal Employment Opportunities for Persons with Disabilities through Legislation: Guidelines* (Geneva, 2014).

Persons with disabilities are listed as rights holders in employment equity and non-discrimination laws in a majority of countries in the region through disability-specific laws and/or laws concerning the population as a whole.[55] Some of these laws focus on employment while others apply to all aspects of society.

In some employment equity and non-discrimination laws, explicit provisions have been made to address the situation of specific subgroups of persons with disabilities who may face more barriers to employment due to the nature of their disability or intersecting disadvantages, such as gender and ethnicity.

Box 15
Provisions for women with disabilities and persons with severe disabilities in the Act on the Employment Promotion and Vocational Rehabilitation of Persons with Disabilities in the Republic of Korea

In the **Republic of Korea,** the Act on the Employment Promotion and Vocational Rehabilitation of Persons with Disabilities includes specific clauses targeting women with disabilities and persons with severe disabilities (article 3). Business owners who employ or intend to employ women with disabilities and persons with severe disabilities are entitled to preferential treatment when applying for relevant loans or subsidies granted by the Minister of Employment and Labor (articles 21 and 22). In addition, business owners hiring women with disabilities and persons with severe disabilities may receive enhanced employment incentives determined by the Minister (article 30).

Note: See www.moel.go.kr/english/poli/poliLaw_view.jsp?idx=226&tab=4.

Employment equity and non-discrimination laws are applied differently across the region. They are monitored and enforced through the labour inspectorate, an administrative monitoring system, a national human rights institution or the court system.[56]

Penalties differ across countries, too. In Indonesia, for example, legal sanctions on employers who fail to provide reasonable accommodation and accessible facilities start with a written warning in the first instance, followed by termination of operational activities and then suspension of the business permit and then revocation of the business permit.[57] In the Philippines, errant employers may be fined or, in the case of repeating or multiple violations, subject to imprisonment of between two and six years.[58]

There are frequent calls for more rigorous implementation and enforcement of employment equity and non-discrimination laws and for amendments to these laws to allow persons with disabilities to pursue cases of discrimination more easily. In some countries, it is up to an individual with a disability to lodge a complaint of discrimination experienced and to prove that discrimination occurred. Where the burden of proof lies with the plaintiff, there has been difficulty in accessing the necessary evidence to prove the case. In some countries globally, the burden of proof in employment discrimination cases has shifted to the employer: Once the plaintiff provides facts from which it may be presumed that discrimination has taken place, the employer must prove that discrimination did not occur, drawing on information at their disposal.[59] Such a shift has improved the effectiveness of anti-discrimination laws in practice.[60] However, many complaints are resolved through conciliation rather than through the courts.

55 See Annex E for a mapping (not exhaustive) of non-discrimination laws in the Asia-Pacific region.
56 ILO, *Achieving Equal Employment Opportunities for Persons with Disabilities through Legislation: Guidelines* (Geneva, 2014).
57 CRPD/C/IDN/1.
58 Philippines, *Magna Carta for Disabled Persons (R.A. No. 7277)*, Section 44 (Manila, 1992).
59 European Union, Council Directive 2000/78/EC.
60 ILO, *Achieving Equal Employment Opportunities for Persons with Disabilities through Legislation: Guidelines* (Geneva, 2014).

Box 16
Grievance-redressal mechanism in India

In **India**, the Rights of Persons with Disabilities Act, 2016 stipulates that no government establishment can discriminate against persons with disabilities in any matter relating to employment. All government establishments are to provide reasonable accommodation and an appropriate accessible environment for employees with disabilities.

The Act calls for every government establishment to appoint a grievance redressal officer to support the employment of persons with disabilities, especially for their vocational training and self-employment. Any person aggrieved by the non-compliance of the provisions may file a complaint with grievance-redressal officers. These officers are required to investigate the matter within two weeks of the registration and suggest corrective actions. If an aggrieved person is not satisfied with the response, they may then approach the district-level Committee on Disability.

Additionally, the Chief Commissioner and the State Commissioners for Persons with Disabilities can inquire, even without the request of a party, about the deprivation of rights of persons with disabilities and recommend remedial measures. According to available data, 985 complaints were registered in 2019–2020 with the State Commissioner for Persons with Disabilities in the Government of Delhi. On his own initiative, the State Commissioner pursued 543 cases. Last but not least, district-level Special Courts have been established for speedy trials of any offence under the Act.

These measures are specified within the Rights of Persons with Disabilities Act. They were brought about by the Indian Government's commitment to implementing the Convention on the Rights of Persons with Disabilities, coupled with strong advocacy by civil society groups and an awareness of the inadequacy of its 1995 Persons with Disabilities Act in eradicating discrimination due to the lack of penalty provisions and enforcement mechanisms.

India's experience in designing and implementing its grievance-redressal mechanism for persons with disabilities underscores the centrality of the following factors in countering discrimination:

Rights-based legislation, aligned with the Convention on the Rights of Persons with Disabilities, that contains provisions for penalties

Strong commitment at senior levels in the disability focal department to operationalize the Act and grievance mechanism

A clear road map or action plan to operationalize the grievance mechanism

Merit-based recruitment of autonomous and accountable grievance-redressal authorities

Easy access to courts and redress mechanisms that are within reach for persons with disabilities

A clear understanding of rights-based laws by duty bearers and rights holders, including through capacity-building and sensitization efforts

Source: T. D. Dhariyal, "Establishing robust grievance redressal mechanisms to promote anti-discrimination in the labour market: India's Rights of Persons with Disabilities Act, 2016", Presentation at ESCAP Expert Group Meeting on Promoting Inclusive Employment for Persons with Disabilities in Asia and the Pacific, 2021. Available at www.unescap.org/events/2021/expert-group-meeting-promoting-inclusive-employment-persons-disabilities-asia-and.

3.2 Laws, policies and programmes that support the employment of persons with disabilities

3.2.1 Employment quota schemes

Quota systems obliging companies to employ persons with disabilities as a specified percentage of their workforce are in place in at least 25 countries of the Asia–Pacific region and are being considered in one other country.[61] Of them, only 10 schemes were in place prior to 2006. The majority of quota systems were introduced when countries in the region began applying the principles of non-discrimination and inclusion in employment policies following ratification of the Convention on the Rights of Persons with Disabilities.

Quotas can apply to either public or private employers, or both, usually above a specified minimum size of the workforce. The size of quota obligation in the region varies from 1 to 5 per cent, with most requiring either 3 or 5 per cent of jobs in a company's workforce to be filled by persons with disabilities.[62] Where the quota applies to both public and private employers, the size of quota obligation for public employers is often larger than for private employers.

Box 17
Implementing quota schemes in Japan

Originally introduced through the Physically Disabled Persons' Employment Promotion Law, 1960, the Government of **Japan** quota scheme is reviewed every five years in terms of the number and employment situations of persons with disabilities.

As of 1 March 2021, private employers with 43.5 employees or more had a quota obligation of 2.3 per cent, while public entities had a quota obligation of 2.6 per cent. A part-time employee with disabilities working between 20 and 30 hours per week is counted as half a worker. Each person with a severe physical or intellectual disability is counted as two workers under the quota scheme.

Private employers who fail to meet their quota obligation are subject to penalties. An order from Hello Work, the Government's employment service centre, is first issued to request the non-compliant company to develop a two-year hiring plan. Should the plan not be well implemented, further guidance is then provided. Private employers with more than 100 regular employees must pay a levy of 50,000 yen per month for each unfilled quota position.

Companies that meet their quota obligation are awarded a monthly incentive of 27,000 yen per worker with disabilities exceeding the quota. Additional financial support is also available for small and medium-sized enterprises with 100 or fewer employees. Subsidies and allowances are provided to support employers in adjusting workplaces and offering reasonable accommodation.

In 2020, the employment rate of persons with disabilities in private companies was nearly 2.2 per cent on average, with 48.6 per cent of private employers meeting the statutory quota rate. For public employers, the employment rate of persons with disabilities reached 2.8 per cent at the national level, 2.7 per cent at the prefecture level and 2.4 per cent at the municipal level. Most national and prefecture public entities achieved their quota obligation.

The Ministry of Health, Labour and Welfare is responsible for the enforcement and regular review of the quota scheme, including compiling and publishing data on quota compliance. The Japan Organization for Employment of the Elderly, Persons with Disabilities and Job Seekers collects and disburses the levy payments.

Source: Tokyo Labor Bureau, "The statutory employment rate for persons with disabilities will be raised from 1 March 2021" (in Japanese), web page. Available at https://jsite.mhlw.go.jp/tokyo-roudoukyoku/hourei_seido_tetsuzuki/shokugyou_shoukai/houteikoyouritu_00630.html; Ministry of Health, Labour and Welfare, "Aggregated results of employment status of persons with disabilities, 2020" (in Japanese), web page. Available at www.mhlw.go.jp/stf/newpage_16030.html; VERYBEST Law Offices, "From 1 March 2021, the statutory employment rate for persons with disabilities will be raised. What should companies do?" (in Japanese), 5 April 2021. Available at https://corporate.vbest.jp/columns/4314/; ILO, *Promoting Employment Opportunities for People with Disabilities Quota Schemes*, vol. 1 (Geneva, 2019).

61 See Annex F for a non-exhaustive mapping of quota schemes in the Asia–Pacific region.

62 In some cases, quota requirements differ between public and private employers: In one instance, the quota only applies to the public sector and to private sector companies benefiting from public concessions (Islamic Republic of Iran); in others, obligations apply only to the public sector (Bangladesh, India, Malaysia and Sri Lanka); in another, only private sector employers are subject to the requirement (Kazakhstan). See ILO, *Promoting Employment Opportunities for People with Disabilities Quota Schemes*, vol. 2 (Geneva, 2019).

Where binding quotas are introduced as part of national legislation, there is sometimes a requirement for companies to pay a levy for each unfilled position. These payments usually go to a fund created to promote employment opportunities for persons with disabilities that a relevant government ministry administers. Such arrangements are in place in at least six countries in the region. In two countries, a warning or penalty is imposed (Kazakhstan and the Russian Federation). Where quota schemes are enforced, the labour inspectorate of the ministry in charge of employment is usually responsible for checking that employers are in compliance with their obligations.

Information on the effectiveness of quota schemes for improving employment opportunities is rarely publicly available in the region's countries. In the absence of such information, it is difficult to gauge the direct impact of quotas on the employment rate of persons with disabilities.

Available evidence suggests that in many cases, employers meet their quota obligations in part rather than in full. They opt to pay the levy fee to the fund rather than recruit workers with disabilities.[63]

In an attempt to strengthen employer involvement and support, additional ways to encourage companies to meet their quota obligation have been introduced. In some countries, for example, as a way of partially meeting the quota obligation, private companies may accept trainees with disabilities; outsource work to designated workshops or centres employing persons with disabilities; or reach a company-wide agreement to promote recruitment, training, integration and retention of persons with disabilities.[64]

Quotas have been subject to considerable debate and controversy. Proponents of quota systems are of the view that, without their obligation, employers would not give persons with disabilities the opportunity to demonstrate their work capacity. Critics consider this policy measure to be a form of discrimination because the imposition of a quota implies that persons with disabilities cannot find jobs on their own merit. Countries where this critical view prevails usually promote

Box 18
Supporting the implementation of quotas through private sector actors: Yishengwuyou agency in China

In 2015 in **China**, the Ministry of Finance, the State Administration of Taxation and the China Disabled Persons' Federation jointly issued the Measures for the Administration of the Collection and Use of the Employment Security Fund for Persons with Disabilities. The directive stipulates a quota obligation of at least 1.5 per cent for both public and private employers. Employers failing to meet the quota obligation must pay a levy to the Employment Security Fund, which in turn supports the livelihood of persons with disabilities. In 2019, a master plan was announced to enhance the workings and implementation of the fund.

Yishengwuyou is a private employment agency for persons with disabilities. It has been a one-stop shop for companies seeking to understand and adhere to their quota obligation. Yishengwuyou maintains a comprehensive database of up-to-date national and provincial policies related to the quota obligations and provides tailored services for its customers in preparing an effective compliance plan.

In collaboration with the China Disabled Persons' Federation and its subnational branches, Yishengwuyou links job and outsourcing opportunities to persons with disabilities through job fairs and an online employment and crowdsourcing platform. It also provides on-demand training for new recruits with disabilities.

As of October 2021, Yishengwuyou has supported more than 5,000 companies in meeting their quota obligation and more than 16,000 persons with disabilities in gaining formal employment with proper social protection benefits. This includes placement in data auditing, customer service and online marketing.

Note: For more information on Yishengwuyou's work, visit: www.55yisheng.com/ (in Chinese).

63 ILO, *Decent Work for Persons with Disabilities: Promoting Rights in the Global Development Agenda* (Geneva 2015).
64 ILO, *Promoting Employment Opportunities for People with Disabilities: Quota Schemes*, vol. 1 (Geneva, 2019).

employment opportunities for persons with disabilities instead through employment equity and anti-discrimination laws as well as job retention and return-to-work measures that apply for all citizens.

Considering that quota systems are in widespread operation in Asia and the Pacific, they could be regarded – in the framework of employment equity and non-discrimination laws – as affirmative action measures that promote equality of opportunity for persons with disabilities in the workforce by setting employment targets. While the Convention on the Rights of Persons with Disabilities does not mention quotas, it does require States parties to promote the employment of persons with disabilities in the private sector through appropriate policies and measures, including affirmative action programmes, incentives and other measures.

3.2.2 Preferential contracting

A quota imposes an obligation on hiring entities to recruit persons with disabilities. But preferential contracting through public procurement seeks to incentivize prospective government contractors (varying from private firms to non-profit organizations) by awarding public contracts to firms and organizations that employ persons with disabilities in inclusive and accessible labour market settings.

Commonly used preferential contracting strategies include:[65]

- Set-asides: whereby a share of government contracts is reserved for a targeted category of bidders.
- Bid price preferences: to discount the bid price of an eligible business that meets the preference criteria by a given percentage to make it more competitive or to add a certain percentage to the bid price of those businesses that do not meet preference criteria.
- Point schemes: when awarding contracts, additional points are given to bidders who meet the preference criteria.
- Assisting businesses in the procurement process: measures to facilitate the participation of businesses that meet the preference criteria, such as waiving the application fee; implementing an online application process; providing training on management, finance and other operational competencies that would improve a business' competitiveness in the bidding process.

Governments should take caution in ensuring that the design and execution of preferential contracting policies do not perpetuate the exclusion of persons with disabilities. Due diligence needs to be taken to avoid awarding contracts to firms that employ persons with disabilities in segregated settings without regard for labour rights.

A few countries in the region, such as Australia, China, Japan and New Zealand, have introduced preferential contracting strategies to create employment opportunities for persons with disabilities. Further research is required regarding the impact of these strategies on the employment outcomes of persons with disabilities.

Box 19
Considerations for social objectives in procurement rules in New Zealand

New Zealand has sought to further its social objectives, including disability inclusion, into its Government Procurement Rules. For instance, Rule 18A, "Quality employment outcomes", explicitly requests that contracting agencies "consider how they can create quality employment opportunities, particularly for displaced workers and groups with traditionally high rates of unemployment or low labour force participation (specifically women, Māori, Pacific peoples, disabled people and youth)". In addition, it stipulates that sufficient monitoring should be in place to ensure that these employment opportunities promised in the contracts are delivered and reported on.

Note: Government Procurement Rules (Fourth edition), New Zealand is available at www.procurement.govt.nz/assets/procurement-property/documents/government-procurement-rules.pdf.

3.2.3 Job retention and return-to-work provisions

Most countries in Asia and the Pacific cater to employees who acquire a disability while in employment through worker compensation provisions. This typically involves a payment in the settlement of damages caused by an injury or illness, often with the assumption that these workers will no longer return to work. At least eight countries in the region, however, combine such a provision with strategies regarding job retention and the return to work of employees (table 6). In some cases, employers are required to retain workers and employees who acquire a disability; be involved in their rehabilitation; and adapt their original job or find them a new job if necessary. Workers are encouraged to return to work and to retrain if they can no longer perform their previous jobs.

65 World Bank, "Preferential public procurement: policy case studies on inclusive business", Policy Paper (Washington, D.C., 2016).

Table 6
Job retention and return-to-work laws in eight countries*

Country	Law or strategy	Main provisions
Australia	National Return to Work Strategy 2020-2030 (2019)	Aims to minimize the impact of work-related injuries and illness and enable a prompt return to work.[a]
China	Labour Law, 1994 and the Law on Employment Contracts, 2007	An employer cannot terminate an employment contract if the employee contracts an occupational disease or workplace injury during employment and is confirmed to have lost partially or completely the ability to work.[b]
India	The Rights of Persons with Disabilities Act, 2016	Public sector employers are prohibited from terminating or demoting employees who acquire a disability while in employment and are obliged to find another job for them, should they be unable to return to their previous position.[c]
Malaysia	Return to Work Programme, initiated in 2007	Offers comprehensive physical and vocational rehabilitation to employees who have acquired disabilities while in employment.[d] Offers comprehensive physical and vocational rehabilitation[e] to employees who have acquired a disability while in employment, in addition to financial support through social security payments.[f] Links have been established with several large employers to provide work for employees unable to return to their original workplace.[g]
New Zealand	Injury Prevention, Rehabilitation and Compensation Act, 2001	Job retention provisions, including provisions for return to the same employment as before if reasonably practicable and requirement for the employer to assist in vocational rehabilitation of an individual with an acquired disability.[h]
Philippines	Employee's Compensation Commission, established in 1974	Assistance to workers with disabilities to be reintegrated into the economic mainstream with their former employer, in a new job or by setting up a small business (microenterprise or home-based business) through rehabilitation, vocational skills, entrepreneurial training, job placement and assistance in starting an enterprise.[i]
Republic of Korea	Industrial Accident Compensation Insurance Act, 1963	Provides for benefits, such as financial support for returning to the original workplace, workplace adaptation training and rehabilitation consultation.[j]
Thailand	Social Security Act, 1990	Provides for training and medical rehabilitation services, including physical therapy, assistive technology devices, prostheses and counselling as well as training and support in entrepreneurship development.[k]

Source: [a] Safe Work Australia, *National Return to Work Strategy 2020–2030* (Canberra, 2019); [b] see CRPD/C/CHN/1; [c] India, *The Rights of Persons with Disabilities Act, 2016* (New Delhi, 2016); [d] Zero Project, "Innovative policy 2013 on employment: Malaysia's returning to work programme". Available at https://zeroproject.org/policy/malaysia/; [e] A case manager coordinates the rehabilitation with the injured employee, their family, employer, doctor and rehabilitation professionals (across disciplines, as required, such as physical therapy, occupational therapy, counselling and pain management); see WHO, *World Report on Disability* (Geneva, 2011); [f] Zero Project, "Innovative policy 2013 on employment: Malaysia's returning to work programme". Available at https://zeroproject.org/policy/malaysia/; [g] WHO, *World Report on Disability* (Geneva, 2011); [h] New Zealand Legislation, "Injury Prevention, Rehabilitation, and Compensation Act 2001", web page, available at http://www.legislation.govt.nz/act/public/2001/0049/31.0/DLM99494.html; [i] see CRPD/C/PHL/1; [j] see CRPD/C/KOR/1; [k] see CRPD/C/THA/1.
Note: * This list is not intended to be exhaustive.

3.2.4 Social protection

Inclusive social protection is indispensable for the realization of decent work for persons with disabilities. Yet, in low- and middle-income countries, fewer than one in five persons with significant disabilities reportedly has access to disability-related social protection schemes.[66] In countries of Asia and the Pacific with available data, only 21.6 per cent of persons with severe disabilities receive disability cash benefits.[67]

The design of social protection schemes can either support or disincentivize work for persons with disabilities. Universal disability benefits and cost-of-disability allowances provide additional resources that help defray additional costs due to disability, both direct and indirect,[68] that persons with disabilities face when seeking and maintaining employment. Enhancements to social health insurance schemes for persons with disabilities also seek to lower the costs of disability, such as subsidies for premiums and the inclusion of rehabilitation and provision of assistive devices within a universal health care package.

In schemes that include the "incapacity to work" as an explicit or implicit criterion for persons with disabilities to receive benefits, persons with disabilities may find themselves in a "benefits trap", whereby they become reluctant to seek employment for fear of losing their disability benefits and related entitlements, including medical benefits and transportation allowances.

Governments can dismantle the benefits trap by permitting workers with disabilities to retain their disability benefits up to a certain threshold of income earned and to become immediately eligible for the full benefit again, should they lose their employment. Provisions can also be made to provide a top-up to wages when an individual is in a low-paid job. Temporary entitlements plus cost-of-disability components irrespective of work status, more flexible in-work payments and options for putting benefits on hold while trying to work are preferred ways to increase employment. These are particularly important for younger people.[69]

Box 20
Inclusive social protection in Australia, Georgia and New Zealand

In **Australia**, a Mobility Allowance is paid to persons with disabilities aged 16 or older who cannot use public transport without substantial assistance and are required to travel to and from their home to undertake approved activities, which include work, study, training or job search. The individual recipient is free to decide how to use this allowance to meet their mobility needs.

In **Georgia**, a hybrid approach to social protection that is compatible with work is in place. Almost all registered persons with disabilities receive a universal disability benefit, regardless of capacity to work or income level. And they enjoy a higher tax-free income threshold. Assistive devices are also available at subsidized or no cost for eligible persons. Separately, persons with disabilities living in a poor household are also entitled to a share of Targeted Social Assistance as a family member of that household.

In **New Zealand**, a weekly Disability Allowance is available to help cover extra costs regularly incurred due to a disability or illness, such as equipment, transport or medical assistance. The amount paid depends on the additional costs of disability and income level of individual recipients.

Source: Alexandre Côte, "Social protection and support to economic participation of persons with disabilities", Presentation at ESCAP Expert Group Meeting on Promoting Inclusive Employment for Persons with Disabilities in Asia and the Pacific, 2021. Available at www.unescap.org/events/2021/expert-group-meeting-promoting-inclusive-employment-persons-disabilities-asia-and; Alexandre Côte, "Disability inclusion and social protection", in *Handbook on Social Protection Systems*, Esther Schüring and Markus Loewe, eds (Cheltenham, 2021); and ILO, *Assessment of the Social Protection System in Georgia* (Geneva, 2020).
Note: More information can be found on the websites of the Department of Social Services, Australian Government: www.dss.gov.au/disability-and-carers-programs-services-for-people-with-disability/mobility-allowance-mob and Work and Income, Ministry of Social Development, New Zealand Government: www.workandincome.govt.nz/products/a-z-benefits/disability-allowance.html.

66 Alexandre Côte, "Disability inclusion and social protection", in *Handbook on Social Protection Systems*, Esther Schüring and Markus Loewe, eds (Cheltenham, 2021).
67 ILO, *World Social Protection Report 2020-22: Social Protection at the Crossroads – In Pursuit of a Better Future* (Geneva, 2021).
68 Direct costs refer to specific disability expenditures (assistive devices, personal assistance, vocational rehabilitation, workplace modifications, special vehicles, etc.) and extra expenditure on general items (health care, transportation, etc.). Indirect costs include, but are not limited to, fewer employment and education opportunities, lower earnings and loss of earning or education opportunities for family members who are caregivers. See Alexandre Côte, "Social protection and support to economic participation of persons with disabilities", Presentation at ESCAP Expert Group Meeting on Promoting Inclusive Employment for Persons with Disabilities in Asia and the Pacific, 2021. Available at www.unescap.org/events/2021/expert-group-meeting-promoting-inclusive-employment-persons-disabilities-asia-and.
69 WHO, *World Report on Disability* (Geneva, 2011).

3.2.5 Measures to reduce the cost of employment for employers and employees with disabilities

There are additional costs incurred to obtain and maintain the employment of a person with disability on both the part of the employer and the employee with a disability. For employers, these are costs associated with reasonable accommodation. For persons with disabilities, these are costs related to travel and the use of assistive devices.

In some countries, both financial and in-kind support are available to workers with disabilities in the form of wage top-ups, transport allowances and specialized equipment, among others. By reducing the associated costs of employment, these measures help reduce barriers to sustained employment.

Box 21
Financial support for employees with disabilities in Australia

In **Australia**, financial assistance is available from the Employment Assistance Fund to purchase various work-related modifications and services for persons with disabilities who are about to start a job, currently working or seeking employment. Eligible expenses include the cost of modifying the physical work environment or work vehicle, the purchase of information and communication devices and a range of services and awareness training.

Note: More information can be found on the Disability Employment Australia website: http://guide.disabilityemployment.org.au/resources/employer_incentives_and_financial_assistance.

Financial support is sometimes provided for employers as an incentive for the recruitment and retention of workers with disabilities. It can take the form of tax exemption, wage subsidy for a specified period or the coverage of insurance premium costs.

Where there is a requirement on employers to provide reasonable accommodation, measures may include loans and grants to defray additional costs, including grants for workplace adaptation, as well as the provision of specialized equipment.

Box 22
Financial support for employers in Hong Kong (China), Indonesia, Singapore and Viet Nam

In **Hong Kong, China**, the Social Welfare Department provides a one-off subsidy to employers for each employee with a disability to procure assistive devices and/or to adapt the workplace, including accessories or adaptive equipment for a computer, an optical magnifying device, hearing and assistive devices, braille products and handrails. Additionally, the Government incentivizes the employment of persons with disabilities in social enterprises through the provision of seed funding under the project Enhancing Employment of People with Disabilities through Small Enterprise. Initiated in 2001, it aims to expand genuine employment opportunities for persons with disabilities in a carefully planned and friendly working environment. For businesses to be eligible for funding support, persons with disabilities must make up at least 50 per cent of their workforce.

In **Indonesia**, the Government provides awards and incentives for employers to foster their involvement and also seeks to encourage collaboration with employers who regard disability issues as part of their corporate social responsibility or diversity policies, in addition to meeting their legal obligations.

In **Singapore**, the Special Employment Credit scheme seeks to incentivize the employment of older persons and persons with disabilities through credits provided to employers in the form of wage subsidies, with more than 8,000 employers benefiting from this scheme and hiring more than 8,300 persons with disabilities up to 2015.

In **Viet Nam**, many provinces support the employment of persons with disabilities through funding allocation from the Disability Employment Fund. Preferential loans are provided from the National Employment Fund for small and medium enterprises, cooperatives, cooperative groups and household businesses employing a large number of persons with disabilities.

Note: See the website of the Social Welfare Department, Government of the Hong Kong Special Administrative Region: www.swd.gov.hk/en/index/site_pubsvc/page_rehab/sub_listofserv/id_vocational/id_sped/; CRPD/C/IDN/1; CRPD/C/SGP/1; and CRPD/C/VNM/1.

Technical support is also provided to employers in the form of advisory services, including job analysis and job matching, as well as the identification of modification requirements and advice on reasonable accommodation, technical aids and assistive devices.

> **Box 23**
> **Advisory services in Australia and Singapore**
>
> In **Australia**, the Employment Assistance Fund finances sign language interpretation, awareness training on disability, deafness and mental health services and specialist services for employees with specific learning disorders and mental health conditions. All of these services are designed to benefit people with disabilities in seeking, gaining and retaining employment.
>
> In **Singapore**, the Open Door programme offers a variety of job placement and support services to individuals with disabilities and their employers, including job re-design, workplace modifications, training, job placement and support services.
>
> ***Note:*** See the website of JobAccess, Australian Government: www.jobaccess.gov.au/employment-assistance-fund-eaf; also see CRPD/C/SGP/1.

3.3 Training to equip persons with disabilities for the labour market

3.3.1 Vocational training

TVET and skills development programmes should enable persons with disabilities to obtain relevant skills and qualifications required for the modern labour market. Yet, in Asia and the Pacific, persons with disabilities often have limited access to these programmes. The average participation rate of persons with disabilities in government-funded training is 3.4 per cent in countries for which data are available. There is considerable variation across countries, from 0.1 per cent in Bhutan to 72.5 per cent in Thailand.[70]

To equip learners with disabilities with the requisite skills for the labour market, an overarching framework needs to integrate disability-inclusive approaches to the TVET system and sufficient resources must be allocated to achieve these ends. A coordinated twin-track approach is required: There is a need to strengthen TVET institutions catering specifically to learners with disabilities to ensure relevance to the needs of the job market. In addition, provisions must be made for learners with and without disabilities to train alongside one another in general TVET institutions. To ensure that women with disabilities also have access to TVET programmes, gender perspectives should be mainstreamed at all levels of the TVET system.

Integrating disability inclusion into TVET sector planning

Disability-inclusive approaches can be integrated at the sector-planning level. This can be done either through the direct insertion of disability-specific provisions into TVET sector policies and strategies or through the development of a separate disability inclusion policy and/or strategy to guide TVET sector development (alongside the country's TVET sector policy and strategy).

Strengthening the relevance of TVET institutions

Global studies indicate that TVET programmes targeted at persons with disabilities are not always linked to local, regional or national employment opportunities.[71] For TVET institutions to adequately equip learners with disabilities with the requisite skills to obtain and maintain employment, it is crucial that they offer courses relevant to the needs of the labour market. This must cover both technical and transferable skills and be delivered with the appropriate pedagogy, including internships and hands-on practice. Partnerships with employment service providers, organizations of persons with disabilities and businesses can further support learners with disabilities in obtaining job placements and managing smooth school-to-work transition.

Empowering learners with disabilities to participate in mainstream TVET schools

In addition to ensuring the relevance of TVET institutions, the mainstreaming of disability inclusion into TVET institutions calls for: accessible physical environments; adapted entry criteria, teaching methods, teaching materials and evaluation methods that suit the needs of persons with diverse disabilities; capacity of the TVET workforce to train persons with disabilities alongside their counterparts without disabilities; and ongoing support services, including reasonable accommodation.[72]

70 ESCAP, *Building Disability-inclusive Societies in Asia and the Pacific: Assessing Progress of the Incheon Strategy* (Bangkok, 2018). It is not clear from the available information whether these vocational training programmes were disability-specific or mainstream programmes.
71 ILO, "Making TVET and skills systems inclusive of persons with disabilities", Policy Brief (Geneva, 2017).
72 ibid.

Box 24
Disability inclusion and TVET sector planning in Vanuatu

In **Vanuatu** and in line with the National Disability Policy and Plan of Action 2008–2015,* the National Disability Inclusion Policy for the TVET Sector 2016–2020** has been developed to mainstream disability inclusion into the TVET sector.

The policy seeks to integrate disability inclusion into the sector through the following measures:

- provide support to service providers in offering training that is inclusive of and accessible to persons with diverse disabilities;
- conduct training for trainers to improve their competencies in delivering disability-inclusive programmes;
- conduct awareness-raising and outreach activities to encourage the enrolment of persons with disabilities from urban, rural and remote areas;
- offer ongoing counselling and support to trainees with disabilities to enable successful completion of training and facilitate work placement and/or business development; and
- provide funding to facilitate reasonable accommodation.

The Ministry of Education and Training leads the policy implementation, in collaboration with a Steering Committee, consisting of the Ministry of Justice, the Vanuatu Qualifications Authority, the Vanuatu Institute of Teacher Education and civil society organizations. The latter include organizations of persons with disabilities, representatives of training providers, the private sector and others as appropriate.

Source: Ministry of Education and Training, *National Disability Inclusion Policy for the TVET Sector, 2016–2020* (Port-Vila, 2015); Sherol George, "Integrating disability inclusion into TVET sector planning-the case of Vanuatu", Presentation at ESCAP Expert Group Meeting on Promoting Inclusive Employment for Persons with Disabilities in Asia and the Pacific, 2021. Available at www.unescap.org/events/2021/expert-group-meeting-promoting-inclusive-employment-persons-disabilities-asia-and.
Note: * The Vanuatu National Disability Inclusive Development Policy 2018–2025 was issued to further enhance the commitment to promoting disability-inclusive development. ** As of September 2021, the National Disability Inclusion Policy for the TVET Sector 2016–2020 was still in effect.

Box 25
Providing relevant skills training in disability-specific TVET institutions in Hong Kong (China) and Japan

In **Hong Kong, China**, the Caritas Vocational Training Centre provides different training modes that suit the diverse needs of persons with disabilities. This includes vocational training, supported employment, job attachment and retraining. Trainees select their desired course from a range of offerings that include catering, servicing, business, logistics, informational technology, arts and general studies.

To ensure that skills are effectively imparted to learners, the centre consults educational psychologists on its training and teaching and provides simulated or real workplace settings for trainees to practise their skills. It also offers courses on transferable skills, such as planning and prioritization, metacognition, working memory, sustained attention, affect regulation and response inhibition.To assist graduates in making a smooth transition from school to work, the centre has developed a three-tier employment support model comprising day-to-day workplace support, group support and customized individual support.

The centre has also built strong partnerships with various business partners who offer internship opportunities to trainees and advise on curriculum development. Mutual visits between the centre and business partners are frequently arranged.

In **Japan**, the National Vocational Rehabilitation Centre conducts vocational evaluation, guidance and

Box 25 (continued)

training through a unified system with vocational counsellors and vocational training instructors, in partnership with the National Rehabilitation Center for Persons with Disabilities. Its programmes comprise in-centre courses and practical training at workplaces, job hunting assistance and support for job retention. The services have been developed in close cooperation with companies looking to hire persons with disabilities. Courses are available for persons with diverse disabilities and differing levels of disability in mechanical drawing, electronic drawing, technical operation, architectural design, DTP/web operations, office automation systems and accounting. In fiscal year 2020, 83 of the 112 graduates were employed within three months after completing the training. On average, more than 80 per cent of graduates have found employment every year.

The Osaka City Vocational Rehabilitation Center also offers an array of courses ranging from one- or two-month skills upgrading programmes to year-long training on specific skills ranging from book-keeping and accounting to cleaning and nursing care assistance, product assembly and soldering. In addition to acquiring vocational skills, trainees participate in a cross-course curriculum that includes basic skills required in the workplace (such as asking questions, reporting and respecting peers), assertiveness training and communication skills. The centre offers training through a variety of mediums: It has been coordinating with local centres and companies to enable persons with disabilities to receive vocational training within their community. Online skills improvement courses are available for persons who prefer remote training.

Source: Nicky Chan, "Providing relevant skills training for the labour market in disability-specific TVET schools and education institutions – the case of Caritas Lok Mo Integrated Vocational Training Centre", Presentation at ESCAP Expert Group Meeting on Promoting Inclusive Employment for Persons with Disabilities in Asia and the Pacific, 2021. Available at www.unescap.org/events/2021/expert-group-meeting-promoting-inclusive-employment-persons-disabilities-asia-and; and email correspondence with Fumihiro Kojima, Vocational Rehabilitation Department, JEED and Kyoko Sakai, Executive Director, Osaka City Vocational Rehabilitation Center.

Box 26
Measures to support the participation of learners with disabilities in mainstream TVET institutions in Singapore and Viet Nam

In **Singapore**, the Learning Accessibility Office has been established at each Institute of Technical Education to support students with diverse disabilities in receiving a holistic education and obtaining work skills for meaningful employment upon graduation. Services available for students with disabilities include but are not limited to transition support, access to facilities, advice on assistive technology devices, course counselling, provision of reasonable accommodation during tests and examinations,* career counselling and industrial attachment. Full-time Singaporean students with a diagnosis statement from a medical professional of physical, hearing or visual impairment can apply for the Special Education Needs Fund under the Ministry of Education to purchase assistive devices or support services. Examples of such devices or services comprise, among others, braille displays, computer pointing devices, text-to-speech devices, note-taking service and sign language interpretation service.

In **Viet Nam**, vocational training is available for persons with disabilities in 200 mainstream training centres and 55 specialized vocational training centres. Disability-inclusive mainstream centres are entitled to government financial support to invest in facilities and training equipment and to lease land to set up premises at locations suitable for persons with disabilities. Other measures to support the participation of persons with disabilities in vocational training include meal and travel allowances for trainees with disabilities in both rural and urban areas.

Note: More information can be found on the ITE website: www.ite.edu.sg/life-at-ite/student-services/learning-accessibility; also see CRPD/C/VNM/1. * Examples of reasonable accommodation include allowing the use of assistive technology devices as well as adjustments to the following items: assessment settings (preferential seating), assessment timing (extended time and frequent breaks), presentation methods (large print and alternative colours) and response formats (written and multiple-choice questions).

Evidence indicates promising results when disability-inclusive approaches are mainstreamed at all levels of a TVET system in Bangladesh. The country saw a sixfold increase in the enrolment of trainees with disabilities within three years following a reform that comprehensively mainstreamed disability inclusion into its TVET system.

Although good practices on disability-inclusive TVET can be found, there is limited information on vocational training provision that is comparable across countries at the regional level, in terms of the profile of service providers; the scope, nature and quality of course offerings; and the impact of such training on employment outcomes for persons with disabilities. It would thus be timely to conduct a comprehensive review of the landscape of vocational training provision in the Asia–Pacific region and identify gaps in skills for employment. Such an exercise would be important for informing further development of disability-inclusive TVET programmes of governments, organizations of persons with disabilities and other stakeholders, especially given the changing contexts in the world of work discussed in Chapter 4.

Box 27
Features of disability-inclusive TVET in Bangladesh

1. Disability-inclusive policymaking

Following the ratification of the Convention on the Rights of Persons with Disabilities in 2007 and its Optional Protocol in 2008, the Government of **Bangladesh** issued the National Skills Development Policy in 2011. It then followed with the National Strategy for Inclusion of Persons with Disabilities in Skills Development in 2016. It also enacted the Rights and Protection of Persons with Disabilities Act in 2013, which includes a call for action to promote disability-inclusive education and training and to educate teachers and employers on disability issues.

The National Skills Development Policy makes recommendations on disability inclusion, with one objective being to improve access to skills development for various groups of citizens, including persons with disabilities. In particular, the policy established a 5 per cent enrolment quota for persons with disabilities across all skills development programmes and mandated the provision of reasonable accommodation and the accessibility of TVET institution buildings.

To support policy implementation, the Directorate of Technical Education (DTE), under the Ministry of Education, developed guidance and resources on disability inclusion for TVET institutes run by the Department of Technical Education. The DTE also established a Disability Inclusion Advisory Group to guide policy formulation on disability budgeting and the implementation of disability-inclusion measures in TVET institutions. The Advisory Group comprises members from DTE, the Bangladesh Technical Education Board, organizations specialized in training for persons with disabilities and various ministries.

2. Institutional capacity-building

The DTE appoints a senior official in TVET institutions as a focal point to ensure disability inclusion in annual work plans, procurement plans, budgets, performance appraisals and data monitoring. Disability-inclusion guidelines for TVET managers and instructors have been developed to enhance the skills and capacity of staff in the TVET system. Training of trainers and refresher courses on disability inclusion are arranged for vice-principals and chief instructors so that they can further train other instructors.

3. Partnerships and network-building

The DTE issued an office order to encourage TVET institutions to establish partnerships with organizations of persons with disabilities and non-governmental organizations working on disability issues. Several memoranda of understanding have been signed to assist the implementation of the 5 per cent enrolment target for persons with disabilities.

4. Monitoring

The DTE created a database of students with disabilities in TVET institutions to monitor enrolment and the drop-out and pass out rates. The data are disaggregated by 12 types of disabilities. The data support management decision-making and relevant policymaking.

Source: ILO, "Disability inclusion in the Bangladesh skills system", Brochure (Dhaka, 2017); ILO, "Good practices for inclusion of persons with disabilities: a replication guide for Technical and Vocational Education and Training (TVET) Institutions", Brochure (Dhaka, 2017); ILO, "Major achievements of the Bangladesh Skills for Employment and Productivity (B-SEP) Project", Brochure (Dhaka, 2017); and ILO, *Including Persons with Disabilities in Technical and Vocational Education and Training: A Guide for Administrative and Instructors to Disability Inclusion* (Dhaka, 2016).

3.3.2 Job coaching

Job coaching is increasingly used as a tool to facilitate the employment of persons with disabilities in Asia and the Pacific. It involves a "place and train" approach linked to supported employment. This is in contrast to the "train and place" approach traditionally used by vocational training centres involving placement of a person to a job upon completion of training. Job coaching was initially introduced by training centres and non-governmental organizations as an effective way of developing the skills of persons with intellectual disabilities using real work in practical situations to the extent possible.[73] It is now widely accepted as an approach to provide employment and employability support to persons with diverse disabilities and supported by public funds.

Box 28
Role of a job coach and the job coaching process

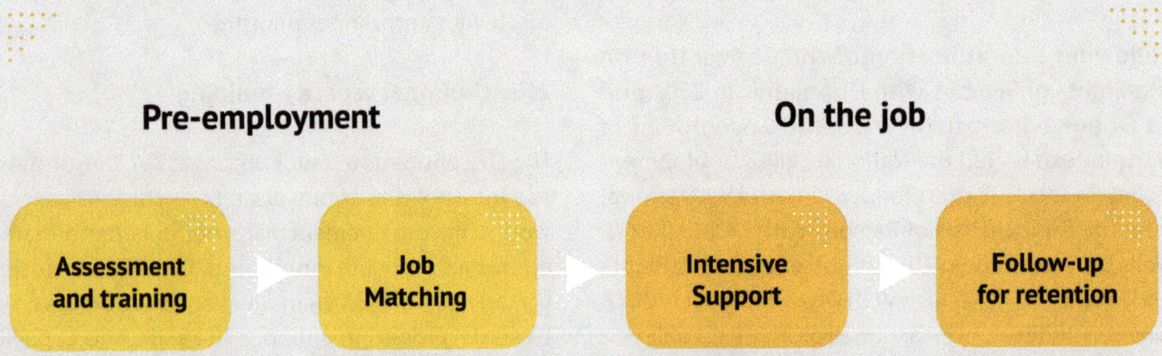

- Prior to the placement of a jobseeker with a disability on a job, a job coach conducts pre-employment assessments and training and then matches the jobseeker with a suitable job opportunity. In parallel, the coach discusses opportunities for a supported-employment placement with potential employers.
- Upon placement, the next step involves reaching an agreement with an employer that the worker with a disability can be trained in the workplace. If there is no supervisor in the workplace who can provide the training, the job coach steps in.
- The job coach works alongside the worker with a disability, providing training on the job and continuing to assist with job tasks until the individual can perform the job independently.
- The job coach also helps prepare the workplace for greater disability inclusion, including conducting disability awareness sessions for co-workers and supervisors.
- Once the placement process is complete, the job coach may visit the workplace from time to time to ensure that everything is going smoothly and to resolve any problems that emerge, for the worker or the employer.

Source: Yeo Swee Lan, "Job coaching for the promotion of sustainable open employment", Presentation at ESCAP Expert Group Meeting on Promoting Inclusive Employment for Persons with Disabilities in Asia and the Pacific, 2021. Available at www.unescap.org/events/2021/expert-group-meeting-promoting-inclusive-employment-persons-disabilities-asia-and; and ILO, "Supported employment and job coaching", Information Sheet (internal document, unpublished).

73 ILO, "Promoting training and employment opportunities for people with intellectual disabilities: International experience", Employment Working Paper No. 103 (Geneva, 2011).

Job coaching offers several advantages for a worker with a disability, including increased relevance of training to the employer's needs as well as gaining experience in an actual mainstream work environment with current and up-to-date working conditions, work processes and machinery. For the employer, the job coaching process also offers the opportunity to observe the work capacity of trainees with disabilities in the process, without having to make an advance commitment to recruit.[74]

Box 29
Job coaching in Malaysia

The Job Coach Network Malaysia was established by the Department of Social Welfare under the Ministry of Women, Family and Community Development in 2008 to facilitate information sharing and partnership among job coaches hired by the Government, non-governmental organizations and the private sector. It operates to promote sustainable employment for persons with disabilities in **Malaysia.**

From 2010 to 2020, 2,773 participants from government departments, community-based rehabilitation centres, civil society organizations, private companies and other organizations attended the job coach training. A total of 1,387 persons with disabilities were supported by job coaches sponsored by the Department of Social Welfare from 2012 to 2020. Persons with learning disabilities accounted for 66 per cent of service receivers.

More can be done to further promote job coaching as an integral tool for supported employment. At present, many job coaches in Malaysia are not working on a full-time basis due to the limited resources of civil society organizations and community-based rehabilitation programmes. It is essential to build partnerships between civil society organizations and the private sector to help all actors leverage resources.

Many employers still do not possess the awareness and experience in promoting disability-inclusive employment through job coaching. There is a need to raise awareness of the role of job coaching in businesses and for the Government to further incentivize employers to create inclusive workplaces.

Source: Yeo Swee Lan, "Job coaching for the promotion of sustainable open employment", Presentation at ESCAP Expert Group Meeting on Promoting Inclusive Employment for Persons with Disabilities in Asia and the Pacific, 2021. Available at www.unescap.org/events/2021/expert-group-meeting-promoting-inclusive-employment-persons-disabilities-asia-and.

3.3.3 Jobseeking skills

In addition to technical skills, skills for seeking employment, including the ability to write application letters, complete application forms and perform well in job interviews, are crucial for gaining employment. Some initiatives and programmes have strengthened the provision of training in jobseeking skills, in addition to vocational skills, in the region in recent years.

74 ILO, "Supported employment and job coaching", information sheet (internal document, unpublished).

Box 30
Jobseeking skills training in China and Indonesia

Standard Chartered Bank in **China** launched and funded the project Path to Success: Creating a Strong Ecosystem for Persons with Disabilities in the Labour Market. It aims to improve the vocational skills and employability of persons with disabilities aged 18–30, with a particular focus on persons with visual disabilities. The project has organized 40 online courses through the WeChat platform that deal with job preparation and soft skills, such as interview preparation, résumé writing and career development. Around 1,800 persons with disabilities participated in the first six-month period after the online courses became available. During the COVID-19 lockdown, this initiative was expanded to a coalition of disability organizations and NGOs to support persons with disabilities, many of whom are facing economic challenges or lost their job due to the crisis. In addition, a training camp was organized in three cities for around 200 students, volunteers and staff from other companies. To date, the project has resulted in more than 50 young persons with disabilities gaining employment.

In **Indonesia**, Puspadi Bali, a training service operated in large part by persons with disabilities, provides personal and professional development courses to jobseekers with disabilities. Alongside vocational training, Puspadi Bali offers soft skills training, including communication skills, personal effectiveness, creative problem-solving, strategic thinking, negotiating, team building and personal care. On completion of training, graduates are offered work experience stints in the form of three-month internships with collaborating companies, supported by access to accommodation, transport and on-the-job training.

Note: More information can be found on the Easy Inclusion website: www.easyinclusion.cn/ and Puspadi Bali website: www.puspadibali.org.

3.4 Employment services to facilitate the implementation of measures supporting disability-inclusive employment

Employment services can be a key link between jobseekers and employers. They are central to implementing and operationalizing active labour market policies. In the context of promoting disability-inclusive employment, employment services fulfil the following functions:

- provide comprehensive information to jobseekers about vacancies and facilitate job referrals and placements;
- facilitate vocational assessment, pre-placement guidance, skills training, job coaching services and on-the-job training or work trials;
- provide information and advisory services to employers on job analysis, design and matching; legal requirements and financial subsidies; workplace modification options, reasonable accommodation and the provision of specialized equipment, technical aids and assistive devices; and
- provide useful follow-up support to workers with disabilities and employers when problems arise.

In Asia and the Pacific, employment services for persons with disabilities are provided through an array of modalities, ranging from those that are government-funded and managed to those that are fully owned and run by civil society organizations and private businesses. Some entities provide disability-specific employment services under a larger umbrella organization catering to all jobseekers, while others are fully dedicated to supporting persons with disabilities. To facilitate enhanced access by persons with disabilities to employment services, a one-stop shop approach has been increasingly applied in the region to deliver employment services to persons with disabilities through employment service centres.

To ensure that persons with disabilities can fully access both general and disability-specific employment services, efforts are required to increase the access of persons with disabilities to such services by improving the physical accessibility of facilities; addressing negative attitudes and stereotypes among service providers; and raising awareness of such services within the disability community. Additionally, employment services, both mainstream and disability-specific, should integrate gender dimensions into all their processes to ensure that women with disabilities can access employment services.

Box 31
Modalities of disability employment services in Asia and the Pacific

Mainstream employment service entities that integrate disability-specific employment services in Japan and Viet Nam

The Japan Organization for Employment of the Elderly, Persons with Disabilities and Job Seekers (JEED) was established by the Government of **Japan** in 2003* as a special administrative organization to promote employment of older persons, persons with disabilities and jobseekers who need assistance. With the merging of several government-affiliated organizations into one single body, administrative costs for the provision of employment services have been reduced. With the employment services for older persons, persons with disabilities and the general population housed under the same organization, JEED is able to take an integrated approach to collaborate with employers to create and sustain employment opportunities for different target populations.

JEED prepares persons with disabilities for employment through vocational assessment, individualized training, employment placement and job coaching. It supports employers in developing plans to create and sustain jobs for persons with disabilities, organizes workshops to equip employers with knowledge and skills to manage persons with disabilities in the workplace and lends (free-of-charge) assistive devices to employers for a fixed period. JEED also advises local employment support organizations, collects levies, provides grants and raises public awareness on disability-inclusive employment.

In **Viet Nam**, job counselling, employment referral, job placement services and job fairs are available for persons with disabilities through a network of mainstream employment service centres. These centres exist in each province and, depending on the specific circumstances of each locality, can be managed by the Ministry of Labour, Invalids and Social Affairs, mass organizations such as trade unions, the Women's Union, farmers' associations and private businesses.

Government entity dedicated to implementing employment services for persons with disabilities: Korea Employment Agency for Persons with Disabilities

The **Korea** Employment Agency for Persons with Disabilities (KEAD) is a government organization established under the Ministry of Employment and Labour that seeks to connect persons with disabilities and companies. KEAD partners with a range of stakeholders from the private sector to support persons with disabilities in finding and securing decent jobs. It also promotes a disability-inclusive environment in the world of work through policy research and awareness-raising activities.

The employment services provided by KEAD include employment counselling and planning, vocational competency development, intensive job placement, the provision of assistive devices, personal assistance services and commuting assistance services. In response to such issues as the rapid increase in the number of older persons with disabilities, the Fourth Industrial Revolution and the rising of the "untact economy",** KEAD is now focusing on job security, job diversification and productivity enhancement for persons with disabilities.

Government-affiliated entity providing disability-specific services, including those concerning employment: SG Enable

In **Singapore**, SG Enable is an agency established by the Ministry of Social and Family Development but registered as a company limited by guarantee and an institution of public character. Its functions include empowering persons with disabilities and caregivers via timely access to information and referral services, grants and support; enhancing employability and employment opportunities for persons with disabilities seeking assistance; and engaging families, communities and other stakeholders in enabling persons with disabilities as integral members of society.

SG Enable applies a one-stop shop approach in the provision of employment services to persons with disabilities. It first prepares persons with disabilities through internships, mentoring, curriculum vitae clinics and training courses. Potential candidates then explore career opportunities from inclusive employers via the Disability Employment Jobs Portal or a job coach. After workers find employment, SG Enable offers support for workplace integration and encourages persons with disabilities to enhance their competencies and skill sets through the SkillsFuture Study Awards. For employers, SG Enable builds

Box 31 (continued)

up their skills and confidence in disability-hiring and defrays the cost of supporting employees with disabilities. Enabling Mark and Enabling Mark Awards have been launched to recognize disability-inclusive business practices. SG Enable strengthens the capabilities of disability employment professionals, such as school teachers, occupational therapists, job coaches and social entrepreneurs who hire persons with disabilities to improve the quality of support services they can provide to persons with disabilities.

Private entity partially funded by government that runs disability-specific employment services alongside vocational training and social enterprises: Thailand

In **Thailand**, the Redemptorist Foundation for People with Disabilities operates schools and community employment centres to provide education and vocational training for persons with disabilities. It also runs social enterprises to offer internship programmes to trainees with disabilities to generate income for the foundation and to provide products or services for internal use. Funded by the Government (30 per cent) as well as businesses and individuals (70 per cent), the foundation works in synergy with government entities, civil society organizations, private sector organizations and other stakeholders, such as the National Human Rights Commission of Thailand and the Lawyers Council of Thailand.

The Foundation has shifted its priorities over the past few decades. From 1984 to 1999, the focus was vocational training. The Foundation worked with employers to develop curriculum and provided skills development programmes according to market demand. Direct contacts with employers were established for job placement. From 1999 to 2012, awareness-raising among employers became a priority. The Foundation conducted accessibility audits in workplaces and offered soft skills training to jobseekers with disabilities and to companies. The emphasis on decent work led to a low turnover rate of persons with disabilities. The Foundation has been expanding its services to support more persons since 2010 due to the high demand for employees with disabilities partially in response to strong enforcement of the quota system.

Source: Phyllis Choo, and others, "Roundtable: Designing and operationalizing needs-relevant employment support services", Presentations at ESCAP Expert Group Meeting on Promoting Inclusive Employment for Persons with Disabilities in Asia and the Pacific, 2021. Available at www.unescap.org/events/2021/expert-group-meeting-promoting-inclusive-employment-persons-disabilities-asia-and; email correspondence with Fumihiro Kojima, Vocational Rehabilitation Department, JEED; ILO, Employment-related Services for Persons with Disabilities in Vietnam (Bangkok, 2009); and CRPD/C/VNM/1.
Note: More information is available on the websites of DEA: https://disabilityemployment.org.au/; KEAD: www.kead.or.kr/english/home/main.do; SG Enable: www.sgenable.sg/Pages/Home.aspx; Redemptorist Foundation for People with Disabilities: www.fr-ray.org/redemptorist-foundation-for-people-with-disabilities/; and JEED: www.jeed.go.jp/english/index.html. * The Japan Organization for Employment of the Elderly, Persons with Disabilities was established in 2003. It was later renamed as the Japan Organization for Employment of the Elderly, Persons with Disabilities and Job Seekers in 2011, absorbing part of the business of the dissolved Employment and Human Resources Development Organization of Japan. See JEED website: www.jeed.go.jp/english/about_jeed/index.html. ** The "untact economy" is a newly coined term that means non-face-to-face social and economic activities.

In countries with multiple employment service providers supporting persons with disabilities, the establishment of an industry body can enhance coordination, information and experience-sharing, as well as organize joint activities such as training and policy advocacy among these providers.

Box 32
Coordinating disability employment services in Australia

In **Australia**, the Disability Employment Australia is a peak industry body that represents, supports and extends resources to the providers of disability employment services. It advises and trains its members on trends, good practices and innovative approaches concerning the disability employment sector, with a focus on government policies, issues impacting the viability of the industry and barriers to workforce participation that persons with disabilities face. It also educates the public on issues related to disability inclusion in the world of work and provides inputs to government consultations and reviews concerning disability employment.

Source: Rick Kane, "Roundtable: Designing and operationalizing needs-relevant employment support services", Presentations at ESCAP Expert Group Meeting on Promoting Inclusive Employment for Persons with Disabilities in Asia and the Pacific, 2021. Available at www.unescap.org/events/2021/expert-group-meeting-promoting-inclusive-employment-persons-disabilities-asia-and.

3.5 Laws, policies and programmes that support entrepreneurs with disabilities

Because persons with disabilities in Asia and the Pacific are predominantly employed in the informal economy (and mainly in self-employment), legislation, policies and programmes to support the entrepreneurship endeavours of persons with disabilities are in place in some countries of the region. These include measures to facilitate the provision of business development skills training;[75] microcredit, loans, grants and business equipment; and support to access markets and business networks.

General policies and services to promote enterprise development can potentially benefit entrepreneurs with disabilities as long as they are disability-inclusive and accessible. For example, websites with information on these schemes and application platforms should be in accessible formats, and the built environment of relevant service centres should be physically barrier-free. And government personnel providing such mainstream services should be aware of and practise the principles of non-discrimination in their interactions with entrepreneurs with disabilities.

Box 33
Legislation, policies and programmes to support entrepreneurs with disabilities in China, the Republic of Korea and Viet Nam

In **China**, the China Disabled Persons' Federation, along with the National Development and Reform Commission, Ministry of Civil Affairs and 12 other government entities, jointly issued the Opinions on Supporting Employment and Entrepreneurship of Persons with Disabilities* in 2018. It specifies preferential administrative, taxation and financial measures to support persons with disabilities in starting and operating a business. For example, it stipulates that reasonable accommodation and priority should be given to entrepreneurs with disabilities in the business registration process. The income taxes and business taxes of entrepreneurs with disabilities may be reduced in accordance with national and provincial taxation policies. Persons with disabilities can apply for subsidies and subsidized loans to increase capital for running their business. China also has adopted a series of policies to support entrepreneurship development of persons with disabilities in a comprehensive manner. Such policies include Notice on Preferential Value-Added Tax Policies for Promoting Employment of Persons with Disabilities, Notice on Policies for Government Purchase of Products from Employers of Persons with Disabilities and the Programme on Employment Skill Improvement for Persons with Disabilities.

The **Republic of Korea** enacted the Act on the Facilitation of Entrepreneurial Activities of Persons with Disabilities** to facilitate business start-ups and entrepreneurial activities of persons with disabilities. It obliges the national and local governments to preferentially invest in and grant loans for enterprises run by persons with disabilities. Public institutions are to facilitate purchases of products made by entrepreneurs with disabilities. In addition, enterprises of persons with disabilities can benefit from tax concessions.

The Act also provides for the establishment of the Korea Association of Disabled Entrepreneurs. The association undertakes activities to empower entrepreneurs with disabilities, such as providing training programmes, facilitating information-sharing, assisting joint purchases and sales and expanding overseas markets for enterprises of persons with disabilities.

In **Viet Nam**, more than an estimated 15,000 persons with disabilities were working in more than 400 businesses owned by entrepreneurs with disabilities in 2018. To support entrepreneurs with disabilities in accessing credit, the Government established the National Employment Fund to encourage the entrepreneurship of persons with disabilities through subsidized loans. The Viet Nam Bank for Social Policy provides loans for entrepreneurs with disabilities at a preferential interest rate of 3.96 per cent. According to national decrees, the lending interest rate for persons with disabilities is calculated at half of what it is for persons from near-poor households. The maximum loan for a self-employed person is 100 million Vietnamese dong, with a repayment term of up to 120 months.

The Viet Nam Bank for Social Policy, in partnership with the Nippon Foundation, is also disbursing small loans to businesses employing, serving or owned by persons with disabilities under the auspices of a technical cooperation project. The total outstanding loans

75 While persons with disabilities may have attended vocational training and acquired specific technical skills, they are less likely to have acquired entrepreneurship skills and may need support in assessing market needs, identifying marketable products or services, seeking funding, selecting raw materials, deciding on the location of a business premise and accessing markets. See FAO, *A Handbook for Training of Disabled on Rural Enterprise Development* (Bangkok, 2003).

Box 33 (continued)

reached 8.8 billion dong, with 158 active borrowers at the end of 2019.

Research indicates that, in practice, entrepreneurs with disabilities still may face difficulties in accessing subsidized loans despite their eligibility due to existing prejudices and stereotypes. Further actions are required to enhance the access of entrepreneurs with disabilities to such credit.

Source: CRPD/C/CHN/2-3; State Council Information Office of the People's Republic of China, *Equality, Participation and Sharing: 70 Years of Protecting the Rights and Interests of Persons with Disabilities in the PRC* (Beijing, 2019); CRPD/C/KOR/1; CRPD/C/VNM/1; UNDP, *Improving Employment Opportunities for Persons with Disabilities in Viet Nam* (Hanoi, 2020); Viet Nam Bank for Social Policy, *Annual Report 2019* (Hanoi, n.d.); and Viet Nam Bank for Social Policy, "Lending interest rate". Available at https://eng.vbsp.org.vn/lending-interest-rate.
Note: * The Opinions on Supporting Employment and Entrepreneurship of Persons with Disabilities (in Chinese) is available at www.cdpf.org.cn/zwgk/zcwj/wjfb/c97c15ce00d14ea296a303f1f8c59cd4.htm. ** The Act on the Facilitation of Entrepreneurial Activities of Persons with Disabilities is available at https://elaw.klri.re.kr/eng_service/lawView.do?hseq=49156&lang=ENG).

In addition to government support, private sector initiatives, including those of employer associations, have assisted entrepreneurs with disabilities in Asia and the Pacific.

Box 34
Initiatives to support entrepreneurs with disabilities in Australia and Sri Lanka

In **Australia**, the pilot project IgniteAbility Small Business Start-ups is supporting new enterprise formation by persons with disabilities. It provides support to aspiring entrepreneurs with disabilities through capacity-building and networking in product development, marketing and financial management. It works with individuals to overcome barriers they face. IgniteAbility builds on the findings of a study of the experiences of entrepreneurs with disabilities, which examined their needs in business development, the dynamic of their business enterprises, the economic and social contributions made and barriers faced. Entrepreneurs reported that the lack of entrepreneurial education was at the root of start-up mistakes, costing them money, time and energy. They also faced difficulties in networking to foster the exchange of information and ideas critical to business development. Compliance with regulation agencies was cumbersome and laborious, tending to stifle entrepreneurial activity. Attitudinal barriers sometimes constrained them from fostering relationships with consumers, contractors, funders and other key individuals. And the support provided at many levels by family and friendship networks was central to the development of their enterprises, particularly when microenterprise activities were involved. These findings could also contribute to the development of disability-inclusive entrepreneurship programmes across the region.

In **Sri Lanka**, the Specialised Training and Disability Resource Centre of the Employers' Federation of Ceylon offers free-of-charge training programmes to persons with diverse disabilities who are willing to join the labour market or start their own business. Training targeted at women entrepreneurs with disabilities is conducted on a regular basis. Examples of courses that facilitate entrepreneurship skills development include but are not limited to writing business plans, "technopreneurship" for social change and managing stalls to market products. The centre also supports entrepreneurs with disabilities in product upgrading, provides interest-free loans and works closely with relevant stakeholders, such as family members of persons with learning disabilities. Based on the centre's experience, it has summarized the areas needing further action in promoting entrepreneurship of persons with disabilities in Sri Lanka:

- deliver training and services to the doorsteps of persons with disabilities;
- support persons with disabilities in diversifying sources of income;
- strengthen cooperation between local businesses and entrepreneurs with disabilities;
- facilitate community integration; and
- ensure representation of entrepreneurs with disabilities in decision-making processes at all levels on matters concerning them.

Source: Settlement Services International, "IgniteAbility Small Business Start-ups". Available at www.ssi.org.au/services/ignite-ability-small-business-start-ups; Simon Darcy and others, *Australia's Disability Entrepreneurial Ecosystem: Experiences of People with Disability with Microenterprises, Self-employment and Entrepreneurship* (Sydney, 2020); Manique Gunaratne, "Supporting entrepreneurs with disabilities", Presentation at ESCAP Expert Group Meeting on Promoting Inclusive Employment for Persons with Disabilities in Asia and the Pacific, 2021. Available at www.unescap.org/events/2021/expert-group-meeting-promoting-inclusive-employment-persons-disabilities-asia-and.

3.6 Measures to create an enabling social environment

3.6.1 Accessibility

Access to the built environment, public transportation, movement to and within workplaces, knowledge and ICT are enablers for promoting employment and entrepreneurship opportunities among persons with disabilities.

Accessibility features strongly in both the Convention on the Rights of Persons with Disabilities and the Incheon Strategy, with a stand-alone article and goal, respectively. The Convention requires States parties to develop minimum accessibility standards and guidelines; ensure that facilities and services take into account the access requirements of persons with different types of disabilities; provide training on accessibility issues; promote access to ICT and systems, including the internet; and provide guides, readers and professional sign language interpreters as well as other forms of live assistance and intermediaries to facilitate access to buildings and other facilities open to the public. It also includes a general obligation on States parties to promote the development of universally designed goods, services, equipment and facilities (including transportation), information and communication, requiring the minimum possible adaptation and the least cost to meet the specific needs of a broad range of users, including persons with disabilities.

Yet, standards of accessibility vary across the region and do not always take into account the barriers faced by persons with different disabilities. Several countries in the region have not developed formal accessibility standards. Although some countries report high levels of accessibility of the built environment, it often applies primarily to wheelchair users and persons with other mobility impairments and seldom reflects the experiences of persons with other types of disabilities.[76]

With the advent of the gig economy and rapid technological advancements, the accessibility of ICT has become more important in the promotion of employment opportunities for persons with disabilities. An evaluation of digital accessibility rights in countries around the world found mixed performance in the region.[77] Urgent action is required by countries to strengthen the implementation of policies and programmes on ICT accessibility, followed by the need to strengthen institutional capacity for more effective implementation.

Despite universal design-based accessibility being strongly desirable and recommended by the Beijing Declaration, including the Action Plan to Accelerate the Implementation of the Incheon Strategy, universal design remains an emerging area of investment in the region. According to the findings of a 2019 ESCAP survey, at least 10 countries recognize by law the concept of accessibility through universal design.[78] There is still much to be done to incorporate universal design principles into projects and actions to improve accessibility across countries.

3.6.2 Awareness-raising

A major barrier to the employment of persons with disabilities stems from mistaken assumptions and stereotypes about their working capacity on the part of employers and the public. These perceptions are sometimes internalized by persons with disabilities themselves, leading to poor self-image and low levels of self-confidence. Women with disabilities are doubly disadvantaged due to the intersectionality of gender and disability.

There is thus an acute need to increase the awareness throughout society – including at the family level – of the capabilities and contributions of persons with disabilities, to foster respect for the rights and dignity of persons with disabilities and to combat stereotypes, prejudices and harmful practices.

Examples of measures to be undertaken include public awareness campaigns to promote recognition of the skills, merits and abilities of persons with disabilities and of their contributions to the workplace and the labour market. The media should also be mindful of portraying persons with disabilities in a manner consistent with the Convention on the Rights of Persons with Disabilities, such as persons with long-term impairments who are hindered by various barriers from participating fully and effectively in society on an equal basis with others.

The Convention's provisions on awareness-raising in article 8 require States parties to adopt immediate, effective and appropriate measures upon ratification. It is thus of concern that there is still a lack of public awareness-raising campaigns, a persistence of the medical approach to disability in measures introduced and continuing negative attitudes, stereotypes and prejudices against persons with disabilities in society.[79]

76 ESCAP, *Building Disability-inclusive Societies in Asia and the Pacific: Assessing Progress of the Incheon Strategy* (Bangkok, 2018).

77 See Annex I for the Digital Accessibility Rights Evaluation Index 2020.

78 ESCAP, *Disability at a Glance 2019: Investing in Accessibility in Asia and the Pacific – Strategic Approaches to Achieving Disability-inclusive Sustainable Development* (Bangkok, 2019).

79 Based on concluding observations by the Committee on the Rights of Persons with Disabilities on the initial reports of States parties in the Asia and Pacific region. The States parties reports can be found at OHCHR, "CRPD, State Parties Reports", UN Treaty Body Database. Available at https://tbinternet.ohchr.org/_layouts/15/treatybodyexternal/TBSearch.aspx?Lang=en&TreatyID=4&DocTypeID=29.

Chapter 4

Changes in the world of work and associated impacts on employment of persons with disabilities

The world of work is evolving rapidly. Technological advancements, the rise of the gig economy and the COVID-19 pandemic have brought about significant changes to the way people work. In turn, the changes have created new opportunities and challenges for the employment and livelihoods of persons with disabilities.

4.1 Technological advancements

Technological changes in recent years have led to a fundamental transformation in the way work is carried out and have resulted in mixed impacts on the employment situation of persons with disabilities.

Increased automation, having rapidly displaced low-skilled jobs involving routine and repetitive tasks,[80] has generally had a negative effect on employment opportunities for persons with disabilities in labour-intensive occupations.

At the same time, new jobs have emerged. For example, where automation has led to declining working hours, the demand for leisure-related activities has increased, giving rise to new leisure industries and services and the creation of jobs in sports, health, recreation, tourism, restaurants, computer games and the do-it-yourself movement.[81]

Importantly, the combination of computers with robotics, algorithms and other forms of artificial intelligence brought forth by the latest wave of technological development, often referred to as the Fourth Industrial Revolution, has unlocked the potential to expand employment possibilities for persons with disabilities in the manufacturing and service sectors. While it is still unclear what these innovations will eventually lead to, there are promising indications that the potential of robots to assist with physical tasks can be tapped to increase employment opportunities for persons with disabilities.

Advances in ICT have also increased telework, commerce and distance learning options, thereby improving employment, entrepreneurship and training prospects. These advancements include the increased availability of small, powerful, affordable and accessible personal computers and smart ICT devices; the growth in public access to the World Wide Web and its enhanced accessibility through new accessibility standards;[82] and new

Box 35
AQUAS Project in Germany and Experimental Cafe in Japan

In the manufacturing sector, the AQUAS project in **Germany** illustrates the potential of service robots as assistants to persons with severe disabilities in performing physically demanding manufacturing tasks. The service robot enables persons with severe disabilities to focus on higher-quality aspects of their jobs, such as work-step preparation, quality control and person-to-person communication. To implement this pioneering robotics technology, the workplace has been adjusted to suit the manufacturing environment. The robot can flexibly adjust to different table heights, and its sensor skin allows it to function without the need for a safety barrier – if a worker comes too close, the robot automatically stops without any contact.

The AQUAS project is jointly conducted by Robert Bosch GmbH, the Fraunhofer Institute for Industrial Engineering IAO, the Fraunhofer Institute for Manufacturing Engineering and Automation IPA and ISAK GmbH. Funding is provided by the German Federal Ministry of Education and Research.

In the services sector, the Nippon Foundation in **Japan** has pilot-tested an approach using robotic technology to enable persons with significant physical disabilities to work. In an experimental cafe, visitors are served by robot waiters, each of which is equipped with a camera and a speaker to help it interact with customers and deliver coffee. The robots are remotely controlled by persons with severe physical disabilities. Following this pilot, there are plans to open a permanent facility in the near future.

Source: Robotics & Automation, "Robotics to aid people with disabilities at work", 5 October 2018. Available at https://roboticsandautomationnews.com/2018/10/05/robotics-to-aid-people-with-disabilities-at-work/19340/; Nippon Foundation, "Serving customers with robots remotely operated by persons with disabilities", 28 November 2018. Available at www.nippon-foundation.or.jp/en/news/articles/2018/20181128-19640.html.

80 McKinsey Global Institute, *Jobs Lost, Jobs Gained: Workforce Transitions in a Time of Automation* (New York, 2017).

81 ibid.

82 See the W3C Web Accessibility Initiative website: www.w3.org/WAI/.

ways of transmitting and searching for information on the internet.[83] As a result, persons with mobility impairments are now able to study and work remotely using accessible computers and software applications, in localities where the ICT infrastructure allows. New entrepreneurship options have emerged, for instance, in China, where persons with disabilities have capitalized on accessible digital technologies to operate personal online stores on WeChat selling local produce or disability-related products.[84]

Improvements in assistive devices that facilitate mobility, communication and orientation have also enabled persons with disabilities to live and work more independently than in the past.[85] The proliferation of universal design – whereby products, environments, programmes and services are developed to be usable by everyone without the need for adaptation – has also made employment opportunities more accessible to persons with disabilities.

The cost of ICT equipment and sophisticated assistive devices remains prohibitive, however, for many persons with disabilities, particularly those living in developing countries. Inaccessible communications infrastructure and inaccessible built environments remain barriers to accessing employment in the region as well.[86]

Rapid technological advancements, coupled with the growing realization that the population of persons with disabilities globally constitutes an emerging market larger than the size of China and potentially worth more than $13 trillion in disposable income[87] has also led to the creation of new jobs for persons with disabilities to support the development of accessible, disability-inclusive technologies, as well as relevant products and services to capture the "disability market".

Box 36
Innovators with disabilities build inclusive and accessible products

A Google programme manager with visual impairment leads a team to make Chrome accessible for all – including users with disabilities – by integrating accessibility into the development processes and developing assistive technologies like magnification options, braille support and dictation in Chromebooks. One of the company's software engineers, a wheelchair user, was inspired by his own experience navigating around cities and teamed up with colleagues to develop accessible routing and offer wheelchair-friendly transit directions on Google Maps.

Microsoft's team of talent with disabilities built the Xbox Adaptive Controller (a controller that connects devices that help make gaming more accessible) and Immersive reader (a free tool built into Office 365 and several other products that implement assistive techniques like text-to-speech).

Source: Google Careers, "Our commitment to hiring people with disabilities". Available at https://careers.google.com/programs/people-with-disabilities/; *Forbes*, "Microsoft reveals 6.1% disability representation for the first time", 21 October 2020. Available at www.forbes.com/sites/denisebrodey/2020/10/21/in-bold-benchmarking-move-microsoft-reveals-61-disability-representation-for-the-first-time/?sh=6fde45d514b0.

4.2 Gig economy

Another significant transformation in the world of work stems from the proliferation of short-term contracts and casual work arrangements for self-employed persons and freelance workers, either individually or as part of crowdwork arrangements. Jobs range from location-based service delivery requiring the use of physical labour (such as driving, running errands, making deliveries or cleaning houses) to digital work delivered through online platforms (such as desk-top publishing, software development, web development, translation, transcription, data analytics, design, administrative support and sales and marketing).[88] For the latter set of assignments in a crowdwork arrangement, the overall tasks are divided into microwork, such as data entry, interpretation of content, completion of surveys and finding of information.[89]

83 In particular, the development of the hypertext transfer protocol (http) around 1990 became the foundation of data transmission on the World Wide Web and the development of Yahoo, Google and similar search engines.

84 Mercator Institute for China Studies, "China's digital economy offers employment for disabled people", 3 December 2018. Available at https://merics.org/en/analysis/chinas-digital-economy-offers-employment-disabled-people.

85 See, for example, World Economic Forum, "What the Fourth Industrial Revolution will do for people with disabilities", 18 January 2016. Available at www.weforum.org/agenda/2016/01/the-fourth-industrial-revolution-will-give-us-super-powers/.

86 ESCAP, *Disability at a Glance 2019: Investing in Accessibility in Asia and the Pacific-Strategic Approaches to Achieving Disability-inclusive Sustainable Development* (Bangkok, 2019).

87 Return on Disability Group, *Design Delight from Disability, 2020 Annual Report: The Global Economics of Disability* (Toronto, 2020).

88 Richard Heeks, "Decent work and the digital gig economy: a developing country perspective on employment impacts and standards in online outsourcing, crowdwork, etc.", Development Informatics Working Paper No. 71 (Manchester, 2017).

89 ILO, "Income security in the on-demand economy: findings and policy lessons from a survey of crowdworkers", Conditions of Work and Employment Series No. 74 (Geneva, 2016).

Persons with disabilities often require accessible technologies, relevant assistive devices and access to the internet to enter the gig economy. Digital gig work, through the omission of cues such as disability, age, accent and dressing, can potentially lower discriminatory barriers that frequently prevent persons with disabilities from accessing full-time employment. The nature of jobs in the gig economy also provides persons with disabilities with much-needed flexibility in terms of time and location, coupled with low overhead costs, all of which may not be viable in the context of full-time employment.[90]

Box 37
Break the Silence Project in Malaysia

In **Malaysia**, the Break the Silence project demonstrates the potential of the gig economy in promoting employment for persons with disabilities. Initiated by Grab, a technology company offering ride-hailing and food delivery services as well as payment solutions, the project engages persons with disabilities as drivers and delivery partners. More than 500 persons who are deaf or live with cerebral palsy or motor impairments now earn an income through the app platform. Grab has also appointed 19 service providers with disabilities to the Driver Representative Committee to explore ways of enhancing their work experience. Additionally, Grab is extending support to enterprises of persons with disabilities by introducing their business on the platform.

All Grab drivers and delivery partners, including service providers with disabilities, are eligible for the GrabBenefits Programme, which provides personal accident insurance subsidies and discounts on travel, services and entertainment, among other benefits. A first-of-its-kind benefits programme for platform workers in the gig economy in Malaysia, the programme aims to support the livelihoods and well-being of Grab partners and strengthen their financial resilience.

Source: Grab, "Grab continues to create greater inclusivity for 500 persons with disabilities in Malaysia", 2 October 2019. Available at www.grab.com/my/press/social-impact-safety/grab-break-the-silence-pwd/. For more information on the GrabBenefits Programme: www.grab.com/my/grabbenefits-in-driver-app/ and www.grab.com/my/press/social-impact-safety/.

At the same time, workers in the gig economy might not have employment benefits and protections comparable to those of workers in a traditional employment relationship, including social security coverage, entitlement to sickness and maternity pay or statutory minimum wages.[91] There is therefore a need for policymakers to ensure that employment opportunities available to persons with disabilities yield decent work in the gig economy.

4.3 COVID-19

In the wake of the COVID-19 pandemic and resulting economic downturn, there was a significant loss of working hours[92] in the Asia–Pacific region in 2020, estimated at 7.9 per cent of working hours lost relative to the fourth quarter of 2019, or equivalent to 140 million full-time jobs.[93] Among subregions, Southern Asia experienced the biggest loss of working hours, at 12.7 per cent, followed by South-Eastern Asia, at 8.4 per cent, Eastern Asia, at 4.2 per cent, and Pacific Islands, at 3.7 per cent (figure 19).[94] Workers in the informal economy, comprising 60 per cent of the labour force in the region, have been hardest hit by the lockdown because they are often in vulnerable jobs with little or no social protection. [95] Limited internet access across the region, with only half the population having internet coverage, has restricted the option to work from home. And the nature of the service sector and blue-collar jobs have made these workers less able to work remotely.[96]

Persons with disabilities have been more vulnerable in the pandemic due to their existing disadvantaged circumstances.[97] Large-scale studies have not yet been done. But findings from localized surveys and anecdotal evidence indicate that the pandemic has had a more severe impact on the employment situation of persons with disabilities, especially for persons in vulnerable employment. In India, for example, workers with disabilities in 10 localities became unemployed overnight due to the closure of businesses and factories operating

90 ILO, "The rise of the 'just-in-time workforce': on-demand work, crowdwork and labour protection in the 'gig-economy'", Conditions of Work and Employment Series No. 71 (Geneva, 2016).
91 ILO, *Non-standard Employment around the World: Understanding Challenges, Shaping Prospects* (Geneva, 2016).
92 The loss of working hours encompasses employment losses and reduced working hours for those who remain employed (including those who remain employed but are not working).
93 ILO, "ILO monitor: COVID-19 and the world of work: seventh edition: updated estimates and analysis", Briefing Note (Geneva, 2021).
94 ibid. Please note that the grouping of countries by subregion differs between ESCAP and the ILO.
95 ILO, "ILO monitor: COVID-19 and the world of work: fifth edition: updated estimates and analysis", Briefing Note (Geneva, 2020).
96 ESCAP, "Can this time be different? Challenges and opportunities for Asia-Pacific economies in the aftermath of COVID-19", Issue Paper (Bangkok, 2020).
97 Easy Inclusion, "Making inclusion easier in China", Presentation, ILO Global Business and Disability Network China Chapter, March 2020. Available at http://www.businessanddisability.org/wp-content/uploads/2020/03/HaibinZhou.pdf.

mainly in the informal economy.[98] A study carried out by the National Centre for Promotion of Employment of Disabled People in India found that 73 per cent of people surveyed had faced severe hardship – primarily financial crises and difficulties in accessing food and health care.[99] In China, 81.5 per cent of surveyed massage shops with blind therapists experienced difficulties or had closed during the pandemic, leading to a significant loss of livelihoods for the workers.[100] In the Philippines, 70 per cent of persons with disabilities surveyed in a rapid assessment indicated that their employment was affected by the pandemic due to issues ranging from remote working arrangements to risks of employment loss.[101]

To safeguard income security and the livelihoods of persons with disabilities during the pandemic, at least 41 governments in the region introduced COVID-19-related employment and social protection support concerning persons with disabilities. These include, among other provisions, encouraging flexible working arrangements; subsidizing companies that continue to employ persons with disabilities; supporting the business of persons with disabilities; establishing online training and recruitment service platforms; providing cash transfers and in-kind aid, such as food packages and hygiene kits; and undertaking administrative measures, such as ensuring the timely payment of disability allowances and extending the validity period of disability certificates to ensure the continued receipt of disability-related allowances.[102]

In the private sector, an exploratory survey of members of the ILO Global Business and Disability Network, including 38 companies from Asia and the Pacific, indicated that telework, flexible hours and paid leave have been the most frequently undertaken practices by employers to protect employees with disabilities during the COVID-19 crisis. Additional practices included the provision of reasonable accommodation and facilities to enable employees with disabilities to work from home and having personal protection equipment in place where they are involved in providing a service. These responses were often devised in consultation with organizations of persons with disabilities.[103]

Figure 19
Percentage of working hours lost in Asia and the Pacific in 2020, by subregion

Asia and the Pacific experienced significant working-hour loss in 2020 due to the COVID-19 pandemic.

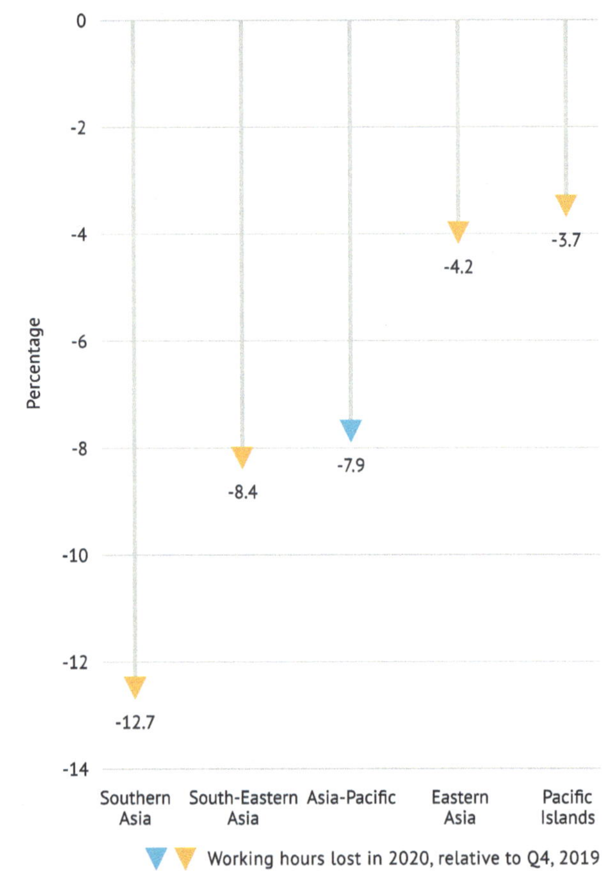

Source: ILO Monitor: COVID-19 and the world of work, 7th edition.
Note: Grouping of countries by subregion differs between ESCAP and the ILO.

98 *Times of India*, "How COVID-19 lockdown has hit disabled people hard", 6 April 2020. Available at https://timesofindia.indiatimes.com/india/how-covid-19-lockdown-has-hit-disabled-people-hard/articleshow/75003358.cms.
99 BBC, "Coronavirus: the disabled Indians losing their livelihoods", 30 September 2020. Available at https://www.bbc.com/news/disability-54188218.
100 CNR News, "Report on the impact of the coronavirus on the massage industry with blind therapists (in Chinese)", 14 March 2020. Available at https://www.cdpf.org.cn/ywpd/xcwh/gzdt6/ffda562c19414d0faac56ccc8dd5c6f5.htm.
101 Jacqueline Veronica Velasco and others, "COVID-19 and persons with disabilities in the Philippines: a policy analysis", *Health Promotion Perspectives*, vol. 11, No. 3 (August 2021).
102 Please see Annex H for the list of employment and social protection related responses by country.
103 While the limited number of participating companies (159) means that the patterns emerging are very tentative, they are nonetheless useful in pointing to examples of good practice that could be promoted more widely. A quarter of the participants were based in the Asia – Pacific region (N=38), with companies from Australia, Bangladesh, India, Indonesia, New Zealand, Philippines and Sri Lanka participating. See ILO, *Disability Inclusion in Company Responses to COVID-19: Results of a Survey among National Business and Disability Networks and Their Members* (Geneva, 2020).

Chapter 5

Recommendations and conclusion

The approaches and strategies featured in Chapters 2 and 3 affirm that progress has been made by the Asia–Pacific region in shifting to a social- and human-rights-based understanding of disability and transitioning from the provision of sheltered employment to the promotion of supported employment. Governments, service providers, organizations of persons with disabilities and other stakeholders have made efforts to strengthen rights-based legal frameworks and develop supportive measures for aspiring and current employees, their employers and entrepreneurs with disabilities.

Yet, large gaps in the employment status of persons with disabilities, compared with the general population, remain. Coupled with the challenges and opportunities brought about by the rapidly changing world of work, the gaps underscore how more needs to be done to promote productive employment and decent work for persons with disabilities.

The following recommendations are proposed to equip Asian and Pacific governments to better implement measures that promote employment for persons with disabilities.

Overarching legislative frameworks

- Governments should ensure that national legal frameworks are harmonized with their international and regional commitments. Although the social and human rights models of disability now dominate in the international instruments, at the national level, rights-based approaches often operate alongside those based on a medical model of disability. This sends mixed messages to individuals with disabilities, employers and the population at large. A review of all relevant laws should be undertaken, with revisions undertaken to address any incompatibility.

- Sector-based laws and policies, particularly those related to education and TVET, labour and employment promotion, entrepreneurship development and the creation of an enabling and accessible general environment, should be reviewed and revised, where necessary, to effectively provide for the inclusion of persons with disabilities.

- Employment equity and anti-discrimination laws should be developed and enforced in countries where these laws do not yet exist, making provision for reasonable accommodation. Such laws are especially critical for minimizing the negative impacts of biases and stereotypes about persons with disabilities that impede their full participation in work and communities, especially during a crisis. Where such laws are already in place, their implementation and enforcement should be strengthened, including a review of the redress and complaints mechanisms and requirements regarding burden of proof in cases where discrimination is alleged to have taken place.

Laws, policies and programmes supporting the employment of persons with disabilities

- The effectiveness of quota schemes as a form of affirmative action to promote the employment of persons with disabilities should be reviewed. Revisions should be made to promote the involvement of employers. Relevant measures should be designed to support employers in employing persons with disabilities and thus meeting their quota obligations (see the recommendations on support for employers). Countries could also introduce alternative ways for employers to meet their quota obligation, such as accepting trainees with disabilities; outsourcing work to designated workshops or centres employing persons with disabilities; or reaching company-wide agreements to promote the recruitment, training, integration and retention of persons with disabilities.

- Where job retention and return-to-work measures are not in place, they should be introduced for employees and workers who acquire a disability while in employment, in addition to worker compensation provisions.

- Social protection measures should be reviewed and revised, where necessary, to ensure that the eligibility criteria for disability-related benefits and entitlements do not create disincentives to employment. Accordingly, the approach to disability assessments also should be reviewed and revised, where required, to ensure that concepts such as incapacity and unemployability do not constitute central elements of the assessment. Disability benefit schemes could be structured such that workers with disabilities retain their disability benefits up to a certain threshold of income earned and become immediately eligible for the full benefit again, should they become unemployed. Wage top-ups for individuals with disabilities in low-paid jobs could also be provided. Additionally, governments could consider rolling out universal disability benefits and cost-of-disability allowances that help defray the additional costs of living with a disability, regardless of employment status.

- The involvement and buy-in of employers in promoting training and employment opportunities for persons with disabilities should be strengthened through the provision of both financial and technical support. Such schemes should be calibrated to address the differing support needs of the different types of employers, ranging from private sector entities to cooperatives and from multinational business to micro, small and medium-sized enterprises. Financial incentives, ranging from tax exemptions to wage subsidies for a specified period and the coverage of insurance premium costs should be introduced to facilitate the hiring and retention of employees with disabilities. Where employers are legally required to provide reasonable accommodation, loans and grants to defray additional costs, including those of workplace adaptation, and the provision of specialized equipment could help employers fulfil their obligations more smoothly. Technical support should be provided to employers in the form of advisory services, including job analysis, matching and placement; on-demand support at the workplace through job coaches; and the identification of modification requirements and advice on reasonable accommodation, technical aids and assistive devices.

Training to equip workers with disabilities

- Regarding TVET, policy nudges, such as changes in funding criteria to TVET centres comprising only trainees with disabilities and to sheltered workshops, could help promote the transition of persons with disabilities to more mainstream forms of training and employment. A comprehensive review of the landscape of vocational training provision at the country level would also better inform the development of TVET for persons with disabilities. Such a review should cover the profile of service providers; the scope, nature and quality of course offerings; and the impact of such training on employment outcomes for persons with disabilities.

- Regarding job coaching, actions should be taken to significantly improve the access of persons with disabilities to on-the-job training with job coaches within the framework of supported employment. There is also a need to raise more awareness among businesses of the pivotal role of job coaching in developing productive work outcomes for employees with disabilities. Civil society organizations and community-based rehabilitation programmes would also do well to partner with private organizations to leverage resources in funding job coaching.

Employment services

- The one-stop shop approach to the provision of employment services for persons with diverse disabilities should be explored as an effective service delivery mechanism. This would include information on employment and training opportunities, referrals and placements, CV clinics and training on jobseeking skills.

- To ensure that persons with disabilities are able to fully access both general and disability-specific employment services, efforts are required to increase their access by improving the physical accessibility of facilities; addressing negative attitudes and stereotypes among service providers; and raising awareness of such services within the disability community. Additionally, employment services, both mainstream and disability-specific, should integrate gender dimensions into all their processes to ensure that women with disabilities have access to employment services.

Support for entrepreneurship development

- Entrepreneurship-support programmes and services tailored to support entrepreneurs with disabilities should be expanded. Such programmes and services may include the provision of business loans, grants, subsidies and equipment with preferential terms, accessible business development skills training catering to the diverse needs of persons with disabilities and tailored support to facilitate access of entrepreneurs with disabilities to markets and business networks.

- Regulations and procedures should be in place, coupled with disability sensitization training, to ensure that eligible entrepreneurs with disabilities are not denied access to credit due to the prejudices of bank and government personnel.

- Mainstream policies, programmes and services to promote entrepreneurship development in the general population should be disability-inclusive, fostering links with dedicated training centres for persons with disabilities and organizations of persons with disabilities to encourage applications. For example, websites with information on these schemes and application platforms should be digitally accessible. The built environment of relevant service centres should be physically barrier-free. Government personnel providing such mainstream services should also be aware of and practice the principles of non-discrimination in their interactions with entrepreneurs with disabilities.

Creation of an enabling social environment

- Accessibility standards regulating the built environment and public transportation as well as the dissemination of knowledge, information and communication should be reviewed and, where required, revised to align with international standards. Where absent, they should be developed. The implementation of accessibility laws and policies should be strengthened, including through improved cross-sector and interministerial coordination at all levels of government.

- Awareness-raising campaigns and sensitization training for policymakers, service providers and the public at large should be designed in collaboration with organizations of persons with disabilities and the media to tackle mistaken assumptions and stereotypes about the work capacity and employment rights of persons with disabilities. Where possible, such campaigns and trainings on disability inclusion should intentionally articulate the gender dimensions of disability and gender gaps to bring attention to the multiple challenges that women with disabilities especially experience.

Disability-disaggregated labour statistics

- Data on the employment status of persons with disabilities should be collected regularly, as part of labour market surveys or employment-related population censuses. And they should be disaggregated by disability type, sex, age, employment type, level and duration and other criteria specific to the context of individual countries (such as ethnicity or migration status). Governments are strongly encouraged to include the Washington Group Short Set on Functioning questions in their collection of labour market statistics to make disability disaggregation possible. Where possible, the use of the Washington Group and ILO Labour Force Disability Module is encouraged to help address these data needs.

- The way disability is defined and classified by type should be consistent throughout the administrative and survey systems of governments to allow disability-disaggregated data to be interoperable across sectoral management information systems, including those of labour, education and social protection.

Leveraging on change – technological advancements

- The evolution of sectors, jobs and the nature of work brought about by technological change has increasing implications for the number and type of employment opportunities catering to persons with disabilities. Government support in the form of grants and joint projects with the private sector is essential to incentivize the development and application of disability-inclusive, accessible and cutting-edge technologies, including further exploration of the potential of robotics and the application of artificial intelligence in improving employment and entrepreneurship opportunities for persons with disabilities.

- Measures are also required to ensure that all persons with disabilities, regardless of socioeconomic status as well as impairment type and level, can access and benefit from technological advances. This must be delivered despite the prohibitive cost of ICT equipment and sophisticated assistive devices for persons with disabilities from disadvantaged socioeconomic backgrounds and/or locations with inaccessible communications infrastructure and built environments. Enabling persons with disabilities to access ICT infrastructure in central locations could be a way around this problem. Financial and in-kind support might also be necessary to allow persons with disabilities with financial difficulties to access the equipment and assistive devices necessary for gaining and retaining employment or setting up a business.

- Focused training in digital literacy for persons with different types of disabilities and different levels of education is indispensable. Training programmes should pay attention to supporting the adoption of technological innovations as they are introduced and provide training on their use.

- Persons with disabilities must be equipped with skills relevant to the job market and the emergence of new jobs and ways of working, especially the increasing demand for digital skills and the digital economy. They should be taken into account when planning and updating vocational training curricula, career advisory programmes and job placement services for persons with disabilities.

Leveraging on change – gig economy

- Policymakers should seek to protect workers with disabilities in the gig economy and ensure that employment opportunities yield decent work. Regulations and other measures should be considered to ensure that at least the minimum wage is paid; working hours are not excessive; working conditions are safe, hygienic and accessible; and that social protection is accessible to all, including persons with disabilities without formal employment contracts and/or working in the informal sector.

Leveraging on change – COVID-19

- The need to roll out emergency measures to protect the livelihoods of persons with disabilities as a result of the pandemic has provided the opportunity for governments to systematically review and, where required, reform policies and institutions to ensure that their employment promotion systems mainstream disability inclusion. Governments should comprehensively study the impacts of the COVID-19 pandemic on the employment and livelihoods of persons with disabilities. They should develop holistic and integrative measures across sectors to empower persons with disabilities and systematically address barriers to their inclusion, beyond temporary measures aimed at mitigating short-term impacts of the COVID-19 pandemic.

Box 38
Engaging organizations of persons with disabilities and other stakeholders in the implementation of policy recommendations

Persons with disabilities should be empowered to actively participate in the decision-making processes concerning them, including those of policy design and implementation. In the context of employment, organizations of persons with disabilities should be encouraged to take an active role as employment-related advisers and service providers.

The involvement of other social partners in promoting the employability and employment of persons with disabilities should also be encouraged, including by mainstreaming disability concerns into the work of these organizations. These partners include but are not limited to trade unions, employers' organizations and civil society organizations advocating for workers' rights.

Conclusion

Evidence demonstrates critical gaps in the employment of persons with disabilities in the Asia–Pacific region. Disability-related barriers to employment often intersect with gender- and rural-based barriers. This consequently puts women with disabilities and those living in rural areas in a further disadvantaged position in the labour market. The unemployment, underemployment and exclusion of persons with disabilities from the labour market impose social and economic losses that could be mitigated by disability-inclusive measures to promote productive employment and decent work.

Investing in productive employment and decent work for persons with disabilities presents an opportunity for governments to make substantial progress on their commitments to inclusive development, such as the Convention on the Rights of Persons with Disabilities and the 2030 Agenda for Sustainable Development, particularly while building back from the COVID-19 pandemic. It also strongly aligns with existing frameworks and efforts to promote disability-inclusive development in the region, including the Incheon Strategy and the Beijing Declaration and Action Plan to accelerate its implementation.

Recent developments in the world of work, especially technological advancement, the evolution of the gig economy and labour market reforms triggered by the COVID-19 pandemic, have presented new challenges. But, more importantly, they have triggered opportunities that the region could leverage to create better employment prospects and conditions for persons with disabilities. Concerted actions are required from governments, businesses and organizations of persons with disabilities to make this happen.

Bibliography

Australian Disability Clearinghouse on Education and Training. Vocational education and training (VET) statistics. Undated. Available at www.adcet.edu.au/inclusive-teaching/understanding-disability/vet-statistics.

BBC. Coronavirus: the disabled Indians losing their livelihoods, 30 September 2020. Available at www.bbc.com/news/disability-54188218.

Cabinet Office of Japan. *The White Paper on Disability.* Tokyo: Government of Japan, 2021.

China Disabled Persons' Federation. *Opinions on Supporting Employment and Entrepreneurship of Persons with Disabilities* (in Chinese). Beijing: 2018. Available at www.cdpf.org.cn/zwgk/zcwj/wjfb/c97c15ce00d14ea296a303f1f8c59cd4.htm.

Chui, C., and others. Work integration social enterprises as vessels of empowerment? Perspectives from employees. *Asia Pacific Journal of Social Work and Development,* vol. 29, No. 2, 2019, pp. 133-148.

CNR News. Report on the impact of the coronavirus on the massage industry with blind therapists (in Chinese), 14 March 2020. Available at www.cdpf.org.cn/ywpd/xcwh/gzdt6/ffda562c19414d0faac56ccc8dd5c6f5.htm.

Committee on the Rights of Persons with Disabilities. *Initial Report Submitted by China Under Article 35 of the Convention.* Beijing: 2010. CRPD/C/CHN/1. Available at https://undocs.org/en/CRPD/C/CHN/1.

_______. *Initial Report Submitted by Republic of Korea Under Article 35 of the Convention.* Seoul: 2011. CRPD/C/KOR/1. Available at https://undocs.org/en/CRPD/C/KOR/1.

_______. *Initial Report Submitted by Thailand Under Article 35 of the Convention.* Bangkok: 2012. CRPD/C/THA/1. Available at https://undocs.org/en/CRPD/C/THA/1.

_______. *Initial Report Submitted by the Philippines Under Article 35 of the Convention.* Manila: 2014. CRPD/C/PHL/1. Available at https://undocs.org/en/CRPD/C/PHL/1.

_______. *Initial Report Submitted by Singapore Under Article 35 of the Convention.* Singapore: 2016. CRPD/C/SGP/1. Available at https://undocs.org/en/CRPD/C/SGP/1.

_______. *Initial Report Submitted by Indonesia Under Article 35 of the Convention.* Jakarta: 2017. CRPD/C/IDN/1. Available at https://undocs.org/en/CRPD/C/IDN/1.

_______. *Combined Second and Third Periodic Reports Submitted by China Under Article 35 of the Convention.* Beijing: 2018. *CRPD/C/CHN/2-3.* Available at https://undocs.org/en/CRPD/C/CHN/2-3.

_______. *General Comment No. 6 (2018) on Equality and Non-discrimination.* Geneva: 2018. CRPD/C/GC/6. Available at https://undocs.org/en/CRPD/C/GC/6.

_______. *Initial report submitted by Viet Nam under article 35 of the Convention.* Hanoi: 2018. CRPD/C/VNM/1. Available at https://undocs.org/en/CRPD/C/VNM/1.

Côte, A. Disability inclusion and social protection. In *Handbook on Social Protection Systems,* E. Schüring and M. Loewe (pp. 354-367). Cheltenham: Edward Elgar Publishing Ltd, 2021.

Darcy, S. and others. *Australia's Disability Entrepreneurial Ecosystem: Experiences of People with Disability with Microenterprises, Self-employment and Entrepreneurship.* Sydney: University of Technology Sydney,2020.

Department of Social Services, Australian Government. *Mobility Allowance (MOB).* Canberra: 2020. Available at www.dss.gov.au/disability-and-carers-programs-services-for-people-with-disability/mobility-allowance-mob.

Disability Data Initiative. Methods briefs. Undated. Available at https://disabilitydata.ace.fordham.edu/method-briefs/.

_______. Results tables. Undated. Available at https://disabilitydata.ace.fordham.edu/.

Disability Employment Australia. Employer incentives and financial assistance. Undated. Available at http://guide.disabilityemployment.org.au/resources/employer_incentives_and_financial_assistance.

Easy Inclusion. Making inclusion easier in China. Presentation, ILO Global Business and Disability Network China Chapter, March 2020. Available at www.businessanddisability.org/wp-content/uploads/2020/03/HaibinZhou.pdf.

European Union. *Council Directive 2000/78/EC.* Brussels: 2000. Available at https://eur-lex.europa.eu/legal-content/EN/TXT/?uri=celex%3A32000L0078.

Food and Agriculture Organization of the United Nations. *A Handbook for Training of Disabled on Rural Enterprise Development.* Bangkok: FAO, 2003.

Forbes. Microsoft reveals 6.1% disability representation for the first time, 21 October 2020. Available at www.forbes.com/sites/denisebrodey/2020/10/21/in-bold-benchmarking-move-microsoft-reveals-61-disability-representation-for-the-first-time/?sh=6fde45d514b0.

G3ict. Digital Accessibility Rights Evaluation Index (DARE Index). Undated. Available at https://g3ict.org/digital-accessibility-rights-evaluation-index.

Google Careers. Our commitment to hiring people with disabilities. Undated. Available at https://careers.google.com/programs/people-with-disabilities/.

Government of India. *The Rights of Persons with Disabilities Act, 2016.* Delhi: 2016. Available at https://legislative.gov.in/sites/default/files/A2016-49_1.pdf.

Government of the Philippines. *Magna Carta for Disabled Persons (R.A. No. 7277).* Manila: 1992. Available at http://hrlibrary.umn.edu/research/Philippines/RA%207277%20-%20Magna%20Carta%20of%20Disabled%20Persons.pdf.

Grab. Grab continues to create greater inclusivity for 500 persons with disabilities (PWD) in Malaysia, 2 October 2019. Available at www.grab.com/my/press/social-impact-safety/grab-break-the-silence-pwd/.

_______. Grab improves GrabBenefits Programme, includes efforts to upskill and drive financial resilience for over 120,000 partners, 4 December 2020. Available at www.grab.com/my/press/social-impact-safety/grabbenefits-programme-upskill-financial-resilience/.

_______. GrabBenefits. Undated. Available at www.grab.com/my/grabbenefits/.

Heeks, R. Decent work and the digital gig economy: A developing country perspective on employment impacts and standards in online outsourcing, crowdwork, etc. Development Informatics Working Paper No. 71. Manchester: Centre for Development Informatics Global Development Institute, SEED, 2017. Available at https://papers.ssrn.com/sol3/papers.cfm?abstract_id=3431033.

Institute of Technical Education, Singapore. Learning accessibility. Undated. Available at www.ite.edu.sg/life-at-ite/student-services/learning-accessibility.

International Labour Organization. *Toolkit for Mainstreaming Employment and Decent Work.* Geneva: ILO, 2007.

_______. *Employment-related Services for Persons with Disabilities in Vietnam.* Bangkok: ILO, 2009.

_______. The price of exclusion: The economic consequences of excluding people with disabilities from the world of work. Employment Working Paper No.43. Geneva: ILO, 2009. Available at www.ilo.org/employment/Whatwedo/Publications/working-papers/WCMS_119305/lang--en/index.htm.

_______. Promoting training and employment opportunities for people with intellectual disabilities: International experience. Employment Working Paper No. 103. Geneva: ILO, 2011. Available at www.ilo.org/employment/Whatwedo/Publications/working-papers/WCMS_167316/lang--en/index.htm.

_______. *Disabilities and Decent Work in the Pacific: The Case for Disability Inclusive Employment.* Suva: ILO, 2012.

_______. *Understanding Deficits of Productive Employment and Setting Targets: A Methodological Guide.* Geneva: ILO, 2012.

_______. *Achieving Equal Employment Opportunities for Persons with Disabilities through Legislation: Guidelines.* Geneva: ILO, 2014.

_______. *Business as Unusual: Making Workplaces Inclusive of People with Disabilities.* Geneva: ILO, 2014.

_______. *Decent Work for Persons with Disabilities: Promoting Rights in the Global Development Agenda.* Geneva: ILO, 2015.

_______. *Statistics on the Labour Force Characteristics of People with Disabilities: A Compendium of National Methodologies.* Geneva: ILO, 2015.

_______. *Non-standard Employment Around the World: Understanding Challenges, Shaping Prospects.* Geneva: ILO, 2016.

_______. *Including Persons with Disabilities in Technical and Vocational Education and Training: A Guide for Administrative and Instructors to Disability Inclusion.* Dhaka: ILO, 2016.

_______. Income security in the on-demand economy: Findings and policy lessons from a survey of crowdworkers. Conditions of Work and Employment Series No. 74. Geneva: ILO, 2016. Available at www.ilo.org/wcmsp5/groups/public/---ed_protect/---protrav/---travail/documents/publication/wcms_479693.pdf.

_______. The rise of the "just-in-time workforce": On-demand work, crowdwork and labour protection in the "gig-economy". Conditions of Work and Employment Series No. 71. Geneva: ILO, 2016. Available at www.ilo.org/wcmsp5/groups/public/---ed_protect/---protrav/---travail/documents/publication/wcms_443267.pdf.

_______. Disability inclusion in the Bangladesh skills system. Brochure. Dhaka: ILO, 2017. Available at www.ilo.org/dhaka/Areasofwork/WCMS_543298/lang--en/index.htm.

_______. *Final Report-Mapping Persons with Disabilities (PWD) in Indonesia Labour Market.* Jakarta: ILO, 2017.

_______. Good practices for inclusion of persons with disabilities: a replication guide for Technical and Vocational Education and Training (TVET) Institutions. Brochure. Dhaka: ILO, 2017. Available at www.ilo.org/dhaka/Whatwedo/Publications/WCMS_596665/lang--en/index.htm.

_______. Major achievements of the Bangladesh Skills for Employment and Productivity (B-SEP) Project. Brochure. Dhaka: ILO, 2017. Available at www.ilo.org/dhaka/Whatwedo/Publications/WCMS_614478/lang--en/index.htm.

_______. Making TVET and skills systems inclusive of persons with disabilities. Policy Brief. Geneva: ILO, 2017. Available at www.ilo.org/global/topics/disability-and-work/WCMS_605087/lang--en/index.htm.

_______. *Women and Men in the Informal Economy: A Statistical Picture (third edition).* Geneva: ILO, 2018.

_______. *Promoting Employment Opportunities for People with Disabilities Quota Schemes,* vol. 1. Geneva: ILO,2019.

_______. *Promoting Employment Opportunities for People with Disabilities Quota Schemes,* vol. 2. Geneva: ILO, 2019.

_______. *Assessment of the Social Protection System in Georgia.* Geneva: ILO, 2020.

_______. *Disability Inclusion in Company Responses to COVID-19: Results of a Survey among National Business and Disability Networks and Their Members.* Geneva: ILO, 2020.

_______. ILO monitor: COVID-19 and the world of work. Fifth edition. Updated Estimates and analysis. Briefing Note. Geneva: ILO, 2020. Available at www.ilo.org/global/topics/coronavirus/impacts-and-responses/WCMS_749399/lang--en/index.htm.

_______. ILO monitor: COVID-19 and the world of work. Seventh edition. Updated estimates and analysis. Briefing Note. Geneva: ILO. Available at www.ilo.org/global/topics/coronavirus/impacts-and-responses/WCMS_767028/lang--en/index.htm.

_______. *World Social Protection Report 2020-22: Social Protection at the Crossroads – In Pursuit of a Better Future.* Geneva: ILO, 2021.

_______. Indicator description: Employment by status in employment. Undated. Available at https://ilostat.ilo.org/resources/concepts-and-definitions/description-employment-by-status/.

_______. Indicator description: Labour force participation. Undated. Available at https://ilostat.ilo.org/resources/concepts-and-definitions/description-labour-force-participation-rate/.

_______. Labour Force Survey (LFS) resources. Undated. Available at https://ilostat.ilo.org/resources/lfs-resources/.

JobAccess, Australian Government. *Employment Assistance Fund (EAF)*. Canberra: 2021. Available at www.jobaccess.gov.au/employment-assistance-fund-eaf.

Korea Legislation Research Institute. *Act on the Facilitation of Entrepreneurial Activities of Persons with Disabilities, Republic of Korea*. Seoul: 2018. Available at https://elaw.klri.re.kr/eng_service/lawView.do?hseq=49156&lang=ENG.

Lamichhane, K. *Disability, Education and Employment in Developing Countries: From Charity to Investment*. Cambridge: Cambridge University Press, 2015.

McKinsey Global Institute. *Jobs Lost, Jobs Gained: Workforce Transitions in a Time of Automation*. New York: McKinsey & Company, 2017.

________. *The Power of Parity: Advancing Women's Equality in Asia Pacific*. New York: McKinsey & Company, 2018.

Mercator Institute for China Studies. China's digital economy offers employment for disabled people, 3 December 2018. Available at https://merics.org/en/analysis/chinas-digital-economy-offers-employment-disabled-people.

Ministry of Education and Training, Vanuatu. *National Disability Inclusion Policy for the TVET Sector, 2016-2020*. Port-Vila: Ministry of Education and Training, 2015.

Ministry of Employment and Labor, Republic of Korea. *[Equal Employment Policy] Act on Employment Promotion and Vocational Rehabilitation for Disabled Persons*. Seoul: Undated. Available at www.moel.go.kr/english/poli/poliLaw_view.jsp?idx=226&tab=4.

Ministry of Health, Labour and Welfare, Japan. *Report on the 2018 Survey on Employment of Persons with Disabilities (in Japanese)*. Tokyo: Ministry of Health, Labour and Welfare, 2019.

________. Aggregated results of employment status of persons with disabilities, 2020 (in Japanese). Tokyo: 2021. Available at www.mhlw.go.jp/stf/newpage_16030.html.

Mitra, S., and J. Yap. *The Disability Data Report 2021*. New York: Fordham Research Consortium on Disability, 2021.

Mizunoya, S., and S. Mitra. Is there a disability gap in employment rates in developing countries? *World Development*, vol. 42, 2013. pp. 28-43.

Nepal Law Commission. *Constitution of Nepal*. Kathmandu: Undated. Available at www.lawcommission.gov.np/en/archives/category/documents/prevailing-law/constitution/constitution-of-nepal.

New Life Psychiatric Rehabilitation Association. Supported employment service. Undated. Available at www.nlpra.org.hk/en/our%20services/ses/32#supported.

New Zealand Government Procurement Branch. *Government Procurement Rules: Rules for Sustainable and Inclusive Procurement*, fourth edition. Wellington: New Zealand Government Procurement Branch, 2019.

New Zealand Legislation. *Injury Prevention, Rehabilitation, and Compensation Act 2001*. Wellington: Undated. Available at www.legislation.govt.nz/act/public/2001/0049/31.0/DLM99494.html.

Nippon Foundation. Serving customers with robots remotely operated by persons with disabilities, 28 November 2018. Available at www.nippon-foundation.or.jp/en/news/articles/2018/20181128-19640.html.

Office of the High Commissioner for Human Rights (OHCHR). CRPD States parties reports. Undated. Available at https://tbinternet.ohchr.org/_layouts/15/treatybodyexternal/TBSearch.aspx?Lang=en&TreatyID=4&DocTypeID=29.

Prince, M. Persons with invisible disabilities and workplace accommodation: findings from a scoping literature review. *Journal of Vocational Rehabilitation*, vol. 26, No.1, 2017. pp. 75-86.

Queensland Government, Australia. Awards and wages. Undated. Available at www.qld.gov.au/jobs/entitlements/wages.

Robotics & Automation. Robotics to aid people with disabilities at work, 5 October 2018. Available at https://roboticsandautomationnews.com/2018/10/05/robotics-to-aid-people-with-disabilities-at-work/19340/.

Safe Work Australia. *National Return to Work Strategy 2020-2030.* Canberra: Safe Work Australia, 2019.

Settlement Services International. IgniteAbility small business start-ups. Undated. Available at www.ssi.org.au/services/ignite-ability-small-business-start-ups.

Shakespeare, T., and N. Watson. The social model of disability: an outdated ideology? *Research in Social Science and Disability,* vol. 2, 2001. pp. 9-28.

Smith, P., and others. Developing open employment outcomes for people with an intellectual disability utilising a Social Enterprise Framework. *Journal of Vocational Rehabilitation,* vol. 48, No. 1, 2018. pp. 59-77.

Social Welfare Department, Government of the Hong Kong Special Administrative Region, China. Support programme for employees with disabilities. Hong Kong: 2021. Available at www.swd.gov.hk/en/index/site_pubsvc/page_rehab/sub_listofserv/id_vocational/id_sped/.

State Council Information Office of the People's Republic of China. *Equality, Participation and Sharing: 70 Years of Protecting the Rights and Interests of Persons with Disabilities in the PRC.* Beijing: State Council Information Office of the People's Republic of China, 2019.

The Laws of Fiji. *Constitution of the Republic of Fiji.* Suva: Undated. Available at www.laws.gov.fj/Home/information/constitutionoftherepublicoffiji.

The Return on Disability Group. *Design Delight from Disability, 2020 Annual Report: The Global Economics of Disability.* Toronto: The Return on Disability Group, 2020.

Times of India. How COVID-19 lockdown has hit disabled people hard, 6 April 2020. Available at https://timesofindia.indiatimes.com/india/how-covid-19-lockdown-has-hit-disabled-people-hard/articleshow/75003358.cms.

Timor-Leste National Statistics Directorate and United Nations Population Fund. *Timor-Leste Population and Housing Census, 2010: Analytical Report on Disability, Volume 10.* Dili: NSD and UNFPA, 2012.

Tokyo Labor Bureau, Japan. The statutory employment rate for persons with disabilities will be raised from 1 March 2021 (in Japanese). Undated. Available at https://jsite.mhlw.go.jp/tokyo-roudoukyoku/hourei_seido_tetsuzuki/shokugyou_shoukai/houteikoyouritu_00630.html.

United States Department of Labor Office of Disability Employment Policy. Spotlight on women with disabilities. March 2021. Research Brief. Washington, D.C.: U.S. Department of Labor Office of Disability Employment Policy, 2021. Available at www.dol.gov/sites/dolgov/files/ODEP/pdf/Spotlight-on-Women-with-Disabilities-March-2021.pdf.

UNESCO Institute for Lifelong Learning. *Fourth Global Report on Adult Learning and Education: Leave No One Behind: Participation, Equity and Inclusion.* Hamburg: UIL, 2019.

UNESCO Institute for Statistics. Education and disability: analysis of data from 49 countries. Information Paper N. 49. Montreal: UIS, 2018. Available at http://uis.unesco.org/sites/default/files/documents/ip49-education-disability-2018-en.pdf.

United Nations. *Report of the Special Rapporteur on the Rights of Persons with Disabilities.* New York: 2015. A/70/297. Available at https://undocs.org/en/A/70/297.

________. *Treaty Series*, vol. 2515, Undated. No. 44910. Available at: https://treaties.un.org/pages/ViewDetails.aspx?src=IND&mtdsg_no=IV-15&chapter=4&clang=_en.

United Nations Development Programmes. *Improving Employment Opportunities for Persons with Disabilities in Viet Nam.* Hanoi: UNDP, 2020.

United Nations Educational, Scientific and Cultural Organization. *Global Education Monitoring Report 2020: Inclusion and Education: All Means All.* Paris: UNESCO, 2020.

United Nations, Department of Economic and Social Affairs. *Disability and Development Report: Realizing the Sustainable Development Goals by, for and with Persons with Disabilities 2018.* New York: United Nations, 2019.

United Nations, Economic and Social Commission for Asia and the Pacific. *Disability at a Glance 2015: Strengthening Employment Prospects for Persons with Disabilities in Asia and the Pacific.* Bangkok: ESCAP,2016.

_______. *Building Disability-inclusive Societies in Asia and the Pacific: Assessing Progress of the Incheon Strategy.* Bangkok: ESCAP, 2018.

_______. *Incheon Strategy to "Make the Right Real" for Persons with Disabilities in Asia and the Pacific and Beijing Declaration including the Action Plan to Accelerate the Implementation of the Incheon Strategy.* Bangkok: ESCAP, 2018.

_______. *Disability at a Glance 2019: Investing in Accessibility in Asia and the Pacific-Strategic Approaches to Achieving Disability-inclusive Sustainable Development.* Bangkok: ESCAP, 2019.

_______. Can this time be different? Challenges and opportunities for Asia-Pacific economies in the aftermath of COVID-19. Issue Paper. Bangkok: ESCAP, 2020. Available at www.unescap.org/resources/can-time-be-different-challenges-and-opportunities-asia-pacific-economies-aftermath-covid.

_______. From indicators to action: Operationalizing the Incheon Strategy indicators to support disability-inclusive development. Technical Guide. Bangkok: ESCAP, 2020. Available at www.unescap.org/kp/2020/technical-guide-indicators-action-operationalizing-incheon-strategy-indicators-support.

_______. Population and development indicators for Asia and the Pacific, 2020. Data Sheet. Bangkok: ESCAP, 2020. Available at www.unescap.org/resources/2020-escap-population-data-sheet.

_______. *Expert Group Meeting: Promoting Inclusive Employment for Persons with Disabilities in Asia and the Pacific.* Bangkok: ESCAP, 2021.Available at www.unescap.org/events/2021/expert-group-meeting-promoting-inclusive-employment-persons-disabilities-asia-and#.

Velasco, J., and others. COVID-19 and persons with disabilities in the Philippines: a policy analysis. *Health Promotion Perspectives,* vol. 11, No. 3, 2021. pp. 299-306.

VERYBEST Law Offices. From 1 March 2021, the statutory employment rate for persons with disabilities will be raised. What should companies do? (in Japanese), 5 April 2021. Available at https://corporate.vbest.jp/columns/4314/.

Viet Nam Bank for Social Policy. *Annual Report 2019.* Hanoi: Viet Nam Bank for Social Policy, 2019.

_______. Lending interest rate. Undated. Available at https://eng.vbsp.org.vn/lending-interest-rate.

Washington Group on Disability Statistics. (2019). *Report of the Washington Group (WG) on Disability Statistics including an Executive Summary of the 19th Annual Meeting.* Meeting Report. Hyattsville: Washington Group on Disability Statistics, 2019. Available at www.washingtongroup-disability.com/fileadmin/uploads/wg/WG19_Executive_Summary_final.pdf.

_______. *WG ILO Labor Force Survey Disability Module (LFS-DM).* Undated. Available at www.washingtongroup-disability.com/question-sets/wg-ilo-labor-force-survey-disability-module-lfs-dm/.

Work and Income, Ministry of Social Development, New Zealand Government. Disability allowance. Undated. Available at www.workandincome.govt.nz/products/a-z-benefits/disability-allowance.html.

Workability International. *Customized Employment Guidelines.* Bangkok: Workability International, 2019.

World Bank. Preferential public procurement: Policy case studies on inclusive business. Policy Paper. Washington, D.C.: World Bank, 2016. Available at www.inclusivebusiness.net/sites/default/files/inline-files/Preferential%20public%20procurement_for%20web_final_0.pdf.

World Economic Forum. What the Fourth Industrial Revolution will do for people with disabilities, 18 January 2016. Available at www.weforum.org/agenda/2016/01/the-fourth-industrial-revolution-will-give-us-super-powers/.

World Health Organization. *World Report on Disability.* Geneva: WHO, 2011.

Zero Project. Innovative policy 2013 on employment: Malaysia's returning to work programme. Undated. Available at https://zeroproject.org/policy/malaysia/.

Annex A
Technical note regarding the use of data in Chapter 1

This technical note provides details regarding the use of data sets, employment indicators and technical terms in Chapter 1.

1. Choice of data sets

Chapter 1 analyses the employment status of persons with disabilities in Asia and the Pacific using data from two repositories: ILOSTAT and the Disability Data Initiative (DDI).

The principal data sources for ILOSTAT are the Labour Force Surveys and Household Income and Expenditure Surveys. The data sources for DDI are censuses and surveys with questions on functional difficulty.

Further details regarding the definitions, methodology and collection of data for the ILO and DDI repositories can be found at https://ilostat.ilo.org/ and https://disabilitydata.ace.fordham.edu/.

The decision to use data from ILOSTAT stems from the fact that the ILO Department of Statistics is the focal point to the United Nations for labour statistics. It collects comprehensive international data from the national statistical offices of governments, including those of the Asia–Pacific region. Among all available data sets on similar employment indicators, ILOSTAT contains disability-disaggregated data on employment indicators from the most number of Asian and Pacific countries.

The decision to use data from the DDI stemmed from the fact that its data sets comprise census or household survey data that are based on internationally comparable disability questions. Hence, it allows for the comparability of data across countries. The DDI provides results across several work-related indicators and disaggregation by type and extent of functional difficulty, sex, urban–rural classification and age. It offers the scope to explore the employment situation of persons with disabilities in detail.

The presentation of both datasets side by side is meant to provide the reader with a broader, more comprehensive picture of the employment situation of persons with disabilities. While the results of both datasets are not meant to be directly comparable, both clearly underscore the consistent existence of disability gaps in employment-related indicators.

2. Choice of indicators

Chapter 1 uses the following employment related indicators.

Indicator	ILOSTAT	DDI
Employment-to-population ratio	ESCAP calculations based on employment and working-age population numbers (in thousands) from ILOSTAT	Available
Labour force participation rate	ESCAP calculations based on labour force participation and working-age population numbers (in thousands) from ILOSTAT	
Proportion of adults in informal work		Available
Youth idle rate		Available
Proportion of women in managerial positions		Available

The following factors were taken into consideration in selecting the indicators for analysis:

- relevance in measuring the employment situation of persons with disabilities; and
- availability of data.

In this context, the most detailed analysis centred on the employment-to-population ratio, which is the only outcome indicator for employment within the Incheon Strategy Target and Indicator Framework (Indicator 1.2).[104]

104 The only other employment-related indicator in the Incheon Strategy is Indicator 1.3 "Proportion of persons with disabilities who participate in government-funded vocational training and other employment-support programmes as a proportion of all people trained."

Given that a significant proportion of persons with disabilities remain outside the labour force because of barriers to participation, an analysis of the unemployment rate of persons with disabilities was omitted, despite the availability of data from ILOSTAT and the indicator being a Sustainable Development Goal indicator. This is because the unemployment rate only calculates for persons out of work within the labour force and does not represent an accurate picture of the employment situation of persons with disabilities, the majority of whom are outside the labour force.

The following table compares the indicators used in Chapter 1 with those of the Sustainable Development Goals.

Chapter 1 indicators	SDG indicators
Employment-to-population ratio (or employment rate) measures the share of the adult population who work for pay or profit (self-employed).	**Indicator 8.5.2:** Unemployment rate, by sex, age and persons with disabilities. The unemployment rate conveys the percentage of persons in the labour force who are unemployed.
Labour force participation rate is a measure of the proportion of a country's working-age population who engage actively in the labour market, either by working or looking for work.	
Adults in informal work measures the share of the adult population who do informal work: self-employed, working for a microenterprise of five or fewer employees or in a firm that is unregistered, and persons who have no written contract with their employer. Family workers without pay are included as informal workers.	**Indicator 8.3.1:** Proportion of informal employment in total employment, by sector and sex. This indicator presents the share of employment that is classified as informal employment in the total economy and separately in agriculture and in non-agriculture.
Youth idle rate captures the share of youths aged 15–24 who are not enrolled in school or not employed. Because information on training was not consistently available, it does not reflect whether youths might be in training.	**Indicator 8.6.1:** Proportion of youth (aged 15–24 years) not in education, employment or training. This indicator conveys the proportion of youth (aged 15–24 years) not in education, employment or training (also known as "the youth NEET rate").

3. Terminology

The term "**functional difficulty**" is used when describing observations from the DDI dataset while the ILOSTAT dataset employs the term "**disability**". Disability in the **DDI data set** is measured solely based on selected functional difficulties (in hearing, seeing, mobility, communication, cognition and self-care) and therefore does not capture all persons with disabilities, specifically those with psychosocial and mental health disabilities. This use of terminology is in alignment with that used in all of DDI's analyses.[105] In the **ILOSTAT data set**, "disability" may be defined and measured differently in different countries while approaches used in most countries either explicitly or implicitly rely on international standards, mainly concepts inherent to the International Classification of Functioning, Disability and Health (2001) or its earlier versions, as well as the Convention on the Rights of Persons with Disabilities.[106]

The term "**working-age population**" is employed by the ILOSTAT dataset to refer to all persons aged 15 or older, although this may vary from country to country based on national laws and practices. For the DDI data set, the term "**adult population**" or "**adults**" is used to refer to all persons aged 15 or older.

The term "**disability gap**" is defined as a disadvantage for persons with disabilities (when referring to the ILOSTAT dataset) or functional difficulty (when referring to the DDI dataset) compared to persons without disabilities or functional difficulty. For purposes of this publication, the disability gap exists when there is a percentage point difference between the performance of persons with disabilities or functional difficulty and persons without, to the detriment of persons with disabilities, regardless of statistical significance. Such a definition allows for the discussion of disability gaps in the analysis of both the ILOSTAT and DDI data sets.

105 Disability Data Initiative, "Methods briefs". Available at https://disabilitydata.ace.fordham.edu/method-briefs/.
106 ILO, *Statistics on the Labour Force Characteristics of People with Disabilities: A Compendium of National Methodologies* (Geneva, 2015).

Annex B
Data tables

1. ILOSTAT (last update as of 18 July 2021)

1.1 Working-age population (thousands)

Country or territory	Total	Persons with disability	Persons without disability	Men	Men with disability	Men without disability	Women	Women with disability	Women without disability
Afghanistan	16 558.01	486.06	16 071.95	8 249.42	285.39	7 964.03	8 308.59	200.68	8 107.92
Armenia	2 204.40	168.93	2 035.48	1 024.65	84.11	940.54	1 179.76	84.81	1 094.94
Cambodia	10 685.79	495.35	10 190.45	5 143.75	228.02	4915.73	5 542.05	267.33	5 274.72
Cook Islands	11.45	0.43	11.02	5.58	0.22	5.36	5.87	0.21	5.66
Fiji	593.62	62.39	531.23	293.90	30.99	262.92	299.72	31.41	268.31
Indonesia	201 676.77	2 642.06	199 034.71	100 747.52	1 262.11	99 485.41	100 929.24	1 379.95	99 549.29
Kiribati	76.91	4.56	72.35	37.91	1.89	36.03	39.00	2.68	36.32
Lao PDR	4 758.03	75.67	4 682.36	2 328.09	38.44	2 289.65	2 429.95	37.23	2 392.71
Maldives	317.48	104.35	213.03	147.75	41.57	106.09	169.73	62.78	106.94
Marshall Islands	38.83	8.30	30.52	19.51	4.12	15.37	19.33	4.18	15.15
Mongolia	2 128.11	121.51	2 006.60	987.94	57.75	930.19	1 140.17	63.76	1 076.41
Papua New Guinea	4 100.03	354.40	3745.63	2 087.43	173.17	1 914.26	2 012.60	181.23	1 831.37
Samoa	110.99	3.01	107.99	56.01	1.56	54.45	54.99	1.45	53.54
Sri Lanka	16 196.23	834.65	15 361.59	7 488.32	387.21	7 101.11	8 707.91	447.43	8 260.48
Thailand	49 938.72	1 869.81	48 068.91	23 602.43	958.39	22 644.04	26 336.30	911.42	25 424.88
Timor-Leste	724.46	23.86	700.60	367.17	13.96	353.21	357.28	9.90	347.38
Tonga	63.19	2.16	61.03	29.53	1.05	28.48	33.66	1.11	32.55
Vanuatu	183.46	14.52	168.94	92.31	8.00	84.31	91.15	6.51	84.64

1.2 Labour force (thousands)

Country or territory	Total	Persons with disability	Persons without disability	Men	Men with disability	Men without disability	Women	Women with disability	Women without disability
Afghanistan	6 884.70	151.88	6 732.82	5 514.10	134.95	5 379.15	1 370.60	16.93	1 353.67
Armenia	1 315.34	51.56	1 263.77	732.14	32.98	699.16	583.20	18.58	564.62
Cambodia	8 579.91	242.61	8 337.29	4 459.46	138.15	4 321.31	4 120.45	104.46	4 015.98
Cook Islands	8.06	0.12	7.94	4.34	0.08	4.26	3.72	0.04	3.68
Fiji	341.83	23.23	318.60	226.29	16.06	210.23	115.54	7.17	108.37
Indonesia	135 858.84	319.61	135 539.23	82 161.74	209.43	81 952.31	53 697.11	110.19	53 586.92
Kiribati	27.54	0.60	26.94	16.35	0.26	16.09	11.19	0.34	10.85
Lao PDR	1 940.23	8.49	1 931.74	1 052.38	6.81	1 045.57	887.85	1.68	886.17
Maldives	191.36	50.92	140.45	113.85	27.68	86.17	77.51	23.23	54.28
Marshall Islands	17.27	3.58	13.69	11.89	2.54	9.35	5.38	1.04	4.34
Mongolia	1 250.61	20.62	1 229.99	659.86	12.13	647.73	590.74	8.49	582.26
Papua New Guinea	1 982.08	149.59	1 832.49	1 022.46	71.16	951.30	959.62	78.42	881.19
Samoa	48.10	0.26	47.84	30.80	0.15	30.65	17.31	0.11	17.20
Sri Lanka	8 376.87	125.75	8 251.12	5 461.40	86.52	5 374.88	2 915.47	39.23	2876.23
Thailand	34 816.14	586.40	34 229.73	18 339.61	344.24	17 995.37	16 476.52	242.16	16 234.36
Timor-Leste	485.88	16.52	469.36	266.60	10.53	256.07	219.28	5.99	213.29
Tonga	29.50	0.28	29.23	16.59	0.16	16.43	12.91	0.11	12.80
Vanuatu	92.18	5.54	86.64	50.01	3.36	46.65	42.17	2.18	39.99

1.3 Employment (thousands)

Country or territory	Total	Persons with disability	Persons without disability	Men	Men with disability	Men without disability	Women	Women with disability	Women without disability
Afghanistan	6 078.51	138.58	5 939.93	4 937.78	122.63	4 815.15	1 140.73	15.95	1 124.78
Armenia	1 074.58	42.41	1 032.17	604.01	27.54	576.47	470.57	14.87	455.70
Cambodia	8 520.56	240.54	8 280.02	4 428.74	136.75	4 292.00	4 091.82	103.80	3 988.02
Cook Islands	7.95	0.12	7.83	4.27	0.08	4.19	3.69	0.04	3.64
Fiji	327.07	22.80	304.26	217.92	15.84	202.08	109.14	6.96	102.18
Indonesia	130 044.98	312.57	129 732.41	78 377.93	206.34	78 171.59	51 667.05	106.24	51 560.82
Kiribati	25.17	0.53	24.64	14.96	0.23	14.73	10.22	0.30	9.92
Lao PDR	1 757.73	8.36	1749.38	939.27	6.68	932.59	818.47	1.68	816.79
Maldives	181.14	47.74	133.40	107.43	26.01	81.42	73.72	21.74	51.98
Marshall Islands	16.16	3.39	12.77	11.01	2.43	8.58	5.15	0.96	4.20
Mongolia	1 162.91	19.14	1 143.77	611.81	11.42	600.39	551.11	7.72	543.39
Papua New Guinea	1 942.40	148.23	1 794.17	995.03	70.12	924.91	947.37	78.11	869.26
Samoa	41.14	0.24	40.90	27.53	0.14	27.39	13.61	0.10	13.51
Sri Lanka	8 015.17	122.90	7 892.27	5 300.31	84.75	5 215.56	2 714.86	38.15	2 676.71
Thailand	34 533.32	563.15	33 970.17	18 176.88	331.82	17 845.05	16 356.44	231.33	16 125.12
Timor-Leste	463.25	15.28	447.97	257.69	10.09	247.60	205.56	5.20	200.36
Tonga	28.60	0.28	28.32	16.15	0.16	15.99	12.45	0.11	12.33
Vanuatu	84.86	5.22	79.64	46.64	3.18	43.45	38.22	2.03	36.19

1.4 Labour force participation rate (percentage, ESCAP's calculations based on tables 1.1 and 1.2)

Country or territory	Total	Persons with disability	Persons without disability	Men	Men with disability	Men without disability	Women	Women with disability	Women without disability
Afghanistan	41.58	31.25	41.89	66.84	47.29	67.54	16.50	8.44	16.70
Armenia	59.67	30.52	62.09	71.45	39.21	74.34	49.43	21.91	51.57
Cambodia	80.29	48.98	81.81	86.70	60.59	87.91	74.35	39.08	76.14
Cook Islands	70.39	28.34	72.01	77.80	36.57	79.46	63.35	19.91	64.97
Fiji	57.58	37.23	59.97	76.99	51.82	79.96	38.55	22.83	40.39
Indonesia	67.36	12.10	68.10	81.55	16.59	82.38	53.20	7.98	53.83
Kiribati	35.81	13.08	37.24	43.14	13.79	44.67	28.68	12.62	29.87
Lao PDR	40.78	11.21	41.26	45.20	17.71	45.67	36.54	4.51	37.04
Maldives	60.28	48.79	65.93	77.05	66.59	81.22	45.67	37.01	50.76
Marshall Islands	44.48	43.13	44.86	60.95	61.55	60.84	27.85	24.96	28.65
Mongolia	58.77	16.97	61.30	66.79	21.01	69.63	51.81	13.31	54.09
Papua New Guinea	48.34	42.21	48.92	48.98	41.09	49.70	47.68	43.27	48.12
Samoa	43.34	8.78	44.30	54.99	9.64	56.28	31.48	7.79	32.12
Sri Lanka	51.72	15.07	53.71	72.93	22.34	75.69	33.48	8.77	34.82
Thailand	69.72	31.36	71.21	77.70	35.92	79.47	62.56	26.57	63.85
Timor-Leste	67.07	69.23	66.99	72.61	75.45	72.50	61.37	60.47	61.40
Tonga	46.69	12.77	47.89	56.18	15.63	57.67	38.36	10.07	39.33
Vanuatu	50.24	38.14	51.28	54.18	42.01	55.33	46.26	33.42	47.25

1.5 Employment-to-population ratio (percentage, ESCAP's calculations based on tables 1.1 and 1.3)

Country or territory	Total	Persons with disability	Persons without disability	Men	Men with disability	Men without disability	Women	Women with disability	Women without disability
Afghanistan	36.71	28.51	36.96	59.86	42.97	60.46	13.73	7.95	13.87
Armenia	48.75	25.11	50.71	58.95	32.74	61.29	39.89	17.54	41.62
Cambodia	79.74	48.56	81.25	86.10	59.97	87.31	73.83	38.83	75.61
Cook Islands	69.50	28.34	71.09	76.58	36.57	78.19	62.79	19.91	64.37
Fiji	55.10	36.54	57.28	74.15	51.12	76.86	36.41	22.16	38.08
Indonesia	64.48	11.83	65.18	77.80	16.35	78.58	51.19	7.70	51.79
Kiribati	32.73	11.59	34.06	39.45	12.10	40.88	26.20	11.24	27.30
Lao PDR	36.94	11.04	37.36	40.35	17.37	40.73	33.68	4.51	34.14
Maldives	57.06	45.76	62.62	72.71	62.56	76.75	43.43	34.63	48.61
Marshall Islands	41.62	40.82	41.85	56.44	59.00	55.80	26.66	22.88	27.69
Mongolia	54.65	15.75	57.00	61.93	19.77	64.54	48.34	12.11	50.48
Papua New Guinea	47.38	41.83	47.90	47.67	40.49	48.32	47.07	43.10	47.46
Samoa	37.07	8.08	37.87	49.15	9.00	50.30	24.76	7.10	25.23
Sri Lanka	49.49	14.72	51.38	70.78	21.89	73.45	31.18	8.53	32.40
Thailand	69.15	30.12	70.67	77.01	34.62	78.81	62.11	25.38	63.42
Timor-Leste	63.94	64.05	63.94	70.18	72.24	70.10	57.53	52.49	57.68
Tonga	45.26	12.77	46.41	54.71	15.63	56.14	36.97	10.07	37.89
Vanuatu	46.25	35.94	47.14	50.52	39.79	51.54	41.93	31.22	42.76

2. Disability data initiative[107]

2.1 Employment-to-population ratio

2.1.1 Employment-to-population ratio for all adults (percentage) (disaggregation a)

Country	No difficulty	Any difficulty	Difference	Statistical significance of the difference
Afghanistan	42.50	32.29	10.21	***
Bangladesh	44.44	27.53	16.90	***
Cambodia	78.93	74.84	4.09	**
Indonesia	63.40	43.45	19.95	***
Kiribati	40.58	37.36	3.22	***
Maldives	50.61	51.14	-0.53	NS
Pakistan	33.82	34.42	-0.59	NS
Papua New Guinea	66.63	70.41	-3.78	***
Tajikistan	36.99	26.53	10.45	***
Timor-Leste	34.95	53.33	-18.38	***
Tonga	49.89	37.30	12.59	***
Vanuatu	67.37	68.94	-1.58	***
Viet Nam	77.77	40.49	37.28	***

2.1.2 Employment-to-population ratio for all adults (percentage) (disaggregation b)

Country	No difficulty	Some difficulty	Difference (no difficulty vs some difficulty)	Statistical significance of the difference (no difficulty vs some difficulty)	At least a lot of difficulty	Difference (no difficulty vs at least a lot of difficulty)	Statistical significance of the difference (no difficulty vs at least a lot)
Afghanistan	42.50	34.75	7.75	***	26.80	15.70	***
Bangladesh	44.44	29.68	14.76	***	19.10	25.33	***
Cambodia	78.93	76.81	2.12	NS	56.65	22.28	***
Indonesia	63.40	48.51	14.89	***	19.22	44.18	***
Kiribati	40.58	41.41	-0.83	NS	24.95	15.63	***
Maldives	50.61	52.86	-2.25	NS	47.82	2.79	NS
Pakistan	33.82	35.08	-1.26	NS	31.96	1.87	NS
Papua New Guinea	66.63	74.80	-8.18	***	60.26	6.37	***
Tajikistan	36.99	31.76	5.22	***	6.57	30.42	***
Timor-Leste	34.95	54.03	-19.08	***	42.12	-7.17	NS
Tonga	49.89	44.01	5.88	***	26.19	23.70	***
Vanuatu	67.37	70.32	-2.95	***	40.59	26.77	***
Viet Nam	77.77	46.50	31.27	***	18.33	59.44	***

107 In the DDI data tables, *, ** and *** indicate statistical significance at the 10%, 5% and 1% levels, respectively. NS stands for not significant.

2.1.3 Employment-to-population ratio for males (percentage)

Country	No difficulty	Any difficulty	Difference	Statistical significance of the difference
Afghanistan	68.52	54.51	14.01	***
Bangladesh	78.74	53.05	25.68	***
Cambodia	90.24	87.64	2.60	NS
Indonesia	80.57	60.79	19.77	***
Kiribati	48.74	45.21	3.54	***
Maldives	95.98	90.46	5.52	***
Pakistan	96.90	92.92	3.98	**
Papua New Guinea	66.41	71.01	-4.60	***
Tajikistan	57.04	39.79	17.25	***
Timor-Leste	62.22	79.16	-16.94	***
Tonga	61.29	49.02	12.27	***
Vanuatu	76.72	78.84	-2.12	***
Viet Nam	82.40	48.08	34.32	***

2.1.4 Employment-to-population ratio for females (percentage)

Country	No difficulty	Any difficulty	Difference	Statistical significance of the difference
Afghanistan	15.19	12.31	2.88	***
Bangladesh	10.98	8.31	2.67	***
Cambodia	75.53	71.14	4.39	*
Indonesia	46.18	29.19	17.00	***
Kiribati	33.08	30.57	2.51	***
Maldives	39.57	40.66	-1.09	NS
Pakistan	16.90	22.75	-5.84	***
Papua New Guinea	66.85	69.78	-2.94	*
Tajikistan	17.10	14.43	2.68	**
Timor-Leste	25.74	37.28	-11.54	***
Tonga	39.07	27.13	11.94	***
Vanuatu	57.94	59.70	-1.76	***
Viet Nam	73.32	34.44	38.87	***

2.1.5 Employment-to-population ratio for rural residents (percentage)

Country	No difficulty	Any difficulty	Difference	Statistical significance of the difference
Afghanistan	44.24	32.73	11.50	***
Bangladesh	42.92	25.67	17.25	***
Cambodia	79.76	75.45	4.31	*
Indonesia	68.65	47.62	21.03	***
Maldives	49.64	52.33	-2.70	*
Pakistan	34.40	37.24	-2.84	NS
Papua New Guinea	70.26	71.87	-1.61	NS
Tajikistan	39.61	30.41	9.20	***
Timor-Leste	36.55	53.98	-17.42	***
Tonga	50.59	39.10	11.48	***
Viet Nam	82.76	44.40	38.37	***

2.1.6 Employment-to-population ratio for urban residents (percentage)

Country	No difficulty	Any difficulty	Difference	Statistical significance of the difference
Afghanistan	37.62	31.32	6.30	***
Bangladesh	48.24	33.51	14.73	***
Cambodia	75.11	71.58	3.53	NS
Indonesia	58.27	38.33	19.95	***
Maldives	52.62	48.09	4.53	NS
Pakistan	32.81	29.96	2.85	*
Papua New Guinea	47.80	59.27	-11.47	***
Tajikistan	35.97	24.87	11.10	***
Timor-Leste	31.40	51.84	-20.44	***
Tonga	47.67	31.41	16.25	***
Viet Nam	66.83	28.29	38.53	***

2.1.7 Employment-to-population ratio for adults aged 15–29 (percentage)

Country	No difficulty	Any difficulty	Difference	Statistical significance of the difference
Afghanistan	37.08	31.62	5.46	***
Bangladesh	34.10	20.80	13.30	***
Cambodia	70.69	69.58	1.11	NS
Indonesia	47.93	31.03	16.90	***
Kiribati	30.22	32.85	-2.63	**
Maldives	42.90	42.11	0.78	NS
Pakistan	25.99	27.40	-1.41	NS
Papua New Guinea	55.05	62.39	-7.33	***
Tajikistan	27.81	26.99	0.82	NS
Timor-Leste	23.41	25.08	-1.67	NS
Tonga	33.07	28.74	4.33	**
Vanuatu	58.38	62.26	-3.88	***
Viet Nam	68.82	44.56	24.26	***

2.1.8 Employment-to-population ratio for adults aged 30–44 (percentage)

Country	No difficulty	Any difficulty	Difference	Statistical significance of the difference
Afghanistan	54.14	43.75	10.39	***
Bangladesh	55.14	43.10	12.03	***
Cambodia	87.42	75.91	11.51	***
Indonesia	74.62	58.49	16.14	***
Kiribati	56.85	51.22	5.63	***
Maldives	53.54	49.79	3.75	**
Pakistan	38.92	35.01	3.92	**
Papua New Guinea	82.98	79.97	3.00	*
Tajikistan	48.84	37.76	11.07	***
Timor-Leste	48.47	51.02	-2.55	NS
Tonga	65.61	55.33	10.28	***
Vanuatu	77.19	75.88	1.31	**
Viet Nam	92.39	69.93	22.47	***

2.1.9 Employment-to-population ratio for adults aged 45–64 (percentage)

Country	No difficulty	Any difficulty	Difference	Statistical significance of the difference
Afghanistan	47.18	34.99	12.19	***
Bangladesh	52.43	33.08	19.35	***
Cambodia	88.12	77.65	10.47	***
Indonesia	75.36	58.87	16.49	***
Kiribati	45.60	41.78	3.83	***
Maldives	69.09	59.94	9.15	***
Pakistan	44.67	38.31	6.36	*
Papua New Guinea	78.65	74.96	3.69	*
Tajikistan	44.96	32.77	12.19	***
Timor-Leste	61.46	66.05	-4.60	*
Tonga	65.04	51.67	13.36	***
Vanuatu	77.56	74.64	2.92	***
Viet Nam	81.72	63.41	18.31	***

2.1.10 Employment-to-population ratio for all adults, by functional difficulty type (percentage)

Country	No difficulty	Seeing	Hearing	Mobility	Cognition	Self-care	Communication
Afghanistan	42.50	30.66	27.85	28.60	26.54	18.87	33.16
Bangladesh	44.44	26.24	20.88	18.04	13.37	9.21	11.16
Cambodia	78.93	75.47	81.37	66.90	72.69	-	59.34
Indonesia	63.40	47.45	32.99	24.89	24.39	16.48	-
Kiribati	40.58	39.80	35.17	25.65	27.45	18.19	24.51
Maldives	50.61	52.08	48.12	51.46	41.17	-	64.95
Pakistan	33.82	36.64	40.42	30.60	31.55	30.86	42.38
Papua New Guinea	66.63	70.21	65.69	68.24	65.27	39.06	-
Tajikistan	36.99	28.69	16.12	22.00	19.52	7.10	7.87
Timor-Leste	34.95	56.80	55.53	52.99	47.02	43.20	48.99
Tonga	49.89	38.52	25.57	27.44	18.74	-	30.45
Vanuatu	67.37	69.29	62.13	63.94	60.63	-	-
Viet Nam	77.77	39.44	27.75	25.18	27.03	-	-

2.2 Adults in informal work

2.2.1 Adults in informal work for all adults (percentage) (disaggregation a)

Country	No difficulty	Any difficulty	Difference	Statistical significance of the difference
Afghanistan	79.93	80.07	-0.14	NS
Bangladesh	65.48	74.34	-8.87	***
Cambodia	79.01	88.71	-9.71	***
Indonesia	63.14	80.13	-16.99	***
Maldives	83.71	85.84	-2.13	***
Pakistan	94.46	92.51	1.96	***
Papua New Guinea	52.17	56.28	-4.10	***
Philippines	38.29	48.57	-10.28	***
Timor-Leste	86.40	92.42	-6.02	***
Tonga	43.53	57.33	-13.80	***
Vanuatu	60.22	67.03	-6.81	***
Viet Nam	66.98	85.65	-18.67	***

2.2.2 Adults in informal work for all adults (percentage) (disaggregation b)

Country	No difficulty	Some difficulty	At least a lot of difficulty	Difference (no difficulty vs some difficulty)	Statistical significance of the difference (no difficulty vs some difficulty)	Difference (no difficulty vs at least a lot of difficulty)	Statistical significance of the difference (no difficulty vs at least a lot)
Afghanistan	79.93	80.61	78.50	-0.67	NS	1.43	NS
Bangladesh	65.48	74.62	72.74	-9.15	***	-7.27	**
Cambodia	79.01	87.00	95.85	-7.99	***	-16.84	***
Indonesia	63.14	78.29	90.69	-15.14	***	-27.55	***
Maldives	83.71	83.21	89.52	0.50	NS	-5.81	***
Pakistan	94.46	91.46	94.83	3.00	***	-0.37	NS
Papua New Guinea	52.17	59.65	48.49	-7.47	***	3.68	*
Timor-Leste	86.40	91.85	97.45	-5.44	***	-11.05	***
Tonga	43.53	59.10	52.41	-15.57	***	-8.89	***
Vanuatu	60.22	66.74	77.37	-6.52	***	-17.15	***
Viet Nam	66.98	85.48	87.20	-18.50	***	-20.22	***

2.2.3 Adults in informal work for males (percentage)

Country	No difficulty	Any difficulty	Difference	Statistical significance of the difference
Afghanistan	77.09	76.58	0.52	NS
Bangladesh	68.23	77.42	-9.19	***
Cambodia	51.63	48.89	2.74	NS
Indonesia	52.95	72.51	-19.56	***
Maldives	96.33	96.41	-0.08	NS
Pakistan	91.74	90.98	0.75	NS
Papua New Guinea	47.01	52.78	-5.77	***
Philippines	36.24	46.36	-10.13	***
Timor-Leste	45.05	57.50	-12.45	***
Tonga	42.63	53.90	-11.27	***
Vanuatu	56.99	64.74	-7.75	***
Viet Nam	62.44	81.93	-19.49	***

2.2.4 Adults in informal work for females (percentage)

Country	No difficulty	Any difficulty	Difference	Statistical significance of the difference
Afghanistan	91.06	91.46	-0.40	NS
Bangladesh	48.40	60.60	-12.20	***
Cambodia	45.03	47.11	-2.08	NS
Indonesia	75.15	87.64	-12.49	***
Maldives	17.49	23.91	-6.42	***
Pakistan	37.18	30.64	6.54	NS
Papua New Guinea	57.51	59.89	-2.37	NS
Philippines	43.25	53.81	-10.56	***
Timor-Leste	39.87	32.05	7.82	***
Tonga	44.85	62.70	-17.85	***
Vanuatu	64.53	69.85	-5.32	***
Viet Nam	71.89	89.79	-17.89	***

2.2.5 Adults in informal work for rural residents (percentage)

Country	No difficulty	Any difficulty	Difference	Statistical significance of the difference
Afghanistan	84.79	87.19	-2.41	***
Bangladesh	73.18	83.40	-10.22	***
Cambodia	81.70	90.29	-8.59	***
Indonesia	72.56	85.04	-12.48	***
Maldives	82.72	86.85	-4.13	***
Pakistan	93.96	92.91	1.04	NS
Papua New Guinea	59.94	61.61	-1.67	NS
Timor-Leste	87.71	94.36	-6.65	***
Tonga	50.98	64.46	-13.48	***
Viet Nam	75.65	89.63	-13.98	***

2.2.6 Adults in informal work for urban residents (percentage)

Country	No difficulty	Any difficulty	Difference	Statistical significance of the difference
Afghanistan	63.22	63.76	-0.54	NS
Bangladesh	47.80	50.02	-2.22	NS
Cambodia	66.23	80.20	-13.97	***
Indonesia	54.02	74.55	-20.53	***
Maldives	85.36	82.97	2.38	NS
Pakistan	95.22	91.71	3.50	***
Papua New Guinea	11.92	15.54	-3.62	***
Timor-Leste	83.53	85.73	-2.20	*
Tonga	18.28	28.35	-10.07	***
Viet Nam	43.46	66.16	-22.71	***

2.2.7 Adults in informal work for adults aged 15–29 (percentage)

Country	No difficulty	Any difficulty	Difference	Statistical significance of the difference
Afghanistan	79.77	82.04	-2.28	NS
Bangladesh	51.93	61.57	-9.64	**
Cambodia	76.28	79.45	-3.17	NS
Indonesia	61.32	75.61	-14.29	***
Maldives	85.62	88.86	-3.24	***
Pakistan	96.49	94.72	1.77	NS
Papua New Guinea	45.36	52.03	-6.67	**
Philippines	34.58	38.53	-3.95	***
Timor-Leste	89.27	89.01	0.27	NS
Tonga	34.41	36.62	-2.21	NS
Vanuatu	61.53	61.73	-0.20	NS
Viet Nam	57.08	69.33	-12.25	***

2.2.8 Adults in informal work for adults aged 30–44 (percentage)

Country	No difficulty	Any difficulty	Difference	Statistical significance of the difference
Afghanistan	80.04	80.36	-0.32	NS
Bangladesh	66.86	67.86	-1.01	NS
Cambodia	75.45	76.24	-0.79	NS
Indonesia	58.18	66.31	-8.13	***
Maldives	76.24	69.00	7.24	***
Pakistan	89.67	78.66	11.01	***
Papua New Guinea	60.90	62.03	-1.14	NS
Philippines	35.36	40.65	-5.29	***
Timor-Leste	78.35	79.41	-1.07	NS
Tonga	40.40	40.04	0.36	NS
Vanuatu	55.71	59.09	-3.38	***
Viet Nam	67.53	78.08	-10.55	***

2.2.9 Adults in informal work for adults aged 45–64 (percentage)

Country	No difficulty	Any difficulty	Difference	Statistical significance of the difference
Afghanistan	79.92	79.03	0.90	NS
Bangladesh	77.47	75.55	1.92	NS
Cambodia	90.59	93.55	-2.96	***
Indonesia	67.93	73.88	-5.95	***
Maldives	90.82	90.00	0.82	NS
Pakistan	96.35	95.09	1.26	*
Papua New Guinea	60.51	58.56	1.96	NS
Philippines	43.66	45.95	-2.29	***
Timor-Leste	91.15	93.83	-2.68	***
Tonga	52.64	53.90	-1.25	NS
Vanuatu	63.03	65.00	-1.97	***
Viet Nam	78.35	86.38	-8.04	***

2.3 Youth idle rate

2.3.1 Idle rate for youth aged 15–24 (percentage) (disaggregation a)

Country	No difficulty	Any difficulty	Difference	Statistical significance of the difference
Afghanistan	14.36	19.33	-4.97	***
Bangladesh	37.13	53.37	-16.24	***
Cambodia	9.71	10.51	-0.80	NS
Indonesia	31.10	56.37	-25.27	***
Kiribati	45.38	49.45	-4.07	**
Maldives	8.73	7.17	1.56	*
Pakistan	12.99	13.18	-0.19	NS
Papua New Guinea	18.05	14.99	3.07	NS
Timor-Leste	17.67	22.02	-4.34	NS
Tonga	26.05	33.78	-7.74	***
Vanuatu	26.18	31.70	-5.52	***
Viet Nam	8.21	38.37	-30.15	***

2.3.2 Idle rate for youths aged 15–24 (percentage) (disaggregation b)

Country	No difficulty	Some difficulty	Difference (no difficulty vs some difficulty)	Statistical significance of the difference (no difficulty vs some difficulty)	At least a lot of difficulty	Difference (no difficulty vs at least a lot of difficulty)	Statistical significance of the difference (no difficulty vs at least a lot)
Afghanistan	14.36	18.24	-3.88	**	21.72	-7.36	***
Bangladesh	37.13	51.65	-14.52	***	57.71	-20.58	***
Cambodia	9.71	13.68	-3.98	NS	4.59	5.12	**
Indonesia	31.10	45.93	-14.83	***	79.68	-48.57	***
Kiribati	45.38	51.63	-6.24	***	42.24	3.14	NS
Maldives	8.73	7.95	0.78	NS	5.80	2.93	**
Pakistan	12.99	16.19	-3.20	*	7.24	5.75	***
Tonga	26.05	38.11	-12.07	***	29.93	-3.88	NS
Vanuatu	26.18	29.17	-2.99	**	58.62	-32.44	***
Viet Nam	8.21	21.55	-13.34	***	71.20	-62.98	***

2.3.3 Idle rate for male youths aged 15–24 (percentage)

Country	No difficulty	Any difficulty	Difference	Statistical significance of the difference
Afghanistan	9.62	13.82	-4.20	***
Bangladesh	11.78	30.94	-19.15	***
Cambodia	1.54	3.24	-1.70	NS
Indonesia	22.89	54.62	-31.72	***
Kiribati	43.80	45.74	-1.94	***
Papua New Guinea	17.05	11.98	5.07	***
Timor-Leste	4.75	5.90	-1.15	***
Tonga	21.94	32.13	-10.19	***
Vanuatu	19.32	25.74	-6.42	***
Viet Nam	5.89	38.43	-32.54	***

2.3.4 Idle rate for female youths aged 15–24 (percentage)

Country	No difficulty	Any difficulty	Difference	Statistical significance of the difference
Afghanistan	19	25	-5	**
Bangladesh	60.33	73.35	-13.03	***
Cambodia	18.04	19.31	-1.27	NS
Indonesia	39.38	58.25	-18.87	***
Kiribati	46.96	54.23	-7.27	***
Papua New Guinea	19.14	17.25	1.89	NS
Timor-Leste	31.05	39.98	-8.93	**
Tonga	30.27	35.68	-5.41	*
Vanuatu	32.85	36.71	-3.86	**
Viet Nam	10.58	38.29	-27.70	***

2.3.5 Idle rate for rural residents aged 15–24 (percentage)

Country	No difficulty	Any difficulty	Difference	Statistical significance of the difference
Afghanistan	12.33	17.20	-4.87	***
Bangladesh	37.95	54.01	-16.05	***
Indonesia	33.59	62.47	-28.88	***
Maldives	11.05	8.02	3.03	***
Pakistan	14.48	11.91	2.58	NS
Papua New Guinea	15.47	12.30	3.17	NS
Timor-Leste	19.82	24.35	-4.54	NS
Tonga	26.78	34.84	-8.07	***
Viet Nam	7.06	39.80	-32.73	***

2.3.6 Idle rate for urban youths aged 15–24 (percentage)

Country	No difficulty	Any difficulty	Difference	Statistical significance of the difference
Afghanistan	19.49	23.06	-3.58	NS
Bangladesh	35.16	51.79	-16.64	***
Indonesia	28.87	49.84	-20.98	***
Maldives	4.87	5.39	-0.53	NS
Pakistan	10.56	15.55	-5.00	*
Papua New Guinea	31.01	33.00	-2.00	NS
Timor-Leste	13.78	17.29	-3.50	NS
Tonga	23.70	29.29	-5.60	NS
Viet Nam	10.93	34.75	-23.82	***

2.4 Women in managerial positions

2.4.1 Women in managerial positions (percentage)

Country	No difficulty	Any difficulty	Difference	Statistical significance of the difference
Afghanistan	0.10	0.08	0.02	NS
Bangladesh	0.22	0.14	0.08	NS
Cambodia	0.85	0.62	0.23	NS
Kiribati	1.43	1.28	0.15	NS
Maldives	1.87	0.71	1.16	*
Pakistan	0.07	0.00	0.07	NS
Papua New Guinea	0.22	0.21	0.01	NS
Timor-Leste	0.48	0.69	-0.21	NS
Tonga	6.87	7.40	-0.53	NS
Vanuatu	1.48	1.48	0.00	NS
Viet Nam	0.42	0.27	0.15	***

3. Data sources

Country or territory	ILOSTAT data source	Year	Disability Data Initiative data source	Year
Afghanistan	Labour Force Survey	2020	Living Conditions Survey	2016
Armenia	Household Labour Force Survey	2019		
Bangladesh			Household Income and Expenditure Survey	2016
Cambodia	Household Socio-Economic Survey	2014	Demographic and Health Survey	2014
Cook Islands	Labour Force Survey	2019		
Fiji	Employment, Unemployment Survey	2016		
Indonesia	National Labour Force Survey	2020	Population and Housing Census	2010
Kiribati	Household Income and Expenditure Survey	2019	Population and Housing Census	2015
Lao PDR	Labour Force Survey	2017		
Maldives	Household Income and Expenditure Survey	2019	Demographic and Health Survey	2009
Marshall Islands	Household Income and Expenditure Survey	2019		
Mongolia	Labour Force Survey	2020		
Pakistan			Demographic and Health Survey	2017
Papua New Guinea	Household Income and Expenditure Survey	2010	Household Income and Expenditure Survey	2009
Samoa	Labour Force Survey	2017		
Tajikistan			Survey of Water, Sanitation and Hygiene	2016
Timor-Leste			Demographic and Health Survey	2016
Tonga			Census	2016
Vanuatu			Population and Housing Census	2009
Viet Nam			Population and Housing Census	2009

Annex C
Washington Group Short Set on Functioning[108] and its application in Asia and the Pacific[109]

The way in which disability is classified – and the corresponding methodology in which disability prevalence is captured – has evolved in tandem with changes in the understanding of disability. Specifically, disability classification has shifted from a medical model approach of focusing on medical impairments to an approach that examines functional limitations arising from impairments in different settings.

Disability classification focusing on functional limitations was first introduced in the World Health Organization's International Classification of Functioning, Disabilities and Health (ICF). Based on the ICF framework, the Washington Group on Disability Statistics has since developed tools for governments to use in censuses and surveys to collect standardized and comparable disability data.

The fundamental Washington Group question set is its Short Set on Functioning, comprising six questions. These questions are designed to be culturally neutral; avoid reference to disability, which can result in underreporting; and are based on difficulties people may experience conducting familiar everyday activities.

Six Washington Group Short Set questions:

- [Do/Does] [you/he/she] have difficulty seeing, even if wearing glasses?
- [Do/Does] [you/he/she] have difficulty hearing, even if using a hearing aids?
- [Do/Does] [you/he/she] have difficulty walking or climbing steps?
- [Do/does] [you/he/she] have difficulty remembering or concentrating?
- [Do/does] [you/he/she] have difficulty with self-care, such as washing all over or dressing?
- Using [your/his/her] usual language, [do/does] [you/he/she] have difficulty communicating, for example understanding or being understood?

Response categories to the above questions:

- No difficulty
- Some difficulty
- A lot of difficulty
- Cannot do at all

Use of Washington Group Short Set in Asia and the Pacific

To gather valid and reliable statistics on disability that are comparable worldwide, more than 80 countries have used the Washington Group Short Set on Functioning. It also has been adopted as the way to disaggregate data for the Incheon Strategy in Asia and the Pacific.

The following member States have integrated Washington Group questions into population surveys:

- Samoa: *2016 Population and Housing Census: Disability Monograph*. Available at www.sbs.gov.ws/digi/2018_Samoa_Disability_Monograph.pdf.
- Kiribati: *2015 Population and Housing Census: Disability Monograph*. Available at www.unicef.org/Kiribati_Disability_Report_E-Version.pdf.
- Lao: *2015 Population and Housing Census: Disability Monograph*. Available at https://lao.unfpa.org/sites/default/files/pub-pdf/PHC-ENG-FNAL-WEB_0.pdf.
- Nauru: *2011 Population and Housing Census: Disability Monograph*. Available at http://nauru.prism.spc.int/naurudocuments?view=download&format=raw&fileId=90.
- Timor-Leste: *2010 Population and Housing Census: Disability Monograph*. Available at www.statistics.gov.tl/wp-content/uploads/2013/12/Disability_Monograph.pdf.
- Viet Nam: *2009 Population and Housing Census. Key Findings on People with Disabilities in Vietnam*. Available at https://vietnam.unfpa.org/sites/default/files/pub-pdf/Disability_ENG.pdf.

There are also plans for Kyrgyz Republic and Sri Lanka to use the Washington Group questions in their upcoming censuses.

108 See more information on the Washington Group on Disability Statistics website: www.washingtongroup-disability.com/.
109 ESCAP, "From indicators to action: Operationalizing the Incheon Strategy indicators to support disability-inclusive development", Technical Guide (Bangkok, 2020).

Annex D
International standards and initiatives

International instruments mentioning persons with disabilities

- ILO Employment (Transition from War to Peace) Recommendation No. 71, 1944
- ILO Social Security Convention, 1952
- European Social Charter, 1961
- ILO Human Resources Development Convention (No. 142) and Recommendation No. 150, 1975
- African Charter on Human and Peoples' Rights, 1981
- Additional Protocol on the American Convention on Human Rights in the Area of Economic, Social and Cultural Rights, 1988
- UN Convention on the Rights of the Child, 1989
- Vienna Declaration and Programme of Action, World Conference on Human Rights, 1993
- Copenhagen Declaration and Programme of Action, World Summit for Social Development, 1995
- Beijing Platform for Action, Fourth World Conference on Women, 1995
- European Union initiatives
- Treaty of Amsterdam, 1997
- European Union Charter of Fundamental Rights, 2000
- European Union Directive on Discrimination, 2000
- 2030 Agenda for Sustainable Development, 2015

International initiatives concerning persons with disabilities

- ILO Recommendation concerning Vocational Rehabilitation of the Disabled, 1955
- UN Declaration on the Rights of Mentally Retarded Persons, 1971
- UN Declaration on the Rights of Disabled Persons, 1975
- UN International Year of Disabled Persons, 1981
- World Programme of Action Concerning Disabled Persons, 1982
- UN Decade of Disabled Persons, 1983–1992
- ILO Convention concerning Vocational Rehabilitation and Employment (Disabled Persons) (No. 159) and Recommendations No. 168, 1983
- Council of Europe Coherent Policy for the Rehabilitation of Persons with Disabilities, 1992
- UN Standard Rules on the Equalization of Opportunities for Disabled Persons, 1993
- Asian and Pacific Decade of Disabled Persons, 1993–2002, 2003–2012 and 2013–2022
- Salamanca Statement and Framework for Action on Special Needs Education, 1994
- Inter-American Convention on the Elimination of All Forms of Discrimination Against Persons with Disabilities, 1999
- African Decade of Disabled Persons, 1999–2009 and 2010–2019
- European Year of People with Disabilities, 2003 and Action Plan, 2004–2010
- Council of Europe–Malaga Declaration, 2003, and Disability Action Plan, 2006–2015
- Arab Decade, 2003–2012
- Decade of the Americas for the Rights and Dignity of Persons with Disabilities, 2006–2016
- UN Convention on the Rights of Persons with Disabilities, 2006

Annex E
Non-discrimination laws in Asia and the Pacific

Country	Non-discrimination law	Key provisions
Armenia	Constitution, 2015	Prohibits discrimination, including on the basis of disability.
	Law on Social Protection of Persons with Disabilities, 1993	Requires state policies to grant "favourable conditions and privileges for the realization of their rights and abilities aimed at ensuring opportunities for persons with disabilities that are equal to those of other citizens".
	Labour Code, 2004 & Law on Trade Unions, 2000	Dictates no discrimination with regard to persons with disabilities joining trade unions.
Australia	Disability Discrimination Act, 1992	Makes it unlawful to discriminate against a person in employment and many other areas of public life due to their disability.
Azerbaijan	Constitution, 1995, amended in 2002, 2009, 2016	States all citizens to be equal before the law and prohibits discrimination.
	Law on Employment, 2018	Requires state policy on employment to provide equal opportunities for all citizens to guarantee the right for choosing their labour and employment freely.
	Labour Code,1999	Prohibits assumption of any discrimination upon business qualities of an employee, professional contribution, factors not related to work results, as well as the rights restriction.
Bangladesh	Rights and Protection of Persons with Disabilities Act, 2013	Prohibits discrimination on the basis of disability in relation to employment, provided the person has the requisite qualifications.
China	Law on Promotion of Employment, 2007	Prohibits discrimination against persons with disabilities in the recruitment process by employers.
	Regulations on Employment of Persons with Disabilities, 2007	Prohibits discrimination against employees with disabilities in terms of promotion, performance evaluation and granting of professional qualifications, remuneration, social security and welfare benefits.
Georgia	Law on the Elimination of All Forms of Discrimination, 2014	Prohibits discrimination, including due to a disability.
India	The Rights of Persons with Disabilities Act, 2016	Prohibits discrimination due to a disability.
Indonesia	Law on Persons with Disabilities (No. 8/2016), 2016	Protects the rights of persons with disabilities to be free from discrimination.
Japan	Persons with Disabilities Discrimination Elimination Act, 2013	Prohibits discrimination against persons with disabilities in employment.
	Promotion of the Employment of Persons with Disabilities Law, 1960, amended 2005, 2008 and 2013	Obliges employers to provide reasonable accommodation.
Kazakhstan	Labour Code, 2015	Prohibits discrimination due to a disability, among several reasons, in the sphere of labour (Art. 6).

Country	Non-discrimination law	Key provisions
Mongolia	Law on the Human Rights of Persons with Disabilities, 2016	Prohibits discrimination against persons with disabilities (Art. 6).
Nepal	Constitution, 2015	Prohibits discrimination of any kind on any basis that includes disability.
	Disabled Protection and Welfare Act, 1982 Disabled Protection and Welfare Regulations, 1994	Prohibits discrimination in any form in appointments and promotions to any governmental service or other public service on the basis of disability.
New Zealand	Bill of Rights Act, 1990	Includes an express prohibition of discrimination against persons with disabilities.
	Human Rights Act, 1993	Protects the right of persons with disabilities to freedom from discrimination.
Palau	Disabled Persons' Anti-Discrimination Act, 1992	Prohibits discrimination in employment.
Philippines	Magna Carta for Disabled Persons R.A. No. 7277, 1992	Prohibits discrimination on the ground of disability in employment, education and other aspects of life.
Republic of Korea	Anti-Discrimination Against and Remedies for Persons with Disabilities Act, 2008	Prohibits discrimination on the basis of disability in all aspects of life.
Viet Nam	Law on Persons with Disabilities (Nr. 51/2010/QH12), 2010	Forbids stigmatization of persons with disabilities and discrimination against them.
	Labour Code, 2012	Requires employers to consult with employees with disabilities on issues related to their rights and interests and to provide persons with disabilities with equal pay for work of equal value, suitable working conditions, working tools and safety and health provisions.

Note: The list is not intended to be exhaustive. Many of the examples have been drawn from the following sources: ILO, *Promoting Employment Opportunities for People with Disabilities Quota Schemes*, vol. 2 (Geneva, 2019) and country reports to the Committee on the Rights of Persons with Disabilities; others are drawn from research on individual country laws.

Annex F
Quota schemes in Asia and the Pacific

Binding levy systems (8 countries)	Binding quota systems, no apparent sanction for non-compliance (15 countries)	Quota system introduced by Government Decision, decree (2 countries)
Cambodia	Afghanistan	Bangladesh
China	Armenia	Malaysia
Japan	Azerbaijan	
Pakistan	India	
Republic of Korea	Indonesia	
Russian Federation	Islamic Republic of Iran	
Turkey	Kazakhstan	
Uzbekistan	Kyrgyz Republic	
	Mongolia	
	Nepal	
	Philippines	
	Sri Lanka	
	Tajikistan	
	Thailand	
	Turkmenistan	

Source: ILO, *Promoting Employment Opportunities for People with Disabilities: Quota Schemes, vol. 2* (Geneva, 2019).

Annex G
Steps to plan or revise a quota scheme

1. To determine the level of the quota, gather information on: (i) number of persons with disabilities seeking employment; and (ii) number of companies of different sizes in the labour market.

2. To ensure commitment, organize consultations with key stakeholders, in particular employers' organizations, trade unions and organizations of persons with disabilities.

3. Upon deciding to proceed with the design of a quota system, based on background information and consultation outcomes, develop a policy document in cooperation with the key stakeholders that sets out the legal status and main features of the scheme, including:
   a. whether it should apply to all employers;
   b. profile of beneficiaries, including whether priority should be given to certain jobseekers with disabilities (such as women with disabilities or persons with intellectual, psychosocial or multiple disabilities);
   c. sanctions for non-compliance; and
   d. alternative options for employers in addition to recruitment.

4. If the scheme will involve a levy payment for non-compliance, the uses of the compensatory levy fund should be laid out in the policy document or in associated guidelines.

5. Other measures to support implementation of the quota should be made available, such as financial incentives and advisory services to employers, as well as other means of encouraging employer involvement.

6. Provisions should be made for monitoring the implementation of the scheme.

Source: ILO, *Promoting Employment Opportunities for People with Disabilities Quota Schemes*, vol. 1 (Geneva, 2019).

Annex H
COVID-19-related measures on employment and social protection concerning persons with disabilities in Asia and the Pacific[110]

Armenia	• The Ministry of Labour and Social Affairs has made sure to avoid delays in the payment of pensions and benefits. Pensions and cash benefits have been delivered to beneficiaries' residence.[111] • The Ministry of Labour and Social Affairs provided food and other protective measures for two months for persons older than 50 years and persons with disabilities.[112] • The Government provided financial assistance to lessen the burden of the COVID-19 crisis. For families that receive a family and social benefit, extra support was given in an amount of 50 per cent of the benefit. Within this, 70 per cent was provided in cash along with the benefit, and 30 per cent was a payment for the energy consumed by the receiver.[113] • From April to May 2020, the Armenian Red Cross Society supported 15,000 vulnerable people across the country with basic food and hygiene aid. The list of recipients was provided by the Ministry of Labour and Social Affairs.[114]
Australia	• A one-off deep cleaning payment was funded by the National Disability Insurance Scheme where support workers diagnosed with COVID-19 need to enter a person's home.[115] • One-time cash payment of AU$750 per person was given to persons receiving disability supports and carer payments.[116]
Azerbaijan	• The valid term of disability certificate that expired on 1 March 2020 was extended, until the end of the quarantine period. This measure covered 14,000 people, and NZ$2.6 million was allocated for this purpose.[117] • In cooperation with the United Nations Development Programme, the Government provided 500 persons with disabilities with training and equipment to support them in starting small businesses.[118] • The Government paid 50 per cent of the tuition fees for vulnerable students studying at universities and specialized secondary and vocational schools. The beneficiaries included recipients of targeted state social assistance and persons whose parents have I- or II-degree disabilities.[119] • The Ombudsman supported low-income families in Baku and other regions with food packages to persons aged 65 or older and persons with disabilities who live alone.[120] • The average monthly pension was increased by 27 per cent in the first six months of 2020, reaching $176.40. The beneficiaries included 380,900 persons with disabilities.[121] • Social programmes, such as the self-employment programme, were continued. The Ministry of Labour and Social Protection increased access of persons with disabilities to the labour market and small businesses by developing specialized profile tests, modular training programmes and professional standards.[122]
Bangladesh	• ADD International's COVID-19 Update noted that nearly 13,500 persons with disabilities received assistance, such as emergency grants, from the Government, NGOs or individuals.[123] • Under the social safety net programme, nearly 265 million taka (including allowances paid in advance) was distributed among 8 million beneficiaries that included insolvent persons with disabilities and students with disabilities.[124] • The Ministry of Social Welfare provided food, cash and other expenditures for persons with disabilities.[125] • The coverage of the Old Age Allowances, the Allowances for Destitute Women and the Allowances for Disabled Persons was expanded to include 1.7 million more beneficiaries.[126] • A general cash allowance was extended to persons with disabilities who did not receive disability-specific allowances.[127]

110 Different combinations of keywords, such as "COVID-19", "coronavirus", "persons with disabilities", "disability" and "vulnerable groups" were used to find available online resources. Special attention was paid to the websites of national news agencies, government disability focal points and ministries in charge of health, human rights, or social protection. Additionally, the COVID-19 portals of the International Monetary Fund, the ILO and the KPMG International were checked to complement the existing information. Due to the limited publicity of disability-related responses and the evolving situation of the pandemic, the measures cannot be considered as exhaustive, definitive or in any way binding and do not reflect the views or position of ESCAP. The hyperlinks of each measure are provided; however, we cannot guarantee the accuracy and quality of every resource.
111 See www.gov.am/ru/news/item/9676/.
112 See http://unprpd.org/sites/default/files/Overview%20response_1.4.pdf.
113 See https://home.kpmg/xx/en/home/insights/2020/04/armenia-government-and-institution-measures-in-response-to-covid.html.
114 See www.redcross.am/en/news/coronavirus-arcs-activities.html.
115 See www.ndis.gov.au/providers/price-guides-and-pricing#price-guide-covid-19-response-summary.
116 See https://openknowledge.worldbank.org/bitstream/handle/10986/33635/Social-Protection-and-Jobs-Responses-to-COVID-19-A-Real-Time-Review-of-Country-Measures-April-17-2020.pdf?sequence=1&isAllowed=y.
117 See www.ilo.org/global/topics/coronavirus/country-responses/lang--en/index.htm#AZ.
118 See www.ohchr.org/Documents/Events/GoodPracticesCoronavirus/azerbaijan-submission-covid19.pdf.
119 See www.azernews.az/news.php?news_id=164092&cat=nation.
120 See www.ombudsman.gov.az/en/view/news/1810/ombudsman-office-provided-food-aid-to-low-income-families.
121 See www.azernews.az/news.php?news_id=167417&cat=nation.
122 See www.azernews.az/news.php?news_id=168764&cat=nation.
123 See www.add.org.uk/covid-19-update-6.
124 See www.bssnews.net/?p=410106.
125 See www.internationaldisabilityalliance.org/sites/default/files/ida_south-asian-region-report_02-02-2021_2.pdf.
126 See www.un.org/ohrlls/sites/www.un.org.ohrlls/files/bangladesh_report_on_covid_19_and_way_forward-20_october_2020.pdf.
127 See www.internationaldisabilityalliance.org/-social-protection-covid19.

Cambodia	• The Government launched a monthly cash transfer programme for poor and vulnerable households.[128] • The Ministry of Culture and Fine Arts mobilized an aid programme for the Music Association of the Disabled, including 1,220,000 Cambodian riel, 500 kg rice and other food items.[129] • The Government offered social protection, such as cash transfers and provisions, to persons with disabilities holding an IDPoor Card.[130] • The Ministry of Social Affairs, Veterans and Youth Rehabilitation continued to call on persons with disabilities to register for disability identification cards at district or commune halls.[131]
China	• The Government mandated all allowances to be paid on time, including the allowance for persons with severe disabilities and the nursing allowance. The amount was increased appropriately in areas where the pandemic situation has been serious.[132] • The China Disabled Persons' Federation issued a notice requiring disabled persons' federations at all levels to ensure the employment and basic livelihoods of persons with disabilities. Rent subsidies, living subsidies and relief subsidies were granted to assist disability employment units, such as blind massage workshops, auxiliary employment institutions and individual businesses of persons with disabilities.[133] • The China Disabled Persons' Federation implored enterprises to stabilise the employment of persons with disabilities through job stabilisation measures and recruitment subsidies from the Government.[134] • In Hubei Province, grass-roots working groups assisted persons with disabilities by giving them anti-pandemic materials.[135] • The disabled service centre in Shenyang City, Liaoning Province, set up an online recruitment service platform for persons with disabilities.[136] • More than 35 million Chinese yuan (about $4.94 million) was offered as special allowances to more than 13,000 people living with difficulties in Hubei Province.[137] • The China Disabled Persons' Federation provided 53 billion yuan ($7.5 billion) for a relief package targeting vulnerable groups. The funding formed part of the state benefits to cover basic living expenses.[138] • Guidelines for safeguarding the employment of persons with disabilities in the wake of the pandemic were developed.[139]
Fiji	• Tax deduction for businesses employing persons with disabilities for three consecutive years was increased from 300 to 400 per cent.[140] • The National Council for Persons with Disabilities provided updates on its Facebook page, such as the 20 affected persons with disabilities who received relief packages.[141]
Georgia	• The Social Service Agency continued state transfers, such as state pensions, compensation and social packages.[142] • The Government allocated a total of 3.5 billion Georgian lari ($1.1 billion) for crisis management, of which 1.035 billion lari targeted social assistance. Around 40,000 persons with severe disabilities and children with disabilities received cash assistance of 600 lari.[143]
India	• India has developed a social protection programme under the Pradhan Mantri Gareeb Kalyan Yojana. Free food rations were provided, and wages under the employment guarantee scheme were increased. Further measures include direct cash transfers of $13 to poor pensioners, widows and persons with disabilities.[144] • According to the Comprehensive Disability Inclusive Guidelines for Protection and Safety of Persons with Disabilities, employees with blindness and other severe disabilities in both public and private sectors were exempted from essential service work.[145] • The Nashik Municipal Corporation in the State of Maharashtra deposited 2,000 rupees per person to the bank accounts of more than 512 persons with disabilities. The amount was transferred by the Social Welfare Department under its scheme to provide financial assistance for persons with disabilities.[146] • Tamil Nadu and Himachal Pradesh paid allowances to beneficiaries, including persons with disabilities.[147] • Many people who lost their jobs due to the lockdown turned to the Mahatma Gandhi National Rural Employment Guarantee Act (NREGA) work. The Rural Development Department involved more than 24,582 persons with disabilities in NREGA work under the Scheme 2020–21. Tasks for persons with disabilities include plantation work, distributing water to workers and nursery activities.[148]

128 See www.imf.org/en/Topics/imf-and-covid19/Policy-Responses-to-COVID-19#C.
129 See www.khmertimeskh.com/50729071/charity-program-benefits-people-with-disabilities/.
130 See www.khmertimeskh.com/50757680/disabled-community-calls-for-more-help-during-covid-19/.
131 See www.phnompenhpost.com/national/ministry-urges-people-disabilities-register-id.
132 See www.gov.cn/zhengce/content/2020-03/07/content_5488352.htm.
133 See http://english.cdpf.org.cn/MediaCenter/updates2/202003/t20200316_674242.shtml.
134 See http://english.cdpf.org.cn/MediaCenter/updates2/202003/t20200316_674242.shtml.
135 See http://english.cdpf.org.cn/MediaCenter/updates2/202003/t20200323_674299.shtml.
136 See http://english.cdpf.org.cn/MediaCenter/updates2/202003/t20200323_674299.shtml.
137 See http://english.www.gov.cn/statecouncil/ministries/202004/01/content_WS5e847f4bc6d0c201c2cbff05.html.
138 See http://english.cdpf.org.cn/MediaCenter/updates2/202004/t20200415_674503.shtml.
139 See www.gov.cn/xinwen/2020-05/26/content_5515061.htm.
140 See www.fiji.gov.fj/Media-Centre/Speeches/2020-COVID-19-BUDGET-RESPONSE-ADDRESS-BY-THE-ATTOR.
141 See www.facebook.com/NCPDfiji/posts/101979114866697.
142 See www.ilo.org/global/topics/coronavirus/regional-country/country-responses/lang--en/index.htm#GE.
143 See https://agenda.ge/en/news/2020/1273.
144 See www.ilo.org/global/topics/coronavirus/country-responses/lang--en/index.htm#IN.
145 See http://disabilityaffairs.gov.in/content/page/whats-new.php.
146 See https://timesofindia.indiatimes.com/city/nashik/nmc-deposits-rs-2000-to-bank-a/c-of-512-disabled-people/articleshow/75396235.cms.
147 See http://unprpd.org/sites/default/files/Overview%20response_1.4.pdf.
148 See https://timesofindia.indiatimes.com/city/jaipur/record-engagement-of-disabled-persons-in-nrega/articleshow/77860761.cms.

	• The National Human Rights Council issued advisories to develop and run internet-based platforms to support home-based small-scale commercial activities, particularly for women with disabilities.[149] • The Tamil Nadu government exempted its employees with disabilities from attending office from 6 May to 20 June 2021 due to the surge in COVID-19 cases.[150]
Indonesia	• Cash social assistance was transferred to the accounts of persons with disabilities or delivered by mail.[151] • The Minister of Social Affairs launched basic food assistance for 7,072 persons with disabilities. A total of 11,835 food packages were distributed to older persons and persons with disabilities affected by COVID-19.[152] The Ministry of Social Affairs oversaw the distribution of social assistance to ensure that it reached target groups, such as poor and vulnerable households and individuals.[153] • The National Development Planning Agency worked with the Ministry of Social Affairs and local governments to re-register persons with disabilities who lacked birth certificates and thus did not receive social aid.[154]
Islamic Republic of Iran	• Thus far, 2,500,000 Iranian rial was allocated to 40,000 persons nursing spinal cord-injured patients, beneficiaries of family-centred nursing and persons with severe disabilities.[155] • A total of $4,500,000 was allocated to assist households of persons with severe disabilities.[156]
Japan	• Temporary measures were made for the certification of disability support classification.[157] • The Emergency Economic Package Against COVID-19 comprised cash handouts for every individual and affected firms.[158]
Kazakhstan	• There is now a mechanism to obtain disability status online.[159] • An anti-crisis package included targeted assistance such as cash transfers to vulnerable households.[160] • The payment of disability benefits has continued during the emergency. Also, the disability benefits were recalculated, benefiting more than 22,800 recipients.[161] • An additional 125 billion Kazakh tenge was allocated for COVID-19 measures, of which 30.8 billion tenge was allocated for the provision of food and household sets to certain categories of the population. The recipients included children from 6 to 18 years old, persons with disabilities of 1–3 groups, children with disabilities, persons engaged in caring for a child with a disability and officially registered unemployed people.[162] • Utility costs would be reimbursed for seven categories of socially vulnerable groups, including persons with disabilities of groups 1-3, families raising children with disabilities, and "invalids and participants of the Great Patriotic War, persons equated with disabled people and participants of the Great Patriotic War".[163] • The Enbek State Programme for the Development of Productive Employment and Mass Entrepreneurship for 2017–2021 continued during the state of emergency. In the Pavlodar region, participants were provided with state grants to develop new business ideas. The main beneficiaries included persons from large and low-income families, persons with disabilities and young people.[164] • Food and household kits worth 1,320 million tenge were distributed to 79,155 vulnerable citizens, including persons with disabilities of groups 1–3, children with disabilities younger than 16 years and people raising a child with a disability. Free protective masks worth a total of 160 million tenge were provided to 470,615 socially vulnerable people, including persons with disabilities of groups 1–3.[165]
Kyrgyz Republic	• The Government prepared a package of COVID-19 economic measures, including a food security programme for vulnerable groups.[166] • Approximately 490,000 citizens from socially vulnerable groups received social payments from the Government.[167] • The Ministry of Labor and Social Development extended the period of disability pension payment due to the state of emergency. Also, the validity of disability-related certificates was prolonged.[168]
Malaysia	• The Government allocated a total of 25 million ringgit in the form of food, health care items and shelter to vulnerable groups, such as older persons and children in shelters, persons with disabilities and homeless people.[169]

149 See https://nhrc.nic.in/sites/default/files/NHRC%20Advisory%20on%20Disability.pdf.
150 See https://timesofindia.indiatimes.com/city/chennai/covid-19-in-tamil-nadu-disabled-govt-employees-exempted-from-going-to-office/articleshow/82404612.cms.
151 See https://kemsos.go.id/en/the-efforts-of-risk-reduction-the-impact-of-the-covid-19-pandemic-against-persons-with-disabilities.
152 See www.kemsos.go.id/en/ensuring-that-covid-19-impact-management-reaches-vulnerable-groups.
153 See https://kemsos.go.id/ar/kemensos-terus-kawal-distribusi-bansos-berjalan-cepat-dan-tepat.
154 See www.thejakartapost.com/news/2020/06/12/people-with-disabilities-demand-access-to-information-basic-rights-during-pandemic.html.
155 See www.ilo.org/global/topics/coronavirus/country-responses/lang--en/index.htm#IR.
156 See http://en.behzisti.ir/news/15817/Latest-measure-taken-by-SWO-to-prevent-Coronavirus.
157 See www.mhlw.go.jp/content/000605029.pdf.
158 See www.imf.org/en/Topics/imf-and-covid19/Policy-Responses-to-COVID-19#J.
159 See www.ilo.org/global/topics/coronavirus/country-responses/lang--en/index.htm#KZ.
160 See www.imf.org/en/Topics/imf-and-covid19/Policy-Responses-to-COVID-19#K.
161 See www.coronavirus2020.kz/kz/tzh-kezeninde-mugedekter-buryn-belgilengen-top-boyynsha-zhardemaky-alady_a3639045.
162 See https://primeminister.kz/en/news/press/pravitelstvom-rk-zaplanirovana-rabota-po-postepennomu-snizheniyu-neneftyanogo-deficita-a-smailov-1141040.
163 See https://primeminister.kz/en/news/press/390-mlrd-tenge-na-zhilishchnoe-stroitelstvo-kak-raspredeleny-sredstva-114436.
164 See https://primeminister.kz/en/news/reviews/personnel-training-teaching-basics-of-entrepreneurship-expanding-microcrediting-in-rural-areas-how-enbek-state-program-implemented-in-kazakhstan.
165 See https://primeminister.kz/en/news/reviews/construction-support-for-smes-and-nvestment-how-east-kazakhstan-region-developed-during-the-pandemic.
166 See www.imf.org/en/Topics/imf-and-covid19/Policy-Responses-to-COVID-19#K.
167 See https://home.kpmg/xx/en/home/insights/2020/04/kyrgyzstan-government-and-institution-measures-in-response-to-covid.html.
168 See https://24.kg/english/150625_Period_of_some_social_payments_extended_due_to_state_of_emergency.
169 See www.bharian.com.my/rencana/komentar/2020/04/672084/pelaksanaan-pakej-prihatin-perlu-mesra-oku.

	• The Melaka Social Security Organization disbursed more than 10 million ringgit for social benefits, including temporary disability, permanent disability and dependant benefits.[170] • The Department of Social Welfare transferred a one-off 300-ringgit payment to 300,000 persons with disabilities and single mothers.[171] • The 1.5-billion-ringgit employee recruitment incentive programme aimed to encourage employers to hire workers among persons with disabilities, especially during the pandemic.[172]
Maldives	• The Ministry of Gender, Family and Social Services requested personal sanitation and essential items for persons with disabilities from the World Health Organization.[173]
Federated States of Micronesia	• One-off payments of $500 were given to eligible low-income households, with additional benefits for households of persons with disabilities.[174] • Temporary waivers of medical expenses were provided for older persons, persons with disabilities and survivors of gender-based violence.[175] • The Department of Finance and Administration prepared a new social protection programme for the vulnerable that targeted assistance to persons with disabilities, such as temporary waivers of certain medical expenses and electricity subsidies.[176]
Mongolia	• Social welfare pensions and allowances were increased from 188,000 tugrik to 288,000 Mongolian tugrik, reaching a total of 62,600 people who included persons with disabilities.[177] • The monthly allowance of 100,000 tugrik for children with disabilities who need permanent care was given until the end of 2020.[178] • The United Nations Population fund collaborated with the Ministry of Labour and Social Protection to distribute 400 dignity kits to persons with disabilities.[179]
Nepal	• Provincial and municipal governments distributed food aid, with special priority given to expecting mothers, orphans, persons with disabilities and persons with chronic illnesses.[180]
New Zealand	• Core benefit payments have been increased by $25 (gross) per week for the most vulnerable.[181]
Pakistan	• The Ehsaas Emergency Cash Programme, worth 144 billion rupees, was developed to benefit 12 million vulnerable families affected by the COVID-19 crisis. Ehsaas is a first-of-its-kind poverty-reduction programme for poor women, widows, orphans, homeless people, persons with disabilities, poor farmers, poor labourers and others from low-income backgrounds.[182] • Other government support programmes for persons with disabilities include the Ehsaas Rashan Programme (food rations) and the Sehat Sahulat Programme (medical care).[183] • The United Nations Population Fund partnered with provincial government departments and commissions to distribute dignity kits to women and girls with disabilities in four provinces to help maintain personal hygiene during COVID-19.[184] • The Government launched the Ehsaas Kafaalat Policy for Special Persons as a step towards a disability-inclusive and sustainable post-COVID-19 world. Two million families are receiving a monthly stipend of 2,000 rupees.[185]
Philippines	• The local government in Dumaguete City have provided a rice subsidy for 30,000 indigent families and individuals, including persons with disabilities and older persons.[186] • Valenzuela City launched the City Care Bag for registered children with severe disabilities and impairment. This is in addition to the City Food Voucher and the Valenzuela City Market on Wheels Programme.[187] • The Department of Social Welfare and Development provided initial assistance of 4,764 food packs for residents in the cities of San Jose del Monte, Meycauayan and Malolos, as well as in the towns of Pandi and San Miguel during the quarantine period. This assistance was received by older persons and persons with disabilities.[188] • The Government provided 200 billion pesos for a cash subsidy for affected workers in the informal sector and vulnerable citizens, such as persons with disabilities.[189]

170 See www.malaymail.com/news/malaysia/2020/06/11/melaka-socso-has-disbursed-rm10m-in-benefits-as-of-may/1874666.
171 See www.malaymail.com/news/malaysia/2020/06/12/penjana-grant-for-nursery-operators-will-ensure-sop-compliance-says-group/1874961.
172 See www.malaymail.com/news/malaysia/2020/06/12/penjana-grant-for-nursery-operators-will-ensure-sop-compliance-says-group/1874961.
173 See www.who.int/docs/default-source/maldives/maldives-sitrep-9-july2020.pdf?sfvrsn=6e6e278e_2.
174 See www.adb.org/sites/default/files/publication/662406/pem-december-2020.pdf.
175 See www.adb.org/sites/default/files/publication/662406/pem-december-2020.pdf.
176 See https://gov.fm/index.php/component/content/article/35-pio-articles/news-and-updates/428-social-protection-programming-for-the-elderly-persons-with-disabilities-and-low-income-households-entering-pilot-stage-program-to-be-expanded-in-march-april.
177 See www.zasag.mn/news/view/24959.
178 See https://montsame.mn/en/read/232972.
179 See www.montsame.mn/en/read/245575.
180 See www.nepalitimes.com/latest/nepal-covid-19-relief-package/.
181 See www.treasury.govt.nz/publications/glance/covid-19-economic-package-glance-he-waka-eke-noa-we-are-all-working-together-april-2020.
182 See www.zameen.com/blog/ehsaas-kafaalat-programme-pakistan.html.
183 See www.thenews.com.pk/magazine/us/641844-digital-baithak-covid-19-and-persons-with-disabilities
184 See www.humanitarianresponse.info/sites/www.humanitarianresponse.info/files/documents/files/pakistan_situation_report.-_20200730.pdf.
185 See www.brecorder.com/news/40037157.
186 See www.pna.gov.ph/articles/1097918.
187 See www.valenzuela.gov.ph/article/news/13386.
188 See www.pna.gov.ph/articles/1098474.
189 See www.pna.gov.ph/articles/1098794.

	• The City Social Welfare and Development Office initially released 2.19 million pesos to 438 beneficiaries of the national Social Amelioration Programme in Zamboanga City. The beneficiaries included older persons, single parents, persons with disabilities, distressed overseas Filipino workers, indigent indigenous peoples, underprivileged sectors and homeless citizens.[190] • The Department of the Interior and Local Government emphasized that persons with disabilities should be prioritized in the distribution of relief goods.[191] • The Department of Social Welfare and Development provided increased support on assistive devices. Persons with disabilities could request this support through the Persons with Disability Welfare Programme and Assistance for Individuals in Crisis Situation at the Crisis Intervention Unit field offices.[192] • The Department of Labor and Employment created a survey to assess the impact of the pandemic on persons with disabilities, with the intention of ensuring disability-inclusive recovery in employment and livelihood.[193] • The Department of Agrarian Reform selected 15 female agrarian reform beneficiaries from six provinces to support their livelihood in crisis by providing a livelihood package based on their preferences and capabilities. Women with disabilities undertaking farming activities were one of the primary target groups.[194] • The provincial government of Pangasinan launched a livelihood aid programme, with cash assistance of 400 pesos per person, particularly targeting persons with disabilities.[195] • Around 77.9 billion pesos cash assistance was distributed to 13,000,080 family beneficiaries under the second tranche of the SAP. The beneficiaries included frail older persons and persons with disabilities.[196] • The San Juan City government released cash assistance under the SAP to residents in an indoor stadium, with a special lane for persons with disabilities, pregnant women and older persons to claim their financial aid.[197] • The Employees' Compensation Commission continued the KaGabay programme to facilitate the employment and livelihood of persons with disabilities through cash benefits, occupational therapy and skills training.[198] • The Department of Social Welfare and Development, along with partner agencies, distributed cash aid to local government units under Enhanced Community Quarantine in Visayas and Mindanao. Beneficiaries, such as persons with disabilities and older persons, received 1,000 pesos, with a maximum amount of 4,000 pesos per family.[199]
Republic of Korea	• The Ministry of Health and Welfare provided consumption coupons for 2.3 million low-income households, including families receiving a disability pension.[200] • Around 21.71 million households received emergency disaster relief payments through a universal programme worth 14.3 trillion Korean won ($11.66 billion). Around 2.8 million vulnerable families, such as beneficiaries of national basic livelihood security and disability pensions, received the funds first.[201]
Russian Federation	• Disability status was automatically extended for six months for citizens whose next re-examination was from 1 March to 1 October 2020. The individual rehabilitation programme was extended for six months.[202] • There has been a simplification of the disability status granting process, and the disability status could be obtained remotely until 1 October 2020.[203] The simplification enabled more citizens to access and receive disability pensions during the pandemic.[204] • Veterans and persons with disabilities of the Great Patriotic War, children with disabilities, persons having disabilities since childhood (first category) and other persons with disabilities (first and second categories) would not need to pay for visits by workers of the Federal Service for State Registration, Cadastre and Cartography. The Government covered the expenses.[205]
Samoa	• The Government provided a recovery package worth 500 million Samoan tala. The Samoa Worker's Congress asked the Government to consider certain aspects, including that person with disabilities should be part of the primary target groups of economic support.[206] • Cash grants were made available to vulnerable groups, including persons with disabilities.[207]
Singapore	• The Social Service Office of the Ministry of Social and Family Development extended social and financial assistance to persons in need through the Temporary Relief Fund, the COVID-19 Support Grant and the ComCare assistance schemes.[208] • The Ministry of Social and Family Development moved job support initiatives online as far as possible during the pandemic, with accessibility considerations for persons with disabilities.[209]

190 See www.pna.gov.ph/articles/1099609.
191 See https://dilg.gov.ph/news/DILG-to-LGUs-Prioritize-PWDs-in-distribution-of-relief-goods/NC-2020-1097.
192 See www.dswd.gov.ph/dswd-provides-assistive-devices-to-persons-with-disability/.
193 See www.dole.gov.ph/news/moving-towards-disability-inclusive-recovery-in-employment-and-livelihood-in-the-time-of-covid-19/.
194 See www.pna.gov.ph/articles/1109353.
195 See www.pna.gov.ph/articles/1110210.
196 See www.pna.gov.ph/articles/1112805.
197 See www.pna.gov.ph/articles/1113738.
198 See www.dole.gov.ph/news/pwds-get-livelihood-aid-amid-pandemic/.
199 See www.pna.gov.ph/articles/1148330.
200 See http://ncov.mohw.go.kr/tcmBoardView.do?brdId=&brdGubun=&dataGubun=&ncvContSeq=353818&contSeq=353818&board_id=140&gubun=BDJ.
201 See www.koreaherald.com/view.php?ud=20200504000558&ACE_SEARCH=1.
202 See https://xn--80aesfpebagmfblc0a.xn--p1ai/what-is-done/social-measures/pomosch_lyudyam_s_invalidnostyu.html.
203 See http://government.ru/en/news/39452/.
204 See https://xn--80aesfpebagmfblc0a.xn--p1ai/what-is-done/social-measures/pomosch_lyudyam_s_invalidnostyu.html.
205 See http://government.ru/en/news/39724/.
206 See www.ilo.org/global/topics/coronavirus/country-responses/lang--en/index.htm#WS.
207 See https://samoa.un.org/en/52796-samoas-second-voluntary-national-review-implementation-sustainable-development-goals.
208 See www.msf.gov.sg/media-room/Pages/Ensuring-continued-social-assistance-and-essential-services-for-vulnerable-groups.aspx.
209 See www.straitstimes.com/singapore/govt-agencies-to-help-job-seekers-with-disabilities.

	• SG Enable and its job placement and job support partners reached out to persons with disabilities who stopped working since the start of 2020, encouraging them to sign up for employment support services.[210] • In response to the continued negative impact of COVID-19 on the employment of persons with disabilities, the Ministry of Social and Family Development announced the creation of new job and training programmes for persons with disabilities, as part of the workstream under the National Jobs Council.[211]
Sri Lanka	• Samurdhi (a poverty alleviation programme) beneficiaries and other vulnerable households have received weekly food rations (rice, lentils and onions).[212] • Older persons' allowances and disability allowances were issued via Grama Niladharis (village officers).[213] • The Presidential Task Force provided a one-off cash transfer of 5,000 rupees for vulnerable groups, including 559,109 older persons, 119,300 persons with disabilities and 160,675 farmers insured by the Farmers Insurance Scheme.[214] • The 5,000-rupee allowance was paid a second time to older persons, persons with disabilities and persons suffering from kidney ailments.[215]
Tajikistan	• The Dushanbe Chairman provided 500 tons of essential food products worth more than 2.5 million Tajik somonis for 5,000 needy families, persons with disabilities, patients, orphans and homeless people.[216] • The Government provided a one-time payment equivalent to a month's minimum wage for vulnerable groups, including persons with disabilities.[217]
Thailand	• The Cabinet approved the payment of an extra 1,000 Thai baht to each disability card holder in addition to their monthly allowances, aiming to ease the burden on persons with disabilities amid the COVID-19 pandemic.[218] • The Social Development and Human Security Ministry proposed to the Cabinet to provide cash transfer for vulnerable groups who had not benefited from the Rao Mai Thing Gun cash handout programme of the Ministry of Finance or the campaigns organized by the Ministry of Agriculture and Cooperatives. The primary beneficiaries have been older persons, persons with disabilities and parents of newborn infants.[219] The Cabinet agreed to set aside 39.42 billion baht to finance a new cash handout programme for 13.14 million extremely vulnerable people.[220] • The Office of the Basic Education Commission allocated a budget for food to students who were learning remotely, including students with disabilities and underprivileged students.[221] • The Permanent Secretary of Labour discussed measures to support workers with disabilities affected by COVID-19 with the Association of Persons with Disabilities. The Association proposed to accelerate government agencies' hiring of persons with disabilities.[222] • The Department of Skill Development under the Ministry of Labour has received Labour SIM cards from Huawei Technologies (Thailand) Co. Ltd. to be distributed to persons with disabilities and workers whose lives were disrupted by the pandemic. The initiative allowed receivers to benefit from distance education services offered by the Department.[223]
Timor-Leste	• The Government introduced a package of socioeconomic support initiatives for poor and vulnerable households, including a universal cash transfer system and emergency rice supply.[224]
Tonga	• Around 1.3 million Tongan pa'anga was designated for the Safety and Protection Cluster to increase the welfare scheme for vulnerable people, including persons with disabilities, as well as to support community policing and other activities.[225] • A cash transfer of $100 per person was given to Elderly Benefit and Disability Benefit receivers, in addition to their regular benefits.[226] • The Government increased monthly payments to older persons and persons with disabilities to assist them in mitigating the impact of COVID-19.[227] • The World Bank committed $30 million to aid the Government in supporting the most vulnerable, including persons with disabilities, in the wake of COVID-19 and Cyclone Harold. The funding was used for social welfare payments.[228]

210 See www.msf.gov.sg/media-room/Pages/Impact-of-COVID-19-on-Employment-Prospects-of-Persons-with-Disabilities-and-Measures-to-Raise-Inclusivity.aspx.
211 See www.msf.gov.sg/media-room/Pages/Around-4500-Jobs-And-Skills-Opportunities-In-The-Social-Service-And-Early-Childhood-Sectors-And-For-PWDs.aspx.
212 See www.ilo.org/global/topics/coronavirus/country-responses/lang--en/index.htm#LK.
213 See www.newsfirst.lk/2020/03/23/presidents-secretary-gives-instructions-to-ensure-smooth-operations-of-state-apparatus-during-covid-19-operations/.
214 See http://www.pmdnews.lk/கொரோனா-அச்சுறுத்தலுக்கு/.
215 See www.news.lk/news/political-current-affairs/item/30133-7-4-million-to-receive-rs-5000-allowance-in-april-min-bandula-gunawardhena.
216 See https://eng.khovar.tj/2020/05/dushanbe-chairman-provides-assistance-to-5-000-families-and-road-service-employees/.
217 See https://eng.khovar.tj/2020/06/president-emomali-rahmon-signs-executive-order-to-mitigate-effects-of-covid-19-on-economy/.
218 See www.nationthailand.com/news/30386927?utm_source=category&utm_medium=internal_referral.
219 See www.nationthailand.com/news/30388495?utm_source=category&utm_medium=internal_referral.
220 See www.bangkokpost.com/thailand/general/1924668/b39bn-for-handouts-gets-nod.
221 See www.bangkokpost.com/thailand/general/1928424/remote-learning-to-stay-if-virus-persists.
222 See www.mol.go.th/en/news/association-of-persons-with-disabilities-of-thailand-discusses-alleviation-measures-for-covid-19-impacted-people-with-permanent-secretary-of-labour/.
223 See www.bangkokpost.com/thailand/pr/2136463/huawei-donates-labour-sim-cards-to-help-empower-persons-with-disabilities-and-the-most-vulnerable-during-pandemic.
224 See http://timor-leste.gov.tl/?p=24159&lang=en&lang=en.
225 See www.gov.to/wp-content/uploads/2020/04/COVID-Pamphlet_Final1.pdf.
226 See https://nukualofatimes.tbu.to/2020/04/02/tonga-sets-60-million-paanga-to-counter-coronavirus-impact/.
227 See www.tonga-broadcasting.net/?p=18447.
228 See www.worldbank.org/en/news/press-release/2020/12/16/30-million-in-support-for-tongas-most-vulnerable.

Turkey	• The monthly money transfer to the Social Benevolent and Solidarity Associations was increased to 180 million Turkish lira from 135 million lira, with the aim of protecting the most disadvantaged groups.[229] • The Vefa Social Support Groups provided for basic needs, such as bread for the most vulnerable in self-isolation.[230] Consisting of local governorate officials, police and gendarmerie units, the groups regularly make home visits to people older than 65 and those with underlying health conditions.[231] • Social assistance for older persons and persons with disabilities was distributed without seeking income criteria and severe disability status.[232] • The Ministry of Health ruled that employees with disabilities should be given administrative holidays when the epidemic was at its peak.[233]
Tuvalu	• All citizens of Tuvalu receive financial assistance of more than $17 per month.[234]
Uzbekistan	• Examples of new working arrangements include allowing employees, particularly pregnant women, older persons and persons with disabilities to use distance-working methods with flexible working hours.[235] • The Center for Coordinating Sponsorship Activities was established to provide charitable assistance, such as food and medicine, for families in need and persons with disabilities.[236] According to a decree signed by the president, lonely older persons and persons with disabilities were offered basic food and hygiene items free of charge during the quarantine period.[237] • The system for issuing documents on temporary disabilities has been simplified.[238] • Disability-related benefits were increased.[239]
Viet Nam	• The Government allocated 650 billion Vietnamese dong ($28.2 million) to help poor households and other social beneficiaries through local branches of the Vietnam Bank for Social Policies.[240] • The Ministry of Labour, Invalids and Social Affairs allocated 300 million dong, focusing on supporting social policy beneficiaries and low-income households.[241] • Additional cash transfers of 500,000 dong per month was given to persons with disabilities.[242]
America Samoa	• A third round of COVID-19 stimulus payments included payments for adult dependants with disabilities.[243]
Cook Islands	• The one-off welfare payment of $400 was given to old-age pensioners, caregivers and the infirm and destitute who are registered with the Ministry of Internal Affairs.[244]
Guam	• Disaster Household Distribution was approved,[245] which included providing persons with disabilities with food aid.[246] • Senators approved a bill to distribute $500 cash assistance to each eligible member of a qualified family. Special arrangements were made for persons with permanent disabilities.[247] • Two bills amending the $500 aid programme were passed unanimously by the Legislature.[248] • A third round of COVID-19 stimulus payments included dependants of any age, including college students, those with disabilities and elderly parents.[249]
Hong Kong, China	• Special considerations were made regarding persons in receipt of disability allowance who, owing to the pandemic, had not satisfied residence requirement for social welfare. They were told there is no rush to return to Hong Kong.[250] • In addition to utility, rent and transport subsidies, an extra payment of the Comprehensive Social Security Assistance Scheme standard rate was given to several allowances, including the Old Age Allowance, the Old Age Living Allowance and the Disability Allowance.[251] • The maximum level of support under the Support Programme for Employees with Disabilities was raised to $40,000. The programme was launched in 2013 to provide employers with a one-off subsidy for each employee with a disability.[252]

229 See www.ilo.org/global/topics/coronavirus/country-responses/lang--en/index.htm#TR.
230 See www.dailysabah.com/turkey/vefa-social-support-groups-to-provide-citizens-with-bread-over-curfew-period/news.
231 See www.hurriyetdailynews.com/even-well-off-people-are-calling-social-support-groups-155080.
232 See http://unprpd.org/sites/default/files/Overview%20response_1.4.pdf.
233 See www.erciyesmedj.com/jvi.aspx?un=EMJ-65725&volume=.
234 See www.rnz.co.nz/international/pacific-news/415493/tuvalu-govt-announces-covid-19-relief.
235 See www.ilo.org/global/topics/coronavirus/country-responses/lang--en/index.htm#UZ.
236 See http://uza.uz/en/society/center-for-coordinating-sponsorship-activities-provides-char-03-04-2020?sphrase_id=21367212.
237 See http://uza.uz/en/business/president-shavkat-mirziyoyev-signs-another-decree-to-support-04-04-2020?sphrase_id=21367212.
238 See http://documents1.worldbank.org/curated/en/454671594649637530/pdf/Social-Protection-and-Jobs-Responses-to-COVID-19-A-Real-Time-Review-of-Country-Measures.pdf.
239 See https://cis-legislation.com/document.fwx?rgn=126605.
240 See http://english.molisa.gov.vn/Pages/News/Detail.aspx?tintucID=222477.
241 See http://english.molisa.gov.vn/Pages/News/Detail.aspx?tintucID=222530.
242 See https://asean.org/?static_post=asean-rapid-assessment-impact-covid-19-livelihoods-across-asean.
243 See www.nationaldisabilityinstitute.org/financial-resilience-center/stimulus/.
244 See www.ilo.org/global/topics/coronavirus/country-responses/lang--en/index.htm#CK.
245 See https://fns-prod.azureedge.net/sites/default/files/resource-files/WRO-Guam-COV-DHD-Final-Approval.pdf.
246 See https://ghs.guam.gov/jic-release-no-556-dphss-issues-guidance-memo-2021-04homebound-covid-19-vaccination-schedule-dphss.
247 See www.postguam.com/news/local/senators-ok-10m-aid-health-insurance-choice/article_b41c32f4-aec2-11ea-8826-ab75027d9f71.html.
248 See www.postguam.com/news/local/senators-pass-bills-on-500-aid-program/article_4f1f2306-ecf8-11ea-ac88-1738bcc1f422.html.
249 See www.pncguam.com/this-time-dependents-of-any-age-may-qualify-for-covid-relief-money/.
250 See www.legco.gov.hk/yr19-20/english/panels/ws/papers/ws20200309cb2-652-4-e.pdf.
251 See www.coronavirus.gov.hk/pdf/fund/CE-Measure-12-eng.pdf.
252 See www.news.gov.hk/eng/2020/03/20200326/20200326_123952_011.html.

	• Measures were discussed to encourage social enterprises to hire persons with disabilities through time-limited positions.[253] • NGOs were encouraged to set up more small businesses and create more job opportunities for people with disabilities.[254] • On-the-job training allowance was increased, benefiting persons with disabilities and their employers.[255] • The Work Orientation and Placement Scheme incentivized employers to employ and coach persons with disabilities through the provision of allowances. These allowances were increased in the second half of 2020, raising the maximum amount from $51,000 to $60,000.[256] • Two relief measures were launched for enterprises subsidized by the Enhancing Employment of People with Disabilities through Small Enterprise Project of the Social Welfare Department. The measures involved the advanced payment of operating grant instalments and the provision of supplementary grants.[257] • Recipients of social security benefits and the Individual-based Work Incentive Transport Subsidy received an additional one-off allowance. This measure benefited 150,000 recipients of the Disability Allowance.[258]
Macao, China	• The payment of benefits continued via bank transfer, including disability pensions.[259] • To receive pension payments, all old-age and disability pension beneficiaries must provide proof of life each year. The provision of proof of life was extended to the end of March 2020.[260] • In March, the Social Welfare Bureau gave an extra pay-out to around 3,200 families regularly receiving financial support. In May, the Bureau also granted a special subsidy to single parents, those suffering from chronic illnesses and persons with disabilities.[261] • The Macau Government began issuing its annual revenue-sharing payments early to persons with disabilities among other groups to alleviate the financial impacts caused by the pandemic.[262]
Northern Mariana Islands	• A third round of COVID-19 stimulus payments included payments for adult dependants with disabilities.[263]

253 See www.lwb.gov.hk/tc/blog/post_10052020.html.
254 See www.lwb.gov.hk/tc/blog/post_10052020.html.
255 See www.lwb.gov.hk/tc/blog/post_10052020.html.
256 See www.info.gov.hk/gia/general/202006/03/P2020060300293.htm.
257 See www.info.gov.hk/gia/general/202006/03/P2020060300293.htm.
258 See www.news.gov.hk/eng/2020/06/20200609/20200609_143426_835.html.
259 See www.gov.mo/en/news/122807/.
260 See www.gov.mo/en/news/122807/.
261 See www.macaupostdaily.com/article8732.html.
262 See www.casino.org/news/macau-begins-issuing-wealth-partaking-payments-early/.
263 See www.nationaldisabilityinstitute.org/financial-resilience-center/stimulus/.

Annex I
Digital Accessibility Rights Evaluation Index ranking ESCAP members in Asia and the Pacific 2020[264]

The Global Initiative for Inclusive ICTs (G3ict) assesses digital accessibility in countries around the world. It then provides support for advocates and policymakers in promoting ICT accessibility. It has compiled a Digital Accessibility Rights Evaluation (DARE) Index for more than 130 countries, in collaboration with organizations of persons with disabilities and accessibility experts.

The DARE Index score is based on country assessments in the following three areas: (i) country commitments as reflected in laws, regulations or policy programmes; (ii) country capacity to implement referring to the existence of relevant agencies, the availability of digital and technology resources as well as the adherence to international ICT accessibility standards; and (iii) country actual implementation measured by outcomes achieved in 10 key areas of ICT accessibility, such as web, mobile telephony, inclusive ICT in education and employment, e-government and smart cities, as well as enabling assistive technologies and ICT for independent living.

The latest DARE Index was released in 2020, with ESCAP member States and associate members in Asia and the Pacific achieving overall scores ranging from 2.5 to 80.

ESCAP members and associate members	Overall DARE Index score (score out of 100)	Country commitments (score out of 25)	Country capacity to implement (score out of 25)	Country actual implementation (score out of 50)
Australia	80	25	25	30
Russian Federation	61	20	15	26
India	53	25	15	13
Philippines	53	20	15	18
Tajikistan	52.5	17.5	15	20
China	49.5	22.5	15	12
Azerbaijan	49	25	5	19
Indonesia	48	20	20	8
Turkey	47.5	17.5	15	15
Malaysia	46.5	22.5	10	14
Pakistan	46.5	22.5	10	14
Kazakhstan	43.5	12.5	5	26
Mongolia	42	20	10	12
Fiji	41.5	17.5	5	19
New Zealand	38	10	20	8
Nepal	37.5	17.5	10	10
Sri Lanka	37	20	10	7

264 More information can be found on the G3ict website: https://g3ict.org/digital-accessibility-rights-evaluation-index/.

ESCAP members and associate members	Overall DARE Index score (score out of 100)	Country commitments (score out of 25)	Country capacity to implement (score out of 25)	Country actual implementation (score out of 50)
Japan	36	10	10	16
Singapore	33	5	15	13
Thailand	31	20	5	6
Cambodia	26.5	7.5	10	9
Samoa	26.5	12.5	10	4
Bhutan	26	5	10	11
Georgia	25.5	7.5	0	18
Cook Islands	25	15	10	0
Afghanistan	23	15	5	3
Kyrgyz Republic	23	10	5	8
Bangladesh	22.5	12.5	5	5
Uzbekistan	22	10	5	7
Lao PDR	18.5	7.5	10	1
Maldives	15.5	7.5	5	3
Turkmenistan	15.5	12.5	0	3
Armenia	13.5	7.5	5	1
Papua New Guinea	9.5	2.5	5	2
Tuvalu	2.5	2.5	0	0